Barbara Bush

Building a better library

Library Friends

one book at a time.

In Honor Of

MARY RUELIUS

Mending Bee

DISCARD

MOTHER BENEDICT

ANTOINETTE BOSCO

MOTHER BENEDICT

Foundress of
The Abbey of Regina Laudis

A MEMOIR

IGNATIUS PRESS   SAN FRANCISCO

Cover photograph:
Mother Benedict and the U.S.S. Argentina
All photographs courtesy of the Abbey of Regina Laudis

Cover design by Roxanne Mei Lum

ISBN 978-1-58617-186-5
Library of Congress Control Number 2006936323
Printed in the United States of America ∞

CONTENTS

FOREWORD

Many weeks during the summer of 1996 found Antoinette
Bosco and me greeting one another on our way to our
scheduled rendezvous with Lady Abbess at her "Tower".
This modest two-story log building, made interesting by its
unusual hexagonal shape, is set in the heart of the enclosure, atop the hill that centers the land of the Abbey. Across
from this building stand the stone altars that mark the spot
where, over a half century ago, Lady Abbess and Mother
Mary Aline, O.S.B., buried a medal of Saint Benedict, laying claim in faith to this hill as a future site for a Benedictine Foundation.

Armed with her writing tablet and my tape recorder,
Antoinette and I were deep into the process of seeking out
the story behind the founding of Regina Laudis from the
woman who had started it all. Archbishop Daniel A. Cronin of Hartford had actually asked Lady Abbess to write
her memoirs in 1993, reiterating an earlier request made by
Archbishop John Whealon. The subject was always on her
mind. When anything of importance happened, she would
say, "Remember that for my memoirs." She knew she would
need help because by then she was already a woman in her
eighties who had lived more than several ordinary life stories.

Lady Abbess gave us many interviews over the course of
those months, patiently cutting through anything that might
distort or soften the truth as she has experienced it and
getting right down to the bone, as the true surgeon she
was. Gradually, the significance of all the various seeds of

her own future personality and call, dormant within her genealogy, were brought to life. We witnessed her anguish in recalling the terrible events of the war years at Jouarre and the silent nightmare she endured as age began to dissolve even the most precious memories. I learned from the privileged hours spent together that one does not elicit the facts or truth from a head-on encounter. To discover what is real and genuine in a person's experience comes most often by waiting and observing, watching for the subtle traces each relationship has left behind. Antoinette was patient and loving and never gave up. When Lady Abbess closed her eyes to rest, Toni wrote and then waited however long was needed until something came to consciousness from the deep.

What came always proved worth the wait. This was nowhere more true than in following the arc of Lady Abbess' relationship to the authority of the Church in Rome. From the initial experience of approbation and warm encouragement from Pope John XXIII and Pope Paul VI, to the dark period of questioning and misunderstanding, when her fidelity was gravely tested, her allegiance to Rome never faltered. For this reason alone her memoir has much to say to those for whom the ways of the Church remain a great mystery. For Lady Abbess it was never so. Her love was never timid, her faith as guileless as it was indomitable. As "Mother Benedict", long before she became Lady Abbess, she had the courage to push aside the "swords" of the Swiss Guards at the Vatican and walk past them with confidence that *she* had the right of way. I know because I was ten feet behind her. When I tried to follow, the line of guards closed ranks before me, and she never even looked back. That was the way it was with us. I was always running and ducking, trying to keep up with her capacity to drive forward in order to make known the urgent goodness of what she heard God calling her to do.

When I first met Lady Abbess on the day of her twenty-fifth anniversary of monastic vows, I was in my early twenties, and she would have been twice my age, or more. I came away from our first encounter amazed at how joyful and innocent she seemed. I remember thinking that she must be very naïve about the ways of the world. Only much later did I understand something of this woman who would become the first woman in the United States to be blessed as an abbess and whose rich legacy to the Church of the twenty-first century includes the inestimable gift of bringing to this soil the ancient ceremony of the Consecration to a Life of Virginity. The power of that "wise innocence" continues to transform the lives of all who are touched by it.

It is my greatest honor to present Lady Abbess to the world through the words of our steadfast and loyal friend, Antoinette Bosco.

— Mother Dolores Hart, Prioress, O.S.B.
Abbey of Regina Laudis
Bethlehem, Connecticut

PREFACE

I had the privilege of interviewing Mother Benedict Duss over a period of several years before her death on October 2, 2005, learning her story so that one day it could be told and preserved. This book would never have come about if she had not been told by her Bishop to write her autobiography and the story of the founding and development of the Abbey of Regina Laudis. I can say that, but for her obedience to the Bishop, the book would not have been written. For as I came to know the Lady Abbess (her official title), I found she was a truly private woman, not given to talking about herself and essentially reserved.

In the hundreds of hours I spent with Mother Benedict, it became my privilege to get to know this remarkable woman, who was never pretentious, pious, false or unresponsive to someone in need. If there is one quality that characterized her, it was her availability to the members of the Community. She explained that as Abbess, "you have to turn all your energy toward fulfilling the expectations of each woman who has entered. It is sometimes very difficult, but for the fertility of the life, you always have to give more of your personal substance than you are really willing to do. That is also true for the nuns here. But as the head of the Community, I have to be available all the time. People have a right to barge in, and I must be able to respond to a problem they cannot postpone. Yet, while I listen with empathy and concern for their individual problem, I must pray for the gift of discernment because always, at all times,

I have to be primarily concerned with and open to the needs of the Community."

It was her complete focus on her responsibilities to the Community that made it difficult for Mother Benedict to offer what I once called "a personal profile" of herself to me, an interviewer. She did not like to turn a mirror on self—not ever. She lived the contemplative life, believing that "when the time comes to find out what you are to do, you'll be told." And she was given her marching orders to follow fifty years ago—a call from the Lord to found a Benedictine Community for women in Bethlehem, Connecticut! I asked her once to look back at these past fifty years and tell me how she felt now about all she had accomplished. She looked at me and, in her matter-of-fact, quiet way, answered directly, and perhaps almost a bit impatiently, "*I* didn't do it." This is a woman who doesn't change her story!

Mother Benedict was also one of the most well-balanced persons I have ever met, in her dealings with others, her spirituality and her ability to read and respond to the signs of the times. Her wisdom was formidable, as was her practicality, her faith and her fidelity to the "call" that took root in her and made her the instrument for doing God's work.

I remember asking her how she managed to keep from feeling defeated when she had no money and so many expenses in running an abbey as large as Regina Laudis. She answered, displaying her subtle humor, "I had no special method to do it, except to do it. The secret to keeping this place going was to do the next thing that had to be done— without wasting time on worrying. If you do something concrete, that opens the possibilities. You don't know what God is doing on the other side, but He's doing something.

You have to keep a sense of obligation on the one hand, and trust on the other."

Then, more seriously, she repeated, "To start a Foundation didn't come from me. It was the last thing I wanted to do. But if God wanted it, who was I to say no? Many times I felt humanly discouraged. I was always thinking about money. God knows what money is—I don't. Sometimes it looked like abandonment on the part of God, but I never thought it was so. If I got ten dollars, I thought that was great, even though ten dollars wasn't going to do it. But I appreciated everything.

"Yet, as a matter of fact, we always paid our bills, not a simple thing to do. And there would always be money we had to have for the immediate need. This affirmed me and stabilized me in my vocation. I could see in human terms that none of this made any sense. There had to be other ingredients. It gave me a stronger sense that God was there. Anything negative had to be taken in stride, not seen as an argument that God had ceased to love me, but that He could show His power in another way. God's finger would appear when we were seriously in need. He knows book-keeping without effort."

So often Mother Benedict would use the word "para-dox" to try to explain the journey from France to Bethlehem. She would repeat, "I did not come here to start a Foundation. I could see the impossibility of moving into that sphere. I wasn't fulfilling a dream. I never had a dream. What was revealed to me was what was happening. I had a strong sense of God and could see signs that a Foundation was the Lord's express wish. I submitted to His plan. Experience shows that if God wants something, He wants it! You just have to submit all the time. It's hard to explain and very paradoxical."

While a lay person may not understand how one sees the signs that are from God, signaling the path He would like one to take, Mother Benedict helped me see how a contemplative living a religious life is linked to God in a specific and a different way.

"To be a contemplative is to be aware of the reality of God's presence and of the unlimited power that He has. Yet you don't see anything He's procuring. To live contemplatively means to struggle in faith concretely—about events or needs or obligations or commitments that you make as you go along. It's an education you receive, but you don't know how. You just know it's taking place and it's very different from having your own project.

"Contemplation isn't a state of mind, but a different perspective about what life is about. Contemplation is constantly correcting our perspective. You keep seeing things you weren't seeing. It's very active and yet not unbridled . . . for, always, contemplation has to have the marks of being under faith and carrying out what God wants.

"Within the monastery, contemplation is harder—and easier. For each person, it is a trial—and a solace. And there again is the paradox."

Mother Benedict would admit she had more than her share of problems, the most painful being when a member of the Community would disrupt the balance in the monastery. "Some are masters at that", she said, adding, "Chronic dissenters usually decide to leave." In her ever-honest way, she told me, "Sometimes you can't break through to reach people who just can't get past the point they're stuck on. If you are following Christ, this is not mysterious. He ended on a cross, and the pattern's not going to change. If you're in a stable way, you never get discouraged, or fall into despair, because you know the finger of God is there. The basic objective is to keep the monastery moving. I have felt the pain of the cross, of course, but I must always find solace in the mystery of redemption."

I asked Mother Benedict once what it meant to enter the contemplative religious life. How would a woman know what she was getting into if she knocked on the monastery door? Mother Benedict gave me a hearty smile and answered that, of course, most of the women who ask to enter don't have the foggiest notion of what they're really getting into.

"You don't come with an agenda. You're going to enter a Community and then discover that you're in for a totally new development of how you relate to the world and to people. It's not that you're giving something of yourself up, but that you're going to use it differently. There's a lot of individuality that will be left, but an egocentric way of applying it has to change. You have to be formed so that your individuality is not used for self-interest. You renounce that self-interest to do what you must do for the monastery and also for what you can offer to others coming to the monastery. It turns out that we all have our different talents that intertwine themselves with the fabric of community life, interpreted by the Community as 'You have a gift for that.'"

I asked how often women coming into the monastery with high hopes and expectations would find they had made a mistake, misunderstanding what this life is really about. "Misunderstandings are 100 percent!" Mother Benedict responded. "Very often people think they have a call, but soon you find they have no capacity for this life, which means emptying yourself of yourself. A person has to have a vocation, or there's no way to understand this life. They just speculate endlessly and fruitlessly, focusing on aspects of the life, refusing in hidden and subtle ways to grow in this life. You cannot enter monastic life with a refusal, yet it is so hard to get people to understand how they refuse. Those who left didn't want to obey. They exhibited behaviors the monastery can't tolerate—like jealousy, which is usually pretty flagrant in how it expresses itself, even though the person might not be aware of it.

"To be a Benedictine contemplative, one has to believe in the redemptive life, has to understand Who Christ is. He is the Redeemer of the world, and we all have to participate in this—which means to love, forgive and bear the cross. That's a tall order."

Listening to Mother Benedict talk about women who come to the door of Regina Laudis, I sensed she had very strong feelings for each one. She affirmed this. "You have to have a lot of respect for people, and you can't be oppressive. You pray a lot as you try to guide them in their formation, which means how you go about hopefully bringing each one to the fulfillment of her potential. Yet the formation is not according to all the wonderful things she can do, but rather, according to how she can bring her giftedness to everybody else. You may have to let her be impertinent, in some fashion, because what you have to do with each one is to help her keep internally free before God. Each one has to choose and freely accept her destiny.

"If there are signs that a woman is visibly and clearly concerned mainly about herself, and if that's all she has to sustain her, that's not enough, and she can't be converted to a Benedictine sense. Being a Benedictine is not a simple matter. You can't fake it."

I was curious whether Mother Benedict often could feel immediately that a woman would not make it at Regina Laudis. She responded, "It has happened often that the Community will accept a person, and I know that she doesn't have it. But if everyone accepts her, it is very difficult for me to say no. If I turn her away, where can she go? Some come in and are externally so much above reproach, yet I know they do not have a genuine Benedictine vocation. But you have to give everyone the benefit of the doubt, and so, everyone who truly wants to try out a vocation is welcome. But the habit doesn't make the monk, and when a woman leaves, the Community senses tremendous relief that the tryout is over."

In many cases, a woman who leaves remains in close friendship with Regina Laudis, grateful for the formation and acceptance she received. Some women have credited Mother Benedict with starting them on the right path. She says, "If the freedom of that person shows that God wants her to serve in another way, we are very pleased. We don't put anyone in a cage here."

Like most people, I have always wondered whether men and women who enter religious life really have to deny their sexuality. And so I asked, how is the question of one's sexuality dealt with in a monastery? Again, I received an honest answer from Mother Benedict, who was not at all intimidated by the subject. First she said, "There is no guilt about sexuality. The sexual drives are normal. When you come into religious life, you don't become abnormal. You find a way to channel your sexual energies. How you serve would be involved with your sexuality because your sexual makeup endows you to act in a particular way.

"Men and women are each built in the total image of God, and that means we have the capacity to act as God, even though within our masculinity and femininity there are limitations and imperfections. It's not a simple matter to be yourself. We have to work consciously at taking on the ways and attitude of God—and the sexual dimension is very real for both men and women in discerning what this means."

She explained that sexuality—which should never be defined solely in genital terms—defines one's total being. Therefore, to deny your sexuality would make you cold, impotent, sterile and incapable of birthing the good work God would have you do precisely because He gave each of us His masculine and feminine gifts. She explained, "Pope John XXIII had very feminine characteristics, and Joan of Arc very masculine ones, but they were both doing the will of God. This was not a psychological deficit, you see, but rather, they became more feminine or masculine according to what they were called to do."

I found it informative and refreshing to have this then eighty-six-year-old religious woman talk so openly and fearlessly about the need for women and men to remember they are always sexual beings, a truth that doesn't change when they choose to dedicate their lives to God in celibacy.

Mother Benedict was put through the crucible and came out beautifully refined. I think what I shall most carry away with me from my blessed time with her is how faithfully she carried out the commitment she made when she said yes to the call of the Lord, both to be a religious and a foundress of a monastery that would visibly keep Christ alive in these modern times. Never will I forget how strongly she affirmed the importance of "internal freedom" and faith.

"Somewhere in the structure of a human being are indications that the autonomy of a person doesn't follow being acclaimed or recognized by another, nor is it taken away when you cannot control what goes on in your life", she told me. "Internal freedom has to do with our relationship to God. It is germane to faith—which is also an autonomous gift, placed in me by God as a part of my being.

Because faith is a part of my being, it is therefore the root of my stability. This infused gift—my faith—becomes brighter and more compelling as time goes on. For anyone, faith becomes more intense if you have a habit of honoring this gift."

She affirmed, "I review my life, and having come to this point, I have the joy of knowing that out of the faith infused in me, I can see the Light."

I have no doubts that this is the very same Light that Mother Benedict Duss helped to bring, through her life and her work, to our world.

—Antoinette Bosco
Brookfield, Connecticut

PROLOGUE

That warm sunny day in July 1982, when I first drove up Flanders Road in Bethlehem, Connecticut, determined to find the Abbey of Regina Laudis, home of a community of Benedictine nuns, will always be etched in my memory.

I had first heard of this community back in the late '40s when I was a student at the College of Saint Rose in Albany, New York. I was a premed student and frequently talked about wanting to be a nun-doctor who would take care of abandoned babies. Someone, I can't remember who, suggested that I ought to get in touch with a group of nuns who had come from France to start a Benedictine monastery in this country. She had heard that the leader was a medical doctor. Her information had come from a friend attending a Catholic college elsewhere, where one of these French Benedictine nuns had visited to talk about their new Foundation. I was curious, but not very.

A few years later, news of this monastery came again to my attention, and this time, it was a national story. It seems the founding of this community of nuns was so unusual that Hollywood had picked up on it, making a movie with two of the big stars of the early '50s, Loretta Young and Celeste Holm. Called *Come to the Stable*, the movie was a fictionalized version of how Mother Benedict Duss and Mother Mary Aline Trilles de Warren, through the friendship of artist Lauren Ford, settled in Bethlehem, Connecticut, after leaving their abbey in France to start a Foundation here.

I loved the movie. It was one more reason why it was great to be a Catholic, and I was certainly a dedicated daughter of the Church. This was, actually, the heyday for Catholics. We had been through World War II, and the antidote for the evil we had seen come from warring nations was to return to goodness, family and God's values. Priests and nuns were accepted as being just about perfect, as depicted by Bing Crosby in *Going My Way* and Ingrid Bergman in *Bells of Saint Mary's*, and we were enchanted by and proud of these special people dedicated to God. At my Catholic college, we read Thomas Merton's *Seven Storey Mountain* and applauded his religious conversion and entry into a Trappist monastery as yet one more proof of the glory of Catholicism. The von Trapp family—two decades before gaining icon-status in *The Sound of Music*— came to the college to sing for us, accompanied by their family chaplain, and again, this affirmed the glory of our faith. With *Come to the Stable*, Loretta Young was one more screen nun who made the world a better place in an appealing way. I saw the movie twice, wishing I could one day go to Bethlehem, if only to hear the nuns chanting their prayers.

It was years before I thought of this monastery again, and it was because of a story I read in a newspaper about a young actress, Dolores Hart. Regally beautiful, she had been in movies with actors like Elvis Presley and George Hamilton and been on Broadway with Cyril Ritchard and Cornelia Otis Skinner in *The Pleasure of His Company*. Now, the article said, she was taking on a new role, that of nun. I was glued to the story, astonished that someone could leave such a promising career to enter a monastery, yet full of admiration for someone who would leave fame and fortune in order to follow her soul. To my added surprise, she was going to the monastery in which I now had a more than passing interest, the Abbey of Regina Laudis in Bethlehem.

Well, nearly two more decades went by before I acted on that long-standing desire to "come to the stable". In late '81, I left Long Island, where for twenty-five years I had lived and raised my family and moved to Connecticut to help launch a new newspaper, the *Litchfield County Times*. I didn't have the foggiest notion what area was encompassed by Litchfield County. When I consulted a map, to my surprise I saw Bethlehem. A young photographer, Gary Gunderson, had been hired a few months before me, and I asked him if he had ever heard of an abbey of Benedictine nuns located in Bethlehem. Gary said he had, and he knew a little bit about them: they had animals there and did farm work. I told him I had been wanting to visit there for decades. Simultaneously, we both said, "Wouldn't it be great to do a story on this place?" Truth is, we both were willing to give our eyeteeth to do this story—Gary fantasizing about photographing nuns—with the animals, on the farm and in the chapel—and I dreaming about doing a Pulitzer-prize winner on how the nuns live and work.

That's what was on my mind that July day when I finally drove up the road leading to the Abbey. Somewhat surprised at the rustic look and the evident simplicity of the place, I went to the entrance door, which is in a glass-enclosed, greenhouse-like atrium with a fountain. Impressed with this unusual structure, I entered and rang, and a diminutive nun, in full habit and evidently on in years, came to the door. I introduced myself, asked if I could speak to the Abbess and asked the nun's name. "I am the portress", she said. She told me that the first one anyone speaks to is the guest mistress, and that would be Mother Placid.

My enthusiasm was immediately diminished. Over the years I had become what was sometimes called "progressive", and I was offended by a woman who did not have a name, but called herself "portress". I began to wonder if I would feel terribly out of place here. Were these nuns stuck in some kind of anachronistic time zone? Now I was being told to go to a "parlor" in the next building and to wait there for Mother Placid. I went, feeling quite nervous.

My nerves got worse when I saw the grille. What kind of a barrier would that be, I wondered. Pretty soon a smiling, dynamic woman just about my age came bouncing in and took a seat behind the grille. "I'm Mother Placid", she said, and our conversation began. I knew immediately that I was going to like this woman. We talked about everything, from what it was like growing up Catholic in our generation to how I wanted to be a nun once, but how life went in a much different direction for me—marriage, seven children, a broken marriage, single parenthood, endless work to support the family. She talked about her work as an artist and her "call" to this Benedictine life. Before long she was "the Dempsey girl from Brooklyn", and I was "the Oppedisano girl from Albany". We laughed a lot.

Then I told her why I was really here, that I wanted to do a great story for the *Litchfield County Times*. She smiled and said okay. But first, they would have to get to know me, and then they'd have to trust me. Maybe in about eight years, she said. I was polite, but insulted. Here I was, a known Catholic writer. I felt I could be trusted now. Then, before I could say anything more, Mother Placid had a suggestion. They had a guest, she said. Perhaps I would like to do a story on him. She had already told me that hospitality is a major "work" of a Benedictine abbey, so I was not surprised that they would have a guest there. My antennae went up immediately when she told me who it was.

Their guest was a venerable Japanese professor, Paul M. Tagita, then eighty-five, who had been in Nagasaki when the atomic bomb hit. The thirty-seventh anniversary of that bombing was coming up in a few weeks. As a newspaper editor, it took me about one minute to realize what a timely piece this would be if I could interview Professor Tagita. Mother Placid told me where I could find this fine gentleman. I went to that building, assigned to male guests, and, to my surprise, Mother Placid was there in a few minutes to introduce me to their renowned guest. This was better, I thought, smiling. Now, with no grille between us, I could give that Dempsey girl from Brooklyn a great big hug.

My story, "Bethlehem Visitor Remembers Nagasaki", illustrated with a great photo by Gary Gunderson, ran in the August 20, 1982, issue of the *Litchfield County Times*, and I knew then that I had begun a relationship with the Abbey of Regina Laudis. What surprised me was that I had gotten over my peeve so quickly. It didn't bother me at all that Mother Placid said it might take eight years before I was seasoned enough to write the story I wanted. I had quickly learned that this was a very special place. I also knew I was welcome and that in the interim I would write many stories about Abbey guests, the Abbey's annual monastic fair and the work of individual nuns.

What I didn't know in 1982 was that five years later a hateful media blitz would hit this community. Allegations made against the nuns said they were engaged in "cult-like" practices and were involved in ambiguous business arrangements. When my office at the newspaper received materials "proving" the nuns were "witches", I thought the world had gone haywire. The woman contacting us wanted to know what I thought about her "find". She had gone to the Abbey property and discovered what she said "looked like a castle tower", and what she found inside shocked her: "a giant, five-pointed star". "A pentagram", she said. "I thought, this is occult!" To her the nuns were clearly witches. She included in her materials an "encyclopedic outline of ceremonial magic and sorcery". Apparently it had never crossed her mind that this was not a "pentagram", but the five-pointed Christmas star of Bethlehem!

With the accusations getting that bizarre, Mother Benedict refrained from responding publicly to these denigrating claims, following the advice of Saint Benedict. He said it is better "to be silent than to speak" in the face of discordant chaos and instead turn to restore what "foul malice" destroys. The office of the papal ambassador in Washington, D.C., at the time told me the accusations against the nuns were "totally unfounded".

By this time, I had gotten to know a few of the nuns and found them to be bright, warm, open, friendly, never judgmental. I remember being at the Abbey one summer day, interviewing for a story on the upcoming fair. I was unsettled and worried about my son Peter, who suffered recurring bouts of mental trauma, but I was trying to hide this. As I was going to my car, one of the nuns came to me and said that Mother Dolores wanted to see me. I had not yet actually met this lovely woman. I went to the entrance, where she stood behind the grilled door, looking as youthful and beautiful as she had years earlier on the screen. She put her hands out to hold mine, and when I looked into her eyes, I felt she had somehow known I needed a human touch that day. We spoke a bit, but I didn't need words to tell me why God chooses very special people for His temples.

Most special of all would be the Abbess, who answered the call first and who built this place where women could come to live a life of faith, in relationship with God and as fully human persons, having a reverence for all created things. The life story of Mother Benedict Duss, a truly remarkable woman, reads like a novel. Her grandmother on her mother's side was a Spiritualist, a leader in this religious movement; her father's parents were the last of an experiment called the Harmony Society, a Christian community in which everything was owned in common and people were bonded in fellowship. Her mother was a convert to Catholicism, and so she had her daughter baptized a Roman Catholic at age five. Young Vera Duss was brought to Paris by her mother, who was half French, just before World War I, and they remained in France through her formative years. By the time she was seventeen, she felt a call to the religious life, but her mother would hear nothing of this. Obediently, she continued school, going on to study medicine, earning her M.D. at the University of Paris (the Sorbonne) medical school in 1935.

Vera's longing for the religious life intensified, however, and she was professed as a Benedictine at the Abbey of Jouarre in 1938, taking her perpetual vows in 1941, a time when France was almost completely under German occupation. At this stage of World War II, it was not a good time to be an American in Paris, and Mother Benedict found herself being sought out by the Gestapo. She was well known in the village where the Abbey was located because she had worked there as a physician helping the people, so she had to go into hiding—an inspiring story of courage.

The day that is burned into her memory is August 27, 1944. She had been terribly ill with hepatitis but had managed to get to Vespers (evening prayer), when the nuns heard a rumbling outside. Rumor had it that the Americans were coming and the war would soon be over. She managed, with some of the others, to get to the monastery tower, and they looked down, seeing armored vehicles. But she also saw something on these—a white star and the American flag. At that moment, something stirred in her soul, compelling her then and there to respond to the American general who had liberated them. She felt something of what she could later call "a charge" to do this by starting a monastery in the United States.

She would learn later that it was General George S. Patton, Jr., who had liberated Jouarre, and she credits him with figuring directly in the founding of the Abbey in the United States. In one of those amazing events we call "coincidence", one day, years later, a young woman would come to the Abbey, seeking to enter—General Patton's granddaughter, who is today Mother Margaret Georgina!

The events that led Mother Benedict to her determination to start a monastery in the United States and the path she pioneered to make this dream come true—encountering obstacles that would have defeated most people—are impressive chapters in an unusual story. I once asked her when were some of the times when she was faced with a crisis. Looking at me, with the hint of a smile, she answered, "Every day. Every day."

To get a real sense of what Lady Abbess Mother Benedict founded, one only has to visit Regina Laudis and see the nuns who are there. The spacious church building on a hill in Bethlehem, Connecticut, hardly appears to be a monastery, if one has preconceived, traditional images of what a monastery is supposed to look like. In its architecture, it is more like an invitation to savor simplicity in design and materials and feel how closely worship and nature are linked.

Its walls of raw wood and glass soar to join with a massive cathedral ceiling, a brilliant achievement that leaves one feeling both the comfort of an enclosure and the freedom of the outdoors, and subtly, even the sense of being immersed in both the earth and Heaven.

The altar is centered, resting on a platform adorned with two fixed garden plots holding stone, earth and plants. On one side is a tall, artistically designed, open grille, setting off the space—the enclosure—where the nuns gather for Mass and prayer. The other side is the space welcoming friends and visitors. This section is equipped with chairs, not fixed pews, a kind of hospitality that fits in with the simplicity and freedom emanating from the specific architecture of this sacred place.

Each morning, shortly before eight, the bells ring, sounding a call that Mass will soon begin. The nuns, who wear full habits, emerge from two doors at either side of the enclosure behind the grille, walk in an orderly procession to meet one another at the center of the choir, bow their heads in greeting the Lord in the Blessed Sacrament and proceed to their seats. Then, in their clear and lyrical voices, they begin the chanting of prayers in the Latin that has a long tradition in the Roman Catholic Church but is rarely heard today.

The morning Mass is not the first gathering for the nuns. Already, many of them have come to chapel at 1:50 A.M. to start the day in a communal prayer called "Matins", and at 6:15 A.M. for "Lauds", that is, "praise" for God. Before the Mass at eight, some have had breakfast; some have done the milking of the cows and other chores with the animals; some have begun "household" tasks required for a "family" of some forty persons living in a self-contained community; others have started preparing for hospitality or the manual, artistic or other tasks they must accomplish this day.

When you first experience the Abbey of Regina Laudis, you can't help but wonder if you have entered a time machine, zooming you back to another era, another place, another culture, another set of values. Who are these women, who, in the twenty-first century, wear traditional habits, pray at regular intervals day and night and worship at a Mass in Latin, singing prayers and responses throughout in the time-honored Gregorian chant?

You have to come to the Abbey to find out, and there, once you begin connecting to these women who make up the Community of Regina Laudis, you are in a discovery zone. You find women who are not lost in a past pattern of religious life, but who are avant-garde in their understanding of what it means to be a religious woman today. They are professional women who find no contradiction between higher learning and deeper living, with the latter defined as choosing the path paved by Jesus Christ. And so you find here the current Abbess, Mother David Serna, a formal social worker; Mother Dolores, now Prioress, a former Hollywood and Broadway actress; Mother Maria Immaculata, the Subprioress, who was a lawyer and Connecticut state representative; Mother Placid, an accomplished artist; Mother Catherine of Alexandria, a chemist; Mother Noella, a Fulbright scholar with a doctorate in microbiology; Mother Telchilde, a doctor of animal science; Mother Lucia, with a Ph.D. from Yale—and on and on.

They will tell you no one "falls off the face of a cliff" when they come here. Everyone stays in touch with her field, be it teaching, theater, arts, government work, education, law, medicine, horticulture, guest work, etc., all for the purpose of being better able to relate to others both inside and outside the Community. "I always had the sense from very early on that my purpose was to be a medium of communication, and it never dawned on me that this life would not be an absolute continuity of this", said Mother Dolores.

I have heard some criticize the nuns, saying, if they are so progressive, why do they still wear the habits that many religious orders discarded after Vatican II? I have raised this question and learned that these Sisters find no contradiction here. In the words of Mother Margaret Georgina, "The habit makes us available, readily visible to ourselves and others in the choice we have made and are making each day. It is also a source of encouragement and strength to us. Each element of the habit has significance and has a particular prayer that we say every time we put it on, reminding us of the meaning of our life and our commitment to one another and to God."

The bottom line you reach is the realization that Regina Laudis is one of the few remaining religious communities of women in the United States that is thriving, and more and more I've come to a conclusion about why this is so. Specifically, the women here have dedicated their lives to the praise and service of God according to the Rule of Saint Benedict, a sixth-century monk. The Rule is an amazing document by a man who had a profound understanding of human nature. Because the Sisters have been faithful to the Rule, which recognizes the need to be in step with the times while holding to the stability of eternal values, the Community of Regina Laudis has worked hard to develop and achieve a healthy and valid environment for contemporary religious women in America today.

But each of the nuns will tell you that redesigning themselves according to the Rule of Saint Benedict is more agony than ecstasy, for his Rule requires one be trained for "service in God's army", a soldiering not for sissies. He was, in fact, requiring the creation of a new kind of man or woman. "Religious life is generally misunderstood, mostly by people who never get to know what it's about", said Mother Placid, who has celebrated her golden anniversary as a nun here. "Entering is like the first day of creation for you. You come to find out what God has put you here for. You walk in, and this place will set off all the light and dark places in you. It's a pressure cooker. You will walk into all the trials you need to clean up your act and learn to love."

As to why these women would choose to enter a monastery, each may have her own explanation, but there is a common theme. Each was looking for "something deeper" and to "become more alive". As Mother David expressed it, "Each of us wants to know that what we're doing hooks into something larger."

Mother Praxedes, an artist and a blacksmith, told me of the "emptiness" she had felt in the era of the Vietnam War. "Nothing meant anything to me in the early '70s. I was idealistic, trying to find something—like an ideal marriage—where I could make a commitment for life. But I was not finding it anywhere. When I visited the Abbey, I felt something very solid here. I was struck by the young people coming here and impressed with the depth of meaning they, like myself, were trying to find."

It took awhile, Mother Praxedes said, but then she knew she had found "something much deeper here . . . like a taproot" to the core meaning of life, love, nature, work and relationships. That interior, dynamic structure, bringing a "marriage-like" dimension to one's connection with all of God's creation—"That's what I was looking for."

As I got to know the nuns of Regina Laudis, I began to understand why entering a monastery is perhaps the most

difficult transition a person can undertake. For to be a Benedictine nun means that a woman has to do as Christ asked
and shed the ego and self-centeredness that come with the
human condition. She has to, in effect, "die" to everything
that would keep her forever a "seed", locked into the lim-
itation of herself. She has to believe, as Christ said, that
only if this seed dies can she find the new birth that revital-
izes her with the spirit of God, so that she can bring this
Eternal love and goodness and peace to her Community
and others.

And so she doesn't run away from life. Rather, she begins
a "spiritual transfer", as Mother Dolores expresses it, bringing her to a fuller life, where one becomes the embodi-
ment of God's values, as taught by Christ. And in this living,
she becomes a witness of what a holy place this world could
be if everyone had the courage to become this new person.
She is doing what Saint Benedict asked, bringing Eternity
into time.

But undeniably, to become oneself in the image of Jesus
Christ is a most difficult passage and doesn't happen by
mere wishing. It is a continual, daily challenge of a lifetime. And just as Jesus was misunderstood and attacked in
His life, so are those who have ever followed Him. "Because
monastic life is dedicated to perfection, in a monastery,
everything is magnified, and every form of imperfection
comes out at times", said Mother Dolores. "If you dare to
say you're living a life of holiness, you better be willing to
be challenged. You never know where the next crisis is
coming from. You're living in the middle of a dart board,
always ducking critics who feel they have a duty to 'perfect' you."

Some people think one joins a monastery to run away
from life, to be sheltered and protected from the world.

When you meet the nuns at Regina Laudis, you learn immediately that nothing could be further from the truth. "Our
life is not withdrawal and seclusion. Saint Benedict's vision
of a monastery was a new paradise, or a garden restored. It
is to be a self-sustaining body holding the values of civili-
zation and reflecting God's creation, and a place of hospitality where others can come to find this truth", said Mother
Dolores. "Monastic life pulls you into a crucible, where the
plan of God is revealed. Monasticism is a school of the Lord's
service", where each lesson leads to the same question: "How
do you give your life for someone else?"

Should people think this is just an academic question,
they should come to Regina Laudis. Here they will find
that the charism of the Abbey is hospitality, embracing the
Rule of Saint Benedict, who said, "Let all guests be received
like Christ." Everyone who comes to the door—those who
are troubled, lost, alone, confused or searching for something deeper and more meaningful in their lives—all are
received warmly, no questions asked. Visitors have come
from all over the world, many of them famous—like Father
Pierre Teilhard de Chardin, Charles and Anne Lindbergh,
Maria von Trapp, Dorothy Day, Patricia Neal, Gloria De
Haven and Maria Cooper Janis.

Many, like myself, return again and again to this place
we find to be a refreshing oasis. And why? I think Sister
Angèle gave the best answer. "Initially when I came, I felt
a kind of liberation. For all the supposed freedom we have,
we're always pretty much doing a number for someone else.
But here, I found the freedom to be the person I am and
an atmosphere that could meet the intensity I felt in my
own faith. That was—and remains—the draw."

Where, I would ask, can you go and always be welcomed, never questioned about your accomplishments, and

greeted and helped according to your need? When you come to the Abbey, you feel, perhaps for the first time in your life, that you are unconditionally loved. You find only kindness and see smiling faces. At Regina Laudis, I have experienced a joy not often found in this world.

Over the years, I got to know the incredible woman who founded this wonder. She genuinely respected every living person and every entity in creation. Never was she judgmental, biased or extreme. She was one of the most well-balanced, honest and open persons I have ever met. She founded an abbey that is a model for what the religious life can be for the modern, professional woman. For this Abbey is a dynamic, evolving, life-giving Community that is linked to the world even as it is enclosed, powerfully rooted in tradition and transcendence.

Mother Maria Nugent, who entered in the '60s, described the foundress with these words: "Lady Abbess, by her breadth of vision, combined everything excellent and true of the past with the present because she was equally open to all that is new. There is no Abbey like this. It expresses a movement of the Spirit for the Church. Lady Abbess was gifted with this particular vision for this particular time."

Here, for the first time ever, is her story, told in her own words.

Chapter I

THE EARLY YEARS IN AMERICA

— *Singular Relations*
— *Early Memories*
— *Strain between Her Parents*

Mother Benedict Duss was born in Pittsburgh, Pennsylvania, on November 21, 1910, although later she preferred to celebrate on November 15, the feast of Saint Albert the Great. Her parents were a young couple who had met as students at Stetson University, a private Baptist co-ed college in De Land, Florida. The courtship of Elizabeth Vignier and John Duss, Jr., was greatly aided by their mothers, friends who did what they could to help John and Elizabeth get better acquainted. When the two students decided to marry, they had to do so secretly in order to continue their college studies. Pregnancy, however, brought a major change to their lives, beginning with a move to Pennsylvania, where they took up residence with John's parents in an elegant structure in a village named Old Economy, now the town of Ambridge. The building was called the Great House and was the executive mansion of the Harmony Society, at this time being cared for by John S. Duss, Sr., a trustee, and his wife Susanna. The birth of a baby girl brought joy to the family and new life to the Great House, so long occupied only by adults. John and

27

Elizabeth named their daughter Vera, delighting John's sister, Vera Duss Houston.

Young Vera Duss grew up in a world dominated by adults of remarkable individuality. If it had not been for the birth of her brother, also named John, when she was fifteen months old, she probably never would have had a close relationship with another child. She was a gifted child, precocious, comfortable with the adults, all of whom had much to do with how she was raised. Her memories of these early years are vivid, permanent impressions never forgotten by her. "I had a happy introduction to life", she said. "My world was essentially happy."

Vera Duss' maternal great-grandparents were nonconformists who certainly "did their own thing", unusual for a couple in the mid-to-late 1800s. By the time Vera was born, her great-grandmother, Elizabeth Heard Densmore, was a noted Spiritualist. She lived in Lily Dale, New York, and was an important leader at the Spiritualist camp in Cassadaga, New York, which was just beyond a lake separating it from Lily Dale and connected by a bridge. Her great-grandfather, Emmett Densmore, was a bit of a rogue: brilliant, probably eccentric—and something of a rover when it came to women. He had married Elizabeth Heard in 1854 when she was seventeen, but he divorced her sometime after their children, Ianthe, Darlott, Shelley (who died young) and Percy, were born. Before the divorce, he sent his wife and the three living children to Paris, where they stayed for five years, the children attending French and German schools. During this time, Emmett Densmore went to London to live with a woman named Cora, who was a Spiritualist lecturer. After three years, he came to America, married a woman named Mrs. Barnard from Washington, D.C., divorced her and later married his stenographer.

Emmett Densmore's life story seems to be dominated by a restlessness, perhaps stemming from his creative yearnings. He began his financial enterprises making big money in oil, then investing in a Florida sweet potato ranch, which was a failure. He became a broker on Wall Street, then invented and developed a typewriter, which was contemporaneous with the Remington and after that began his own brokerage business. At age forty-five, he earned a medical degree from a homeopathic college in New York City and became interested in developing "some medical formulas", an interest he shared with Mrs. Barnard. When he married her, she had a recommendation signed by President Garfield that allowed her to market a health product. After the President was assassinated, Emmett Densmore acquired the formula, called it Garfield Tea and for years successfully manufactured that tea.

As he grew older, the attraction of Spiritualism led him to go back to be near his first wife, who by that time was living in Florida in a "sister" town to the one harboring the Spiritualist camp in New York State, this one, too, called Cassadaga. He lived in a cottage near the home where Elizabeth Heard Densmore lived. He often visited her during his last illness. He died at Thanksgiving 1910, a few days after his granddaughter, Elizabeth Vignier Duss, gave birth to his great-granddaughter, Vera Duss. The baby's great-grandmother died, too, shortly after Vera was born. Because Vera never knew her, she could not describe her, other than to say she knew that her mother had "a reverential fear" of her. Vera's mother, Elizabeth, had been brought up in the wilderness of Cassadaga, between Jamestown and Dunkirk in western New York State. She was the only child of Ianthe Densmore and a Parisian, Charles Vignier, Vera's maternal grandparents.

Ianthe Densmore was a very important influence in young Vera's life. She was a notable woman for her times. The newspaper obituary published after her death in November 1930 praised her for her life's activities in literature, language and art, as well as for her personal charm, adding, "She was a graduate of the New York School of Expression. She staged many beautiful pageants, both here and abroad, and was a superior teacher of the French language, and taught in public and private schools, also accompanied many groups of people to France and Germany as interpreter."

The man who stole her heart was Charles Vignier of Paris, but it was a short-lived marriage. They lived together only for a few years. Mr. Vignier belonged to a group of poets, and he was a writer, although he never made any money at this. In those years, his wife supported him. He was also very autocratic. Ianthe separated from him when she became pregnant—but he made her come back with the baby, Elizabeth, who had been born in 1891. Later, Ianthe's father, Emmett Densmore, pressured her successfully to leave her husband, whom he considered to be a deadbeat, and come to stay in America.

Mother Benedict recalls her grandmother as being "a dreamy type of person, who took her desires for realities. She had a strong aesthetic sense that started in a school of modern dance she attended. She would create extremely beautiful positions that would be reminiscent of those seen in Greek statues. She performed in Europe and in the court of the king of Bavaria.

"My grandmother taught me this kind of poise—how to walk, how to move, how to look for symmetry of position, how to do exercises that would give me a poise that would come naturally, so that I would never be self-conscious. I am very grateful to her for giving this to me."

At the same time, there was often static between young Vera Duss and her grandmother. "My grandmother had a marked preference for my brother. I was very aware of that and thought it was probably because she had traveled a lot when her child was young, or maybe because she never had a son of her own. We had a kind of antagonism. She was always finding fault with me, but she took care to see that I always got what I needed. She said I was much too bold, but I was really shy. I didn't know what she meant." Ianthe Densmore Vignier was later to have an even greater role in Vera's life when, as a child not yet four years old, Vera and her brother, then less than two, were brought by their mother to live in France with their grandmother.

Mother Benedict's grandparents on her father's side (John S. Duss, Sr., and Susanna Creese Duss) were the last members of an extraordinary experiment in community living in America called the Harmony Society. It had been founded in Germany in the late eighteenth century by George Rapp, who brought his sect to America in 1804 because he believed he had a prophetic mission to leave Germany and establish the Harmony Society elsewhere. In Germany he had felt the continual movement of oppression between the Lutheran tradition and politics, and he felt impelled to leave and seek a place where there was freedom of religion if his Harmony Society was to flourish.

Shortly after George Rapp came to this country, he was joined by a stalwart, younger man named Frederick Reichart and about six hundred others. Recognized as a genius, Frederick had supervised a Herculean effort to bring these associates with him to America, making sure that each one had a profession important for building a town. They were befriended by the Society of Friends in Philadelphia, who helped them get a tract of land and establish their first

Harmony village. Frederick was elected industrial super-intendent and manager of the Society's external affairs. At the same time, he changed his name to Rapp and became George Rapp's adopted son.

Eventually, the Harmony Society had three settlements, two in western Pennsylvania and one in southern Indiana, all self-sustaining, with thriving industries, and economi-cally sound. From 1825 until 1868, the experiment flour-ished. But in the next twenty years, an emphasis on celibacy caused members who wanted to marry and have families to leave, resulting in a loss of laborers. Among other setbacks—including the death of George Rapp—financial dark times descended. Eventually, the Society had to sell most of what it owned. Lawsuits were rampant as former members sued to get money they felt they had earned. What some had called "a noble experiment" ended with nothing left but the Great House—cared for by John S. Duss, Sr., and his wife, Susanna—and memories.

The history of the Harmony Society was preserved by Mother Benedict's grandfather in a book written in 1943 enti-tled *The Harmonists: A Personal History*.[1] In his preface to the book, E. Gordon Alderfer writes, "The story of the Har-mony Society ... I think, to be one of the truest American illustrations of the meaning of 'Community'. This people was banded together, not necessarily by any kinship or by any common creed, but by eternal ties of fellowship—the fellow-ship of men functioning as a common economic and social unit. ... The members of the Society ... possessed no worldly goods except as a part of the Society which held the prop-erty of all members in common".

How it happened that John S. Duss, Sr., became a mem-ber of the Harmony Society is a story in itself. He was born in Cincinnati in 1860. Both his parents, John Duss and Caroline Kroll, had come to this country from Würt-temberg, Germany. When the Civil War erupted, his father was conscripted into the Confederate Army. "Unwilling to fight at variance with his own convictions, he feigned ill-ness until the Battle of Bull Run. Then he found an oppor-tunity to escape, and to join the Army of the North. Being a deserter from Confederate ranks, upon advice of certain Federal officers, he changed his name to John Rutz, and thereupon became a private in Company H, 75th Pennsyl-vania Volunteers, 11th Corps", wrote his son.[2]

A powerful remembrance in John S. Duss' book is the news of his father, seriously wounded in the Battle of Get-tysburg, July 3, 1863. In his words, "Some days after my father, with a bullet wound in his shoulder, had been removed to a Baltimore hospital, my mother and I experienced a strange psychologic phenomenon. . . . It was late in the night; deep silence had settled on the village. Suddenly my mother and I, asleep in the same room, awoke. The quaint old room appeared strangely illuminated from without the east win-dow. My mother arose and approaching the window, whis-pered, 'Come here quickly.' In the sky there seemed to be a great light, much larger than the moon. Only a few sec-onds it lasted, then faded away. . . .

"Inquiry the next day developed the fact that no one else had any knowledge of the phenomenon, whereupon my mother construed it as an omen in reference to my wounded father. Perhaps she was correct—who knows? At any rate word soon came from the hospital in Baltimore that my father had breathed his last—at about the time we had perceived the light in the sky."[3]

John Rutz, the assumed name of Mother Benedict's great-grandfather, appears on the Gettysburg monument.

Mother Benedict's great-grandmother Caroline was an intensely religious and stern woman. Alone with her young son, she heard of the Harmony Society and their town called Economy through another religious group. On their recommendation, she was invited to come and stay with the Harmonists, the beginning of a lifelong connection for herself and her son.

Encouraged by his mother, John Duss went on to get a college education and to study music, eventually becoming a conductor as well as a performer. Meanwhile, he had met the Creese family, who lived directly across from the schoolhouse at Economy. He worked with Miss Kate Creese, who taught English, while he taught German. Before long he became acquainted with the family, finding Miss Kate's younger sister, Susanna, particularly attractive and lovely. They fell in love, and when he finished college, John and Susanna were married at the home of her brother David in Keokuk, Iowa, on July 17, 1882. In the years that followed, John Duss, in his work with the Harmony Society, became known as a businessman, philanthropist, financier and economist. But more than that, he was respected as a most professional and versatile music conductor, leader of the Economy Band and, later, the Duss Band. His concerts were played on such noble stages as the Metropolitan Opera House and Madison Square Garden, always to rave reviews. His love of music was a legacy passed on to his granddaughter, Vera.

As it was becoming clearer that time was running out for the Harmony Society, sadly, the Dusses were mired in lawsuits by people seeking money from the dissolution of the Society. These legal entanglements increased after 1905 when Mrs. Duss and other members decided to dissolve the Society and, as joint owners of its property, "to distribute the same among themselves", wrote Mr. Duss. While there was nothing illegal or immoral in this action, they were sued, and the need to defend themselves dominated their lives. Mr. Duss wrote that he lost even his music career because of the "waves of legal proceedings which for a quarter of a century had engulfed us". In the end, somehow, the legal conflicts appear to have ended in peace.

The fact that her grandparents were for so long a part of a true community is a memory cherished all her life by Mother Benedict. She freely speculated that her own attraction to community life could be rooted in this spiritual legacy of her grandparents. "My grandfather was still alive when I entered the Benedictine Abbey at Jouarre in France in 1936. He equated this call to live in community as continuity with the Harmony Society and spoke of his granddaughter maturing and taking on the legacy of the Society. In fact, from my childhood I was drawn to the activities of the Harmony Society, which I realized much later really had a Benedictine sensitivity and a monastic schedule." The foundress of Regina Laudis openly revealed that she saw a linkage between herself and her grandparents, who may have laid the groundwork for her call to community, affirming, "The continuity in mission that a family has must be corporate", that is, carried out by the flesh-and-blood members of that family. "It might take generations to fulfill the mission", she reflected, adding that "the process is present in me."

While John and Susanna Duss still occupied the Great House in Old Economy, by the turn of the century, Mrs. Duss was beginning to suffer a decline in health. During the winters of 1903 and 1904, she spent some time in Florida. Finding the climate beneficial, she decided to buy a place in Florida so they could winter there.

Mother Benedict recalled this period, saying, "My grand-mother had glaucoma and heart disease and needed a quiet life, which she found in Florida. They bought property on undeveloped land on the Atlantic beach, scrub land, very solitary, opposite the nearby town of New Smyrna. In addition to a large house, the property also had a bungalow, and that's where my parents came to stay."

But not for long. Theirs was a marriage that was riddled with problems, as little Vera was destined to discover too early in her young life. She dearly loved her father, John Duss, Jr., an attorney, but her mother moved away from him, going to France, taking the children with her when Vera was not yet four.

"I was very close to my father. He and his family doted on me, giving me great affection. After I went to France, I did not see him again for seven years. I missed him. It was very difficult for me. I couldn't share this with my mother. She was having her own problems with him. I think there was some-thing lacking in his ability to relate to others. He was a very staid person who loved living in Florida. He was not ambi-tious as the world would have it. His relationship with his mother was probably responsible for his being unable to assert who he was. She was very controlling of her son and domi-nated him. But I had a devoted relationship with my father. Even the years I was in France, we kept in close touch through many letters.

"And then my relationship with his sister, Aunt Vera, was very important to me. She was a singer. She had no children, so I was very special to her. She was always the one who would stick up for me. She would always defend me, saying, 'She has potential. She needs time to express herself.' "

With her great-grandmother Elizabeth Heard Dens-more, a Spiritualist; her maternal grandmother, a language teacher who was respectfully called Madame Ianthe Vignier; her paternal grandmother, Susanna Duss, a leader in the Harmony Society; her mother, Elizabeth Vignier Duss, a maverick who left her husband and moved to France to raise her two children there; and her aunt, Vera Duss Houston, a musician, and more importantly, a woman who could always be true to herself—Mother Benedict reflected, "The strong women in my life were probably, if unconsciously, a great influence on me."

Though she was only a toddler when she lived in the Great House, Mother Benedict retained a mosaic of memories about this mansion built by the Harmony Society. "It was an impressive, large structure that had a sense of grandeur about it. It was in itself an awesome presence, filled with color. There was something protective about the architecture that gave you a sense of security. It was within an enclosure, making me feel that, here, you could ward off catastrophes." This early experience of "enclosure" at the Great House may have played a role in the later call this child would have for the monastic life.

"The most important person in the background at the Great House was my grandfather, always gracious, gentle and cheerful. But I spent most of my time with my grandmother, who loved me very much. She really was the housewife, the queen of the kitchen, cooking and preparing meals, taking care of the household needs. She always had me near her. I wanted to do what she did. When she was baking, she would give me a piece of dough—proportionate to my size—so I could work, too." Little Vera would imitate her grandmother and then use some of her own creative ideas for shaping the dough. "I made a lot of little dirty cakes, not fit for eating", she said, smiling as she remembered how her grandmother would pretend to bake these.

In this adult-dominated world, she often became the center of attention—and loved it. Whether in the kitchen with her grandmother, or in the garden with Aunt Vera, she "loved to present" herself. "I was an actress at two and a half, and very free ... a freedom that took me many years to get back to", she said, alluding to some of the chapters that were to follow in her life.

Perhaps the major event of her first years on earth was the birth of her brother on February 12, 1912, when she was fifteen months old. Her mother, then twenty-one and very independent, resented the pregnancy, Vera would learn in later years. "My mother had a very restless nature and was very strong-willed. She gave me the freedom to be myself, because that's what she wanted for herself. She believed the system should not determine how you think. I appreciated my mother early. Everything she did was for our good. She had a way of being there for you and spent a lot of time with us. She would go out of her way to make a child happy."

In early 1912, Vera, hardly more than a baby herself, connected to her tiny brother from the first moment she saw the infant. This instinctive love never lessened. Even though later separated by distance, brother and sister remained connected in spirit all their lives, until John Duss' death in March 1990.

"While we were very close, we didn't make a show of this. We behaved the way we wanted to, but kept this quiet. It was our world, where we invented games and took care of each other, but we weren't defiant. We were so different, yet our relationship was definitely another expression of love, even when we would sometimes be in conflict. He was much more vigorous physically than I was. He loved to run, and I couldn't. I'd suffocate in a minute if I tried. Sometimes I think he was more protective of me than I was of him. He was so sensitive, honorable and devoted. And we were never jealous of each other."

The toddlers were too young to realize that trouble was escalating in their home between their mother and father. Some of the conflict was due to their mother, who had become curious about the Roman Catholic Church, due to her friendship with Father Michael Curley, then pastor of the Catholic church in De Land, where she and her husband had attended college. Father Curley was an impressive person, in his midthirties and "friends with everybody—very welcomed, both by Protestants and by Catholics".

"After my mother met Father Curley and began to learn a bit about the Catholic faith, she reasoned that Catholics had something others didn't have. She would say, 'The Catholic Church has something we don't have', even though she was very Protestant in that no one could tell her what to believe!" Mother Benedict said, lightheartedly. "My mother asked Father Curley for instructions, and he was willing. He marveled at how bright she was. Father Curley became a friend and was accepted by the family. He became a frequent guest. My mother's conversion to Catholicism, I think now, was an act of revenge, really, against the family."

Though she was only a two-year-old at the time, Mother Benedict recalled how important Father Curley was to her. "To have someone be a kind of patriarchal figure to you at that age is unforgettable. One of the factors of trust and balance I had in those years came, I believe, from my attachment to Father Curley." Later, when she was baptized Catholic at age five in France, Father Curley was her godfather, by proxy. Mother Benedict remained spiritually close to this priest, who became Bishop of Saint Augustine, Florida, and later, in the 1920s, Archbishop of Baltimore. He died in 1946. "There's a *bonum* [good] that can best be described as the core of innocence that is 'one' with God's life in each individual. I think he recognized, in the innocence of my childhood, who I was and communicated that to me. That was Father Curley's gift to me. I am also convinced that a sense of Eternity comes from certain experiences in very early childhood—and I think that, too, was a gift given to me by Father Curley."

Even this early in the marriage, troubles were heating up between Elizabeth Duss and her husband, and so Elizabeth decided to get away for a while, taking her two children to visit her mother, Ianthe Densmore Vignier. Vera's grandmother now lived in the house that had been her mother's in upstate New York, near the Spiritualist camp in Cassadaga. "It was a lovely house, with a big porch and high columns, on a lake."

"I particularly remember one morning. The room my brother and I slept in was on the lake side, and on this morning, the sun was dawning, reflected on the water. I just watched that whole scene with such fascination, admiration and joy. I felt immense gratitude for how beautiful the world was." And then reality set in. "It suddenly occurred to me that time had passed, and I had gotten no breakfast. I started moaning, 'I need food.' I think my brother did, too. Finally someone heard this moaning. I was very clear about needing attention. In one sense, I was a spoiled brat. Nobody I can remember at that period did anything to train me. It was a very 'ad lib' time for me."

It was also a time of special moments—like the buggy drive with her mother—for this child, not yet three years old. "My mother was a horsewoman. She rode. Her specialty was trotting horses—not galloping—and buggy driving. One day we were both alone in the buggy across the lake from Lily Dale. She was driving a mare called Polly. I thought the horse was somewhat sluggish, and I wanted to see if I could elicit any power from her." She took the whip and touched the mare with it. "I didn't want to hurt her. I just wanted to see if I could get some animation from her. My mother was very tolerant of that. The horse moved faster, and my mother told me this meant she was trying to respond to me. It was a revelation to me that I could 'talk' to an animal that size." This sense of connection with another creature of nature made a profound impression on her at this very tender age.

Upon their return to Florida, another incident made a lasting impression on Vera. "It was a summer evening, around dusk. I was close to three then. My mother was outside, talking to a friend from Pennsylvania who was there. I always loved to talk to adults, so I was out there too, running around. Well, then my brother threw up. I took care of him and settled him down. But then I remember sitting quietly and thinking, 'Is life worth living?'" This was only the beginning of the pattern her life would take, where "metaphysical references", as she expressed it, would erupt, raising questions not to be ignored.

Elizabeth Duss' foray into the Catholic Church, which had caused some discomfort in the family, now had further repercussions. "She insisted that my brother and I have a Catholic education and somehow felt that she had to go to Europe to manage that." But her reasons for making the decision to leave Florida and go to France with her children were much more complex. Certainly the strained relations with her husband were a factor. Then, she also wanted to see her father, Charles Vignier, who still wrote poetry but had developed an interest in importing Oriental art and had become one of the best art critics in Europe.

Financial necessity had been a motivating factor in getting her father, who had a new family, to put his poetry writing temporarily on a back burner while he became a businessman. His younger brother may have been the force behind the change. He had vision and believed that if they became experts in the art of the East, they could start a thriving business. Together they scraped up enough money to go to China and "study the mysteries of the Far East. They became renowned experts in the art world and built a business and a reputation" that brought in considerable wealth. Because of this, his first wife, Ianthe, had been able legally to get a sizeable divorce settlement from him.

With this influx of money, Ianthe had rented an apartment in Paris, large enough to accommodate her daughter and grandchildren, and so Elizabeth Duss packed up and with her children—one only three, the other less than two—boarded a boat to France. This was at the end of 1913. What she didn't know was that a world war would erupt a few months later, dominating their lifestyle and having lasting repercussions.

Chapter 2

CHILDHOOD AND YOUTH IN FRANCE

— *Girlhood in Paris*
— *War Breaks Out*
— *A Troubled Family*
— *Adolescence*
— *Her Surprising Decision to Study Medicine*

The transatlantic trip to France by boat in late 1913 made some lasting memories on little Vera Duss, then an impressionable three-year-old. Mother Benedict would later label those days as "life on the deck". She stayed on the deck almost all day long because she found the one way not to be bored was to look at the sea. She would stare at the water for hours, becoming ever more conscious of how the "sea is constantly different. I would wonder about the hidden life there."

Her brother, almost two, who was restless, would become "a natural projectile". He would be running or finding what could be called child games to play, "none of which I particularly liked", she recalled.

Arrival in this new country was also memorable, with no one at the dock to greet this young mother with her two very young children. While they would be staying eventually with Elizabeth Duss' mother, Ianthe Densmore Vignier had not crossed the ocean with them. She was to leave later to join her daughter and grandchildren in Paris. Hospitality in the meanwhile was to be provided by Aunt Alice Densmore, the sister of Elizabeth's father, Charles Vignier. Aunt Alice's home was the first destination of the trio of travelers just in from the States, and Mother Benedict would recall that her first impression was meeting her cousins, Aunt Alice's two daughters, Marianne and Yvonne, sixteen and eighteen years old, "one more beautiful than the other". She would always speak of this family as being "of tremendous help in getting us organized".

The apartment Elizabeth and the children first lived in was in a place called the City of Flowers, an enclave between two large gardens in Paris, with houses on both sides. Mother Benedict's enduring memory of this place was the flower garden her mother, "a very good gardener", had planted.

In these early months in Paris, Vera and her brother were almost always together. "We'd participate in certain activities we'd make up ourselves. Sometimes these would displease my mother, and she'd scold us. But we were always taking care of each other. One day there was a terrible storm, and my mother was out. My brother and I sat in an armchair, embracing, consoling and supporting ourselves through the storm. My mother came in, looked at us and said this was the most touching thing she ever saw, these two kids protecting each other."

This was the spring of 1914, and it appeared that the coming months would be particularly lovely in Europe that year. On the farms, the animals and crops flourished, and in the cities, commerce was brisk and business boomed. Prosperity and peace seemed to be the order of the day. Yet a terrible rumble was looming as two opposing and powerful military alliances gained strength—Germany and Austria-Hungary, the "Central Powers", on the one side, and France, Britain and Russia, the "Allies", on the other. Europe was becoming an armed camp, soon to be divided against itself.

"I remember a dinner party at our home that spring. My mother had quite a few guests, some from Pennsylvania. She had a circle of red coral around her forehead. Conversation turned to international affairs and rumors of trouble to come. I remember the vague anxieties people began to show. It was a shadowing of events to come", said Mother Benedict. Indeed, World War I erupted a few months later, in August 1914.

Yet, for the moment, being a child, all her attention turned to something that mattered immediately to her—the move to a new apartment, where they would live with her grandmother Ianthe. It was on the third floor of one of the impressive buildings that surrounded a garden near the Eiffel Tower. "Privileged people lived there. Princess Grace of Monaco later had one of these apartments", said Mother Benedict. Their apartment had a big corner window overlooking the garden, and Elizabeth would let the children play there because she could watch them from the window. Vera was drawn to that garden, with its small fruit trees, and spent hours there, "in contemplation and in ecstasy".

Soldiers of all nations, mainly English, Canadian, French and Russian, were constantly around because they attended an institute for training called the "War School" near the Eiffel Tower, which was used as an observation tower by the French Army. "The soldiers admired my brother, who walked around wearing a Russian hat. He had absolutely gorgeous golden hair, naturally curly. The soldiers were entranced by him."

The garden within the boundaries of the apartment buildings came to have a special meaning for the young child

Vera, who loved this "enclosure". She explained, "I think I was drawn from the beginning of my life to enclosures and gardens. This enclosure in Paris was like Paradise to me . . . like a fairyland for a child. I would stand in awe of a flowering tree . . . and the apples that grew and were ripe in the fall." It was sort of an early prophecy or preparation for the life, within the enclosure of a monastery, that would one day beckon her.

That summer of 1914 was idyllic for the children. Elizabeth took them to the coast of Normandy to a lovely place where they could picnic. Vera and her brother were allowed to play with big balls on the adults' tennis courts, and this was an exciting privilege for the youngsters. But the outstanding memory of that time was the discovery of apricots. "They looked like the sun and had such a pleasing taste." Vera was particularly fascinated by the sun at this place. "I remember the sun vanishing, and we would follow it. It was a beautiful experience."

But peace was to be shattered with the declaration of war. Mother Benedict retained a vivid impression of the day war was declared. "It was remarkable. Total silence. Everything stopped. I know there was public transportation to gather youths for military service. But it was done with deadly silence, and it was this quiet which struck me so much. Years later I saw a play called *The Persians*, about the invasion of Greece by the Persians. What struck me in this great play was the stress on the silence when the war was proclaimed. In this ancient tragedy, in this intensity of conflict, there was not a vociferous or loud response, but silence. That stayed with me."

Not long after the announcement of war in Europe, on August 21 as the family had lunch, grandmother Ianthe, a Protestant, remarked that Pope Pius X had died the day before of a broken heart. Mother Benedict related her reaction: "I had no way of knowing who or what a Pope was, but I knew intuitively something of what he was. I felt a real sense of his presence. My grandmother explained that he had made all diplomatic efforts to prevent war and had been defeated. He died with a vision of what this war would cost. I had no frame of reference for understanding this, but I was deeply moved. He spoke to me, and this was not just a child's illusion. It was genuine.

"To this day, that image of Pope Pius X is one of the most significant memories I have. It's connected to the dedication of my whole life. It's quite comprehensible to me that this was why I was given this image. I relate to it as a reality that was authentic, a gift that connected me to him and to each Pope who has come in time.

"His successor was Benedict XV, who made a plea for peace, but was rudely turned down by the French and the Germans. The French would say he was pro-German. To me this was a gross mistake. He was obviously trying to mediate for peace, and they were attributing motives to him that he didn't have. I was convinced he would also die of a broken heart."

The war years were long and full of anxiety for everyone. Elizabeth tried to protect her children from fear and danger. But "everybody was trembling at night. I remember the long corridor in the apartment, and all I saw if ever I looked were profiles of soldiers with spiked helmets."

By the fall of 1915, the Duss children were attending a small private school. School became especially important to Vera because she was learning to write and so could compose her own letters to her father. The separation from her father was becoming ever more painful, since she missed him so much. While her mother worked faithfully to keep the children in touch with their father, Vera learned that letters were an inadequate substitute for presence.

When it came to writing, her little brother was better at it than Vera was. "He had a more disciplined use of his hands", his sister recalled. "He had a great facility for learning. He was so bright. He caught things without having to break his back too much. I had to work for everything I learned in school, like a slave. In music, it was the same way. He could just pick it up. We studied piano for twelve years and gave recitals. He could sight-read Mozart. I couldn't. He became a talented musician, later well known in Florida", where their grandfather John Duss, also a noted musician, lived. "We had a great difference in gifts, and I'm glad he had what he had."

Mother Benedict spoke proudly of her brother, who served in World War II, nearly losing his life when he and others were lost at sea after a bombing attack on his ship. He became an attorney, starting at the bottom of the ladder, but going on to achieve enough to found his own firm. He dedicated his life to his wife and two sons, Robert and John. When his wife became ill with Alzheimer's disease, he stayed by her side till she died. Only then would he leave her to travel to Connecticut two or three times a year to visit his sister at the Abbey she had founded in Bethlehem. John S. Duss III died on March 15, 1990, survived by his sons and four grandchildren.

In the late months of 1915, Elizabeth Duss began to prepare her daughter for an event that would remain forever imprinted in Vera's memory—her baptism as a Catholic. The day chosen for the ceremony was January 6, 1916, and the baptism was to take place at the Church of Saint-Pierre du Gros Caillou (Saint Peter of the "Big Boulder"). Father Michael Curley was to be her godfather, by proxy. To note the occasion, he sent Vera a large picture of himself in episcopal vestments. Her godmother, Lucie Bremonde, was a French painter known to her mother, who was also an artist. Elizabeth had commissioned this woman to do a large portrait of herself and her two children. Vera's brother, John, was to be baptized a year later.

Mother Benedict vividly remembered this event. "It was about a twenty-five-minute walk to the church, and we left about four in the afternoon to get there. Night was already falling, and there was a little rain coming down. I remember being in awe of the darkened church and the ritual. For a child, this was a profound experience. Back home, my mother gave a reception in the living room. She had special candies on a small table. I remember feeling a disproportion between this little celebration and the event itself."

With Europe now entrenched in war, Elizabeth Vignier Duss found her plans for a temporary stay in Paris had gone awry. She had wanted to leave Florida to get away from her husband and mother-in-law for a while. She had to sort out where she was going in life, with the complications of her conversion to Catholicism. She also had a strong urge to reconnect with her father, Charles Vignier, a man she barely knew, and she wanted her children to have at least some contact with their maternal grandfather. But she wanted to save her marriage and had expected to return to the States when she felt ready. She hadn't expected that a war would block her from traveling back home.

Somehow, Elizabeth managed to arrange a trip to the States for herself. She probably decided to go alone for fear there might be danger. She dearly loved her children and protected them at all times. When it came time for her to leave, in the spring of 1916, she left the children with grand-mother Ianthe in charge. "The day she left, she didn't tell us she was going. My grandmother took me and my brother to Bois de Bologne, where there was an exclusive park, a lake and island, a pastry shop and tea room. Things were severely rationed at that time and children, especially, were not supposed to manifest what they'd like. But we were asked that day, and I chose pastry with a syrup of grenadine. I got suspicious that something was wrong when I was offered a second round. When I got home, I found out that Mama had gone to America. This was so treacherous! The party didn't make up for it at all."

Though she longed for her mother and father, Vera accepted what she couldn't change, focusing her attention on her studies at school and on caring for her brother. She had the capacity to adjust to disruptions, perhaps because she was a war child, living with uncertainty every day. But, more importantly, she was gifted in her ability at a young age to be attuned to nature and the beauties of the world, and, while she was lonely for her parents, this kept her from descending into gloom.

That summer grandmother Ianthe took Vera and John to Saint-Aubin, near a small fishing village in Normandy. They visited a basilica, Mont-Saint-Michel.[1] Mother Benedict recalled how she was mesmerized by this magnificent structure that had been a monastery for Benedictine monks. "The solemnity, the magnitude of it impressed me to no end. It was a place of worship, so particularized that it seemed to exist only for itself."

What she loved most was being on the beach, contemplating the sand, the sea and an island. "The sky there was so vast. I had a sense of being between two worlds. It was heavenly, a paradise on earth."

Her mother came back from the States that summer. Vera and John had been on the beach. "When we came back, there were two kiddie carts at the back door, and on each one was a box of gifts. My mother was like that. She returned as she had left, without saying. But I knew she was there—so life was worth living again."

At the end of the summer, Elizabeth, Ianthe and the children returned to the apartment, which had been renovated while they were gone. The children went back to school. Elizabeth continued her study of French, hoping to be able to communicate better with her father if she learned the language well. She was hurting financially, and she thought he would help. Charles Vignier had another family by this time, but the fact that she wanted to meet him again and relate to him with the children touched him. He was shocked that the financial situation had become so critical, and he tried to fill the gaps somewhat. Vera found that her grandfather was very responsive to her, and that pleased her.

Money remained a recurring problem. Elizabeth was a gifted painter and would work, quit and then return to it, so she could never make a living at it. She tried bookbinding for a while, but that failed, too. She depended financially on her mother, Ianthe, and she also received support from the Duss family back in America. Now and then Vera would overhear a conversation between her mother and grandmother that would excite her. It would be talk about her father coming to Paris to visit them. Sadly for the children, he never made it.

Some time after the family returned to Paris, they moved to a smaller apartment. This one was on the ground level, with bright interiors because of its location, on an angle between two streets. The great appeal to Vera was that it had gardens all around. It reminded her of a scene from a Molière play her mother had taken her to see at the Comédie-Française. Elizabeth and her mother were deeply interested in theater, opera and literature and were determined to share these cultural ventures with Vera and her brother. The years in Paris were dotted with visits to museums and libraries and attendance at plays and musical events, experiences that were very unusual for children to have.

With the move to the new apartment, the children were put in a new school. At first Vera was happy there, well adjusted to the schoolwork and delighted with her teacher. But then, after a year, the family made the decision to send her brother to an all-boys' boarding school, Collège Stanislaus de Paris. This was more than a blow to her. "It was a traumatic experience for me. Breaking us up, losing his presence gave me a very hard time. He came home very rarely. I couldn't tell my mother how I felt. She wanted us to get the finest education, and this was her decision to send him there."

But while something was taken away from her, something was also given to her. Their move had brought them close to the Church of Saint Thomas Aquinas. The pastor there was a remarkable old man in his eighties, Canon Cabanoux, a first-rate priest who was greatly responsive to the young. He directed the catechetical program, and Vera was one of his pupils. "He was always very alive. He was extremely vigorous, but also gentle. He had only a positive effect on me. He was a tremendous role model for me. I'm sure he had a great deal to do in shaping the masculine part of me. He was a very holy man, and for me, unforgettable", Mother Benedict said. Later, when he died, "I went to his funeral. You couldn't get into the church for the crowds. He was so beloved. He is buried in the cemetery called Montparnasse. I went often to visit his grave."

Her religious instruction continued with a teacher named Mademoiselle Dode. The celebrations in the month of May, when children brought flowers to the altar, which was lit with candles, were memorable. She got her "first sense of the liturgy" at this time, when she was seven, and recalled how "the Rosary, prayer and song transported me."

By now, 1918, all the talk and yearning in France was for the end of the war to come. The news finally came in November that the armistice had been signed. "Everybody went wild", Mother Benedict said, including the children. Elizabeth didn't make plans to return right away to America. Nor did she make any moves in that direction by the summer of 1919. Instead, she took the children to Brittany, where she rented a house on the beach. Vera's mother also very generously invited the children of an artist, Carlos Schwab, her son John's godfather. Carlos' eldest child, who was about twenty-five, came for a while and made a lasting impression on Vera. "She was a self-appointed mystic and had a book on Saint Thérèse, the Little Flower, with her. She would read this to me. She was so extreme in her stories about ascetics. She told me about a group that would found a community and never again eat salt, and so they would all die. My mother was wild. She couldn't abide that sort of person. But this girl didn't harm me at all. In fact, she did open something for me. She was the first person who made me aware of the existence of Saint Thérèse." [2] Vera's attraction to the saints and religious life was a seed that would take root and grow.

It was the following year, when Vera was almost ten, that Elizabeth Duss left Paris with her two children to return to the States, and to her husband, with the hope of saving her marriage.

❧ ❧ ❧

The child who returned to the United States in 1920 was very different from the one who had left her country nearly seven years earlier. Sensing the magnitude of the terrible conflict, she had lived through wartime in France, and she had known the excitement of 1918, with everyone rejoicing that a peace treaty had been signed. By March 1920, Vera Duss was already something of a sophisticated young lady for a nine-year-old. She had been encouraged by her mother to do a lot of reading, but the books she read were hardly those now considered children's literature. History fascinated her, and she read books full of historical data, documenting the kings of the past and the impact they made in their time. Her interests were further nourished by writers like Shakespeare, and *Hamlet* was her favorite play.

There were times, though, when young Vera would find herself thinking, not of theater, books and dolls, but rather of Saint Thérèse of Lisieux. Vera was curious about what it meant to be called to a life of prayer and contemplation. Something about church, and the events that took place there, attracted her strongly. She would always think of 1920 as a very important year, the year when she began serious catechetical instruction and eventually received her First Communion at the Church of Saint Thomas Aquinas in Paris.

"The whole experience was deeply recollective, no facetiousness or laughing. I was very penetrated by that. When you receive a careful introduction to the liturgy, a communication takes place, and you are prepared to move on in this way. You get on the road. You enter the mystery", Mother Benedict explained.

It was March when nine-year-old Vera, with her mother and brother, boarded the ship that would bring her to the United States for the first time in nearly seven years. "It was a time of enormous excitement for me because I missed my father so much. But almost immediately, young as I was, it was clear to me that I would be facing more squarely the divisions in the family."

Troubles began anew from the time the mother and her two children got off the boat. John Duss had come from Florida to New York to meet his wife and children, but his mother also had decided to come. Elizabeth Duss resented that very much. She had felt that her mother-in-law had essentially ruined her son by making herself indispensable to him. His mother had made it impossible for John to affirm anything on his own or to discover who he was and be himself. He was handsome and had a fine mind, but he never was able to assert himself in a way that might have separated him from his mother. The very presence of the mother-in-law damaged any possibility that Elizabeth and John would be able to rebuild their marriage. "My grandfather was always very pleasant. He didn't challenge his wife to let go of their son, but he always tried to create an atmosphere of friendliness" to soothe over the friction between his wife and daughter-in-law, said Mother Benedict.

For the children, the arrival in New York was like a glorious holiday. For they were greeted not only by their father and paternal grandmother, Susanna, but also by the other adults who gave them attention and love—their paternal grandfather, John S. Duss, Sr., and their maternal grandmother, Ianthe Densmore Vignier, who by then had divorced Charles Vignier and preceded them to New York.

From New York, the children were taken to Florida near New Smyrna, to stay at the home of their father's parents. Two houses were on the property. One was a large one, where Vera's grandparents had received people from the Harmony Society with no home of their own. John and

Susanna Duss took care of these people till the end of their lives. They themselves lived in the other house, the small bungalow.

Vera was happy. Here she was able to spend time with her father, a most attractive person, who was very impressed with his ten-year-old daughter, an avid reader who could quote *Hamlet*. He would say to his father, "I believe this child actually knows what Shakespeare is about."

Her grandfather, in turn, spent even more time with her. He was "the underlying presence" in the house and "very soon appreciated me". Always an individual, Vera decided she would not call him "Grandfather" but would find an appropriate nickname. She did. She called him "Pap" and did so whenever she met him or wrote him over the years, until his death at age ninety-one on December 14, 1951.

Elizabeth and the children did not stay long in New Smyrna. Discord between her parents was escalating. The next thing Vera knew, they were on a train. The first stop was Saint Augustine. Elizabeth was seeking help from the priest who had led her to the Catholic Church and was now the Bishop in this city. "Bishop Curley was on the platform when we got off the train. It was the first time I'd seen him since World War I days. I think he felt my mother's distress and tried to counsel her. I think it was a sadness for him, too. We went to Mass the next morning in Saint Augustine and then left, taking the train to New York."

When they got to the big city, they were to go to the apartment that her grandmother Ianthe was renting at the time, but first they checked in at a hotel. Unexpectedly, Vera's father found them. Her mother's reaction was one of panic. She feared that her husband was going to kidnap the children and take them back to Florida. Yet, it seems he really wanted only to talk to her and his children. He and his parents had taken on much of the financial responsibility for raising the children, and while Elizabeth needed and accepted the money, she demanded the right to make her own decisions when it came to how she and the children would live.

Elizabeth signed out of the hotel and took a taxi with her children to her mother's apartment. Ianthe Densmore Vignier was also helping her daughter financially. She had come into a good amount of money after getting a divorce settlement from her former husband, Charles Vignier. Since she had supported him in the early days of the marriage, she claimed, successfully, it was only fair that when he became well-off from his art business, she should have that money and more given back to her.

As mid-June approached, Elizabeth made plans to take the children to Shadyside, her mother's house in Lily Dale, across the lake from the Spiritualist camp in Cassadaga, New York.

Here at Shadyside, Vera was given a responsibility that made her most joyful. She was asked to help take care of the land, particularly the garden. She was given a special little space for flower beds, "which grew beautifully and caused a great excitement for me".

As summer came to an end, Bishop Curley unexpectedly arrived at Lily Dale. Decades later Mother Benedict would say, "It was always a memorable experience to spend a few days with him and hear about his focal points in the management of his diocese. At this time, the development of schools was uppermost in his mind. He was working on a speech he had to give upon his return. I think he tried to read us his speech. I'm not sure we were fascinated."

By this time it was evident that Elizabeth and John Duss were not going to reconcile. The marriage might exist in name, but in reality, it was over. In late October, Elizabeth and the children were on their way back to France. The visit to America had lasted eight months. From that point on, Vera's father was not in the picture, not destined to be a father who would make a difference in his children's lives. Even so young, Vera knew she just had to get used to this, for there was no hope that the situation would ever be different.

Back in France, Elizabeth reenrolled her daughter in the same Catholic school where she had been before and put her son back in Collège Stanislaus de Paris.

When Vera completed elementary school, her mother enrolled her in a private Catholic high school, the Institute of Saint Clotilde. Here Vera studied general liberal arts, along with highly specialized science, and she graduated at age seventeen. A year later, she got a second degree in philosophy, "in 1928, the year Lindbergh made his solo flight across the ocean".

Many years later, Charles Lindbergh made a visit to Regina Laudis in Bethlehem. Mother Benedict recalls that he was "very pleasant to meet, very affable".

Back in France and needing money, Elizabeth was trying to reconnect with her father, who now was a renowned expert on art. Her mother's motive, Mother Benedict recalled, was "strictly business—meaning, 'How much will you give me?'" Vera had seen her grandfather several times, for he had come to their home at her mother's insistence. On one occasion, Vera opened the door when he arrived, reacting with surprise because she didn't know the person at the door would be her grandfather. She heard him say to her mother, "*Elle est très gentille*" (She is very lovely), and she never forgot that compliment.

"My mother was a very fierce person, who showed her worst tendencies toward her father. She always said what she thought, and she never minced words. She never had any empathy for his position. She could never compromise. Everyone had to meet her standards. My grandfather had another family, and while he didn't seem to want a relationship with my mother, I think he really wanted to see me", Mother Benedict reflected.

Recalling that she had always been "a very religious child", Mother Benedict explained, "The sense of the presence of God was never absent. Perhaps, unconsciously, the acceptance of mystery was the reason. Maybe I felt it would upset the apple cart [of existence] if we had all the answers. I was held by a sense of the providence of God. He didn't give me everything I asked for. But He gave me more—a religious reality that was holding me together"—and, she added, never failed her.

"I had been thinking about religious life considerably. I wanted to be a Carmelite nun, like Saint Thérèse, but when I told this to my mother, she was adamantly against this. She said, 'I will never discuss this with you again.' She had sacrificed a great deal for me and my brother, but she also demanded that we perform. While she had an esteem for a religious vocation, she felt that to have one of us go into religious life would have meant her time and sacrifices would have been wasted. And of course at that point, considering my age and lack of resources, she could stop me.

"So, I began to do some soul-searching. I wanted to do something with my life that would be useful to people. I wanted to have the capacity to serve others in an accurate context, not in one where I'd have to use my imagination to find ways to help others. Between the ages of fourteen and eighteen, I had thought of many things. I was a good student of history, but I didn't believe being a historian would be helpful to people on the street. It was a pure deduction on my part that brought me to consider medicine. I saw this as a profession based on a sense of humanity, where I could serve others in a specific way. I hestitated to say anything about this for a while because I was not good in math and could only get by in science. I knew that studying medicine would be a tremendous risk for me, that I'd have to work constantly. But once I decided to go for it, I never worried about not making it. I knew I'd find a way. I had that kind of temperament.

"When I finally told my mother that I had decided to study medicine, she was surprised and told me I had chosen a very difficult profession, one that would put a great strain on me, but she did not try to change my mind.

"But even as I made plans to go to medical school, the thought of religious life was always there. Yet I knew I'd have a struggle somewhere. Most important to me at this time was the need to establish a context that would satisfy all my interests while I learned the discipline of service. Medical school was so demanding and the training so massive that I didn't have time for much else, yet I never felt discouraged. I felt that so long as I just continued, it would work out.

"I didn't know it then, but medical school was great training for the religious life. It took me a long time to make this connection because medical studies were totally unprecedented as an orientation for entering religion. It has sometimes astounded me that this training has always been with me. Even yet, seeing people in a parlor, what's uppermost in my mind is—how can I help them?

"But going back to my medical school days, studying medicine was, I came to realize later, an astounding choice for a woman of the 1920s to make—and in no way could I have foreseen the consequences of that decision."

Chapter 3

VOCATIONS

— Medical School in Paris
— Entering the Benedictine Abbey at Jouarre

Vera Duss entered medical school at the University of Paris (the Sorbonne) in 1930 after completing two years of premed studies. It didn't take long for her to learn that she had chosen a very hard road with frightfully demanding work. There were about one thousand students in medical school that year, only 3 to maybe 5 percent of them women. Besides dealing with the weight of the studies, a student was faced with the need to get practical work experience, what they called the "externship" phase, and for most students there was very little opportunity for that.

The really important thing was to get into the hospital, and she was competing with one thousand others to get in. To get accepted, one had to take a competitive exam and score high. This was a significant level of challenge for a woman since the prevailing attitude was that the places belonged to the men, because the women would probably marry and not devote their lives to medicine. The mentality was that a female medical student was only taking the spot away from a man. "Yet the men in medical school would accept you, if you were halfway civil to them. Actually, I felt that France recognized the right of a woman to

study medicine more than most countries did at that time",
Mother Benedict would later say.

She achieved externship very soon, but then the second
level was internship, and this required the passing of another
exam. Because of her ranking in the exam, she was given a
provisional internship. As she explained, "I think I could
have done better if I hadn't been dealing with two major
distractions at that time, one being my mother, who was
forever unsettled and getting worse, and the other being
my ever-increasing desire for the religious life. I tried once
more to do better than a provisional internship, but I didn't
make it. I presume I was less interested than others, because
it was not a terrible struggle for me to meet their standards.
And besides, I knew I would always qualify to get my medical degree."

But big problems were looming at her home, and suddenly she found she had to deal with new and serious troubles brought on by her mother. While she had been working
diligently at her early medical studies, her mother had created a serious problem. Angry that her father, Charles
Vignier, would not give her money, she had started writing
letters to officials of the French government, trying to get
them to force her father to give her a financial settlement.
When she was asked to stop doing this, she refused and
kept up the demanding and denigrating letters. Her father,
exasperated, told her to her face, "You're a hyena." Finally,
the French government itself stepped in and told her to go
home to America. "We've seen enough of you, Madame",
they explained.

With no choice but to obey, her mother had to prepare
to leave France. She was only forty-two, but very fragile at
this point and near a nervous breakdown. It was clear to
Vera that her mother could not take the trip alone, and so

she interrupted her studies briefly so as to accompany her back to the States, where her father and his parents could help her mother to become functional. Elizabeth Duss' own mother, Ianthe, had died in 1930. Sadly, before her death, she had lost her lovely home near Cassadaga in New York State.

There was a good side about returning to America for Vera, since it gave her the chance to visit her father and grandparents in Florida. They were very proud that their twenty-one-year-old granddaughter was a medical student, and they said they would provide financial support for her so she could complete her medical studies. She also would get to see her brother John, who had followed through on a decision he had made to settle in Florida, choosing to follow in their father's footsteps, becoming, like him, an attorney in Jacksonville, Florida.

She also wanted to visit Father Curley, her godfather, who was now the Archbishop of Baltimore. But she was unprepared for what happened when she tried to visit him. "I was told he couldn't see me, and that was most painful. He was going blind, and that was very hard on him. He was completely lost. He didn't have the serenity you associate with blind people. I was never able to see him in Baltimore. His housekeepers wouldn't let me in. When he found out about this, he wrote me a very distraught letter. It was very strange. I was devastated by this rejection", Mother Benedict would later say.

The only person who seemed to help put Archbishop Curley at peace and help him gain serenity was his secretary. After he died, she came to see Mother Benedict, to say that he had wanted his secretary to write to his goddaughter. But Mother Benedict had already had a consoling experience. "One night in 1946—I was in Bethlehem in America at this time—I dreamt about him", she said. "I was meeting him somewhere, and when he arrived, he looked very handsome. He told me it was wonderful that he was seeing me. And then he said, 'I'm happy, and I'm going to see you again, but not for a while.' That was a Sunday morning, and at breakfast, I got the word that Bishop Curley had died in the night. What consoled me was the dream I had had. That pristine dream healed my hurt. Something human and comprehensible was restored and returned to me. Shortly after getting this news, I went to pray at his crypt at the cathedral in Baltimore."

After her stay in America, she went back to Paris, returning to her medical studies in earnest. When she had free time, which was rare, she went to the theater, to concerts and to the movies and sometimes visited her grandfather, Charles Vignier. She had many friends, both men and women, and enjoyed the richness of companionship with them. The thought of marriage never entered in. While she could see the wonders of married life and was not averse to this, she never chose the path of a romantic relationship.

When her medical studies were coming to an end, she had to move from the apartment, which was expensive to keep up. Fortunately, a close friend nearby, Antoinette Le Ber, offered her hospitality. This was a welcome invitation because she was now deeply immersed in writing her doctoral dissertation. Mother Benedict explained, "I had chosen a most unusual subject, and it was almost a shock to me that it was accepted. My thesis was titled 'Concerning the Mystical Experience according to Saint John of the Cross'. I had started reading Saint John of the Cross when I was sixteen, and I never stopped. He seemed to me to be a master who could hold you. I wanted to come up with a medical subject relevant to Saint John of the Cross. I was very conscious of the mind-body connection, and I saw clearly that Saint John's work could shed light on how mind-body balance is the path to good health. When I proposed this for my dissertation, eyebrows went up. Actually, I had terrible nerve. I would have to defend this unusual thesis before a group of physicians, and then it had to be accepted by a broader group at the Sorbonne. As it turned out, it was a pleasant experience that I didn't expect. I still remember a Protestant doctor in the jury, who told me he was very interested in my thesis. In actual fact, I came to see that I was decades ahead of my time in defending the position well accepted today—that mind and body are interconnected when it comes to good health—since back then the medical establishment looked mainly to science for answers to illness."

At this time, it was becoming very clear to Vera Duss that her future would be religious life. The summer before she finished medical studies, she had gone to Paray-le-Monial, the place where Jesus, showing His Sacred Heart, had, according to tradition, appeared to Saint Margaret Mary Alacoque in the seventeenth century. "Every religious order, including the Carmelites, wanted to be represented in that town. It was a world of bells. There was always a bell ringing in that town."

"I was still convinced I would enter the Carmelites. My attraction to the religious life was getting ever more pronounced. While my schedule was very busy and my days active, within myself I had a great longing for the contemplative life, which I believed would bring me to finding God in my life in a very concrete and visceral way. By nature, it suited me perfectly. The Lord was undoubtedly leading me to a different religious order, however, because when I knocked at the door of the Carmelites, I soon learned that someone with my scientific bent would not fit in here at all. That mentality was too narrow to welcome me. I knew I had to have a broader container. I attribute the rejection I felt probably to just one stupid Sister, but it was clear I wouldn't make it there.

"The following Holy Week, I was studying intensely and suddenly felt the urge to make a retreat. I had been going to a Benedictine monastery of monks in Paris for Sunday Mass, and so I approached them, asking if they could tell me where there would be a Benedictine monastery of nuns, hoping one would be near Paris. They pointed me to the Benedictine Abbey at Jouarre, and I went there. I was immediately struck by this huge eighteenth-century building with its impressive tower. Later I came to feel a subtle sacredness about this abbey, which was very old and had long been called La Sainte [the Holy].[1] Other abbeys were called the Famous, the Brilliant, or the Rich, but Jouarre was called La Sainte, spoken of as being on sacred ground. My first visit there was life-altering. I'm always looking for a comprehensive view of what's at stake in where you find yourself and whom you meet. The way events unfolded in that retreat affected me profoundly."

Her retreat started on Palm Sunday, and on Tuesday a nun died, an occurrence that touched her deeply in the days to follow as she saw how the Abbey dealt with this. "It was a tremendous encounter with death, where the emphasis was on love and the transformation of this nun's earthly life into her new life with God. It gave me a huge insight to the meaning of monastic life, where the whole cycle of earthly life as part of Eternal Life is the focus.

"During Holy Week, they couldn't have a funeral, so they were able to note her passing only with Vespers for the dead. They had to wait till after Easter to have the Mass.

Then she was given every recognition possible. It was the mystery of the Redemption being celebrated, piece by piece, and for me that was an education in itself. It struck me for the first time how death could be so organic in this Benedictine monastery. Everything was taking place at 'home'. The casket was carried by religious women, strong from their farm work, with all the others in procession, going from the choir to the cloister underground passageway leading to the outside of the building and to the garden that enclosed the cemetery. It was so dignified. It struck me how you lived and died in one place here. I saw it to be all one unit, the cohesion and the coherence. Everything was one. It gave you a sense of timelessness and brought a great deal of peace.

"This was the beginning experience that started to lead me away from the Carmelites and toward the Benedictines. For what I had discovered here in a deeper way was the wonder and mystery of the liturgy, and I was powerfully drawn to this. I also found myself in awe of how the nuns were given to prayer—how they had a serenity, but also an insertion in reality, and how truly they were connected to nature. By the end of my Holy Week retreat, I knew I had been given a true gift of having experienced a part of the richness of the Benedictine life, getting a peek at the 'hidden realities' of what monastic life could be and what it could offer. All this intensified my call to religious life."

Meanwhile, Vera Duss had to complete her medical studies, a choice she would say all her life that she never regretted. For her, it was exactly the thing to do. She would say that it conditioned her "to always look at humanity in a special way, asking, 'How is this person faring? Is this person afflicted with any physical or mental problems?' I think the concern and compassion for people that intensified with my medical training were values that greatly aided me later when I had the responsibility of being in charge of a religious community of contemporary American women."

The big moment for her, when she had finally completed her studies at the Sorbonne, the University of Paris, and was now Vera Duss, M.D., came on June 27, 1936. Since her whole family was in the United States, she celebrated her graduation with friends. "I didn't score any points with my family when I told them I was not going to set up a medical practice—I was going to enter a monastery. They may have had problems with my decision, but I didn't. I believed God had had a hand in leading me there."

She graduated on a Thursday, and on the Sunday following, with her new medical diploma packed away, and, seeking to become a Benedictine nun, she left for the Abbaye Notre-Dame de Jouarre.

Still, as she had come closer to making that final decision, she had strongly realized that it is always very difficult to leave the world. The closer the moment comes, the less one wants to do it.

Yet, hard as it was to leave the life she had been used to, she would always say she really felt that a strong force was leading her away from the secular life. "I felt it was a true call from the Lord. The call is something you experience with a certitude that God is asking you to do this. It is linked to fulfilling God's will. You have been led to believe this is how you will get to God in a more assured way. The principle is that you're not saved alone. The people you meet and relate to are part of the mystery of salvation. Just as Christ was called by God to be the Messiah, we are similarly called, in a very specific way. Our vocation is a subdivision of that call to be one with Christ. God is the only one who can demand this totality. That is the meaning of the call, and if this motivation disappears, then there is no point in what you are doing", Mother Benedict explained.

"Saint Benedict, the founder of the Benedictine order back in the sixth century, appealed to me because he expanded the call by shaping the life", she added. "He said you had to have a particular place to be, so as to be faithful to the call, and the founding of monasteries came out of that. He saw that the daily life needed a liturgical component but also a communal aspect so that the relationships among members could develop healthily as each learned how to relate to the world while being separated from the world.

"Saint Benedict believed you leave the world to dedicate yourself to the salvation of the world. He has been called a 'spiritual architect', because he was somewhat specific in teaching how this would be done by those entering the monastery, writing a Rule that has been declared a masterpiece of common sense. He showed the way to deal with life's contradictions, pointing out the importance of order and moderation in all things, seeing the beauty in creation and having a reverence for all created things. He had a lofty concept of labor and believed every monastery should be a self-supporting economic unit. He saw each as a home of craftsmanship, and he revered nature and the land, seeing all of this as a ladder to the supernatural.

"For the type of call I had, it fit monastic history, unchanged from what Saint Benedict had started back in the sixth century. Yet, true to the spirit of Saint Benedict, while I was very traditional at the time I entered at twenty-five years of age, I understood that the way of tradition is to be open to both the past and the new that has to come in. We have to be open to both and find a way to blend.

Each generation has to rediscover the will of God in a new way. You can't copy what was done before."

Clearly Doctor Vera Duss was different from the other nuns at Jouarre, since few of them had much of an education, and certainly none of them had advanced degrees. She soon suspected her being there would bring something of a change to Jouarre, but as she put on the habit of a Benedictine nun, she had no way of knowing that within a few years a major change in her life would come from outside forces, from the clash of World War II. On that June 30, 1936, she was received by the Abbess and greeted no differently from any other young woman arriving to be a postulant (a candidate for admission) at the Abbey—except perhaps that the Abbess was a bit annoyed that the young doctor came on a Sunday at a time that was inconvenient for them.

"I arrived around twelve, and I was received at the official enclosure door. But I had to wait for the Abbess and Mistress of Novices because they were having lunch. No one had warned me when not to come. When they were ready, they greeted me, and I was given a habit—a simple black serge dress, and two capes, one that covered the shoulders and one covering the arms. For my head covering, there was a little black bonnet made of transparent lace and a black tulle, see-through veil. I was also given a white bonnet, which we had to wear when we were doing work like sweeping, and I was amazed that we had to put that on. It was not flattering. It was humiliating.

"The Mistress of Novices brought me to my room, a small, unheated cell. It had a cot with a straw mattress and wool blankets on a metal frame, a little sink with running water, a small pitcher, a shelf for books and a hook for hanging clothes. There was a prie-dieu (a kneeler), a sort of cupboard with a lower part for shoes and a diminutive chest of drawers for linens, like the wimple, handkerchiefs, stockings, towels and such. There was a cover on top of this that one could pull up, deep enough for a washbasin, glass, toothbrush, soap and any other personal items. The nuns were allowed one picture of their choice on the wall and a crucifix. My room also had a big window, from floor to ceiling, making the room very cold.

"I was told I would have to learn to conform to the bell, which controlled the daily around-the-clock schedule of when to rise, pray, eat, work and rest. The prayers were sung in the church, with the Sisters, behind the grille, since this was a cloistered order. The nuns were called to pray at eight periods in the course of twenty-four hours, chanting the Office, the required prayers for the order, with each time given a name—Matins, Lauds, Prime, Terce, Sext, None, Vespers and Compline. Now that I had joined them, I, too, would be awakened at 2:00 A.M. for the first prayer, Matins. The wake-up call was a ritual that never changed. One nun would be assigned to awaken the others, and she would have to remove the glass and light the wick in her lamp, passing the flame on until all the lamps were lit. Each nun had to take her little lamp with her to see where she was going. The lamps would be put on a table, and the flames extinguished until prayer was over, and then they would be lit again for the return to our rooms.

"Then we had to rise at 6:00 A.M. for more prayer and then Mass. That was followed by a light morning meal, a cup of café au lait and a piece of bread, exactly two ounces, which was taken standing up. The coffee was served in big basins, prepared with the milk and sugar in it. The nuns each had a ten-ounce cup, which they took turns filling with a ladle. Each nun could have one cup of coffee, never two. Sometimes we had a little butter and a piece of cheese. It was a little skimpy for me, as a doctor, and especially as an Anglo-Saxon! By nine in the morning, about all I could think of was food! The noon and evening meals always had two dishes, both vegetarian, one of them a soup. Meat was almost never served.

"One day I was asked how I knew that it was just two ounces of bread served in the morning. I answered that I knew because I was the one who weighed the bread, which were pieces cut from crusty French bread, leaving plenty of crumbs. I told the Sister that having to weigh the bread was my cross. She asked why. And I said I was so hungry that I would have done anything to eat those crumbs. I always had a big pile of crumbs when I was done, and I had to give the crumbs to the chickens! I really had to hang on to that table, I was so hungry. Five minutes after a meal I was still famished and ready to start over, and that condition lasted for a long time. But this was a reality that enforced and confirmed what I knew to be necessary, and I was not offended.

"There were some funny things that happened at mealtimes. I still smile when I think of the day Sister Telchilde was sitting next to me in the refectory. Suddenly, she was totally frozen, staring at her plate. There in her salad was a worm. Without bringing any attention to what was going on, I took the culprit off her plate!

"When it came to after-meal cleanup, everyone took care of her own dishes. Then there was what was called a 'Great Silence' after lunch. It was recommended that we did not choose that time to discuss business or problems. It was actually very refreshing to have this daily bit of free and quiet time."

Vera learned she was not alone in living this difficult daily ritual. Everyone had work to do. Jouarre was a complete

five- or six-acre farm, with cows and a poultry yard. Some
worked on the farm, some at bookbinding, and one nun
made communion hosts. Vera asked to work in the yard,
taking care of vegetables, and received permission, which
made her very happy because she needed to be outside.
The outside work was done in the morning. The bell rang
at 12:00 for Sext (noon prayer), and after that, lunch was
served in the refectory. After lunch, and a free period, they
all went back to work.

"I usually did historical work then, from 2:15 to 4:30. I
had been assigned to work on a history of Jouarre. Twice a
week music classes were held in this afternoon time. Singing made me very happy. I had a distinctive voice that was
noted, but not very much appreciated by the Community", Mother Benedict recalled. "I had been given work
that required writing, but it was difficult to write in my
cell in the winter months. My room was so cold that I
would have a woolen blanket around my legs, and sweaters
and shawls to try to stay warm. To keep my fingers from
getting numb, I had to wear mittens while trying to hold a
fountain pen and write!"

The bell rang for Vespers at 4:30 for a half hour of
prayer and meditation. Just before Vespers, the nuns could
have a snack, a little bread. That would hold them over
until supper, a lighter meal than lunch. This meal was
served at 6:00 P.M. Recreation was obligatory after supper.
The nuns then did craft work or some other task that was
their responsibility. The kitchen would then send them
vegetables to peel, but nobody seemed to mind, doing the
work willingly.

At this time, she was stilled called "Miss Vera", since
postulants are not called "Sister" until after they are "clothed"
and become a "novice".

The way the monastery worked, a woman entering the order was initially a postulant and placed on a brief "probation" period. Then she would take first vows, binding for three years, and would be called "Sister". After three years, she could renew her temporary vows for three more years. However, one could be professed, meaning she could take final vows, earlier if the Abbess determined she was ready, and once professed, her vows would be permanent. She would also from then on be called "Mother".

The time sequence made sense to Miss Vera because she knew no one was obliged to stay in this life. Each one had to make sure she was called to do this, and that meant the human psyche had to be fully ready and able to take on what was required for this particular religious life. That is not a preparation that takes place overnight.

After six and a half months as a postulant, Miss Vera was invested as a novice on January 7, 1937, and given the name Soeur Benoît (the French words for Sister Benedict).[2] The ceremony begins with the petitioning nun wearing a white wedding gown, symbolizing her marriage to God. During the ceremony, the nun leaves to have the gown removed, and she is then clothed as a novice, in a simple black habit, with a white veil. It would be a year later, on January 11, 1941, before Soeur Benoît would take her first vows.

While Miss Vera was still a postulant, Abbess Madame Angèle Bontemps had approached her, telling her that she was being assigned to be the physician for the Community and in charge of the infirmary. This was revolutionary, for novices were never given such authoritative responsibilities. This was not an assignment Soeur Benoît would have chosen, for it pointed out how different she was from the other nuns, most of whom had a minimal education, as was the usual situation for women in those times. She knew it would put her in a delicate position and that she'd probably be caught between obedience to her Abbess and the need to honor professional secrecy of the nuns who would no doubt confide in her. She also knew that giving her this position of authority would create conflicts between the Abbess and the pharmacist, Mother Scholastique. "That venerable nun had been the pharmacist for forty years at that time, in charge of doling out medications, and she was hardly willing to have a novice come along and tell her what to do. So what if this novice was a physician. The question here was authority, not education, skills or competence. But I won her over, and we had a very good relationship", Mother Benedict recounted. Mother Scholastique endured and kept her position as pharmacist until her death at eighty-seven.

"My challenge was complicated by my concern that it would be enormously difficult to be the Community doctor for the some one hundred women at Jouarre and at the same time be a good postulant and novice. I wondered if there might be some jealousy, but I put that worry aside. My responsibility as a doctor was to be faithful to the Hippocratic Oath, and nothing would change that, not even if it meant I had to speak authoritatively to the Abbess. From the very beginning, I was put into a most difficult position, as the nuns would come to me and talk endlessly about their problems. I had such an unusual life, being the medical authority. It was my job to recognize both medical and psychiatric problems and prescribe help. I really tried. I nurtured them; I took care of them. But being responsible for the sick, and still having to do my work, took a toll.

"Looking back, I can honestly see where it was hard to adjust to life at Jouarre. With my medical background, however, I was prepared to take whatever happened in stride. I never wavered, though I wasn't always comfortable or happy in a human sense or enjoying it. But I have a natural sense of peace, and it doesn't topple too easily."

Then, someone new to her, but known to the others, came to Jouarre. She was Mother Mary Aline Trilles de Warren, a beautiful, energetic woman who had been temporarily away to aid another monastery and now returned to Jouarre. Soeur Benoît had no way of knowing, of course, that this nun would become her dear friend and play a crucial and lifelong role in her destiny.

Chapter 4

FRIENDS AND ENEMIES

— Enter Mother Mary Aline
— Life at Jouarre
— World War II Begins, 1939
— The Chaos of the Early War Days
— Return to Jouarre

The arrival of Mother Mary Aline back at Jouarre in early 1938 was an event. No one of the one hundred-plus nuns there could have ignored the grand reentry to the Abbey of this woman, who, at age thirty-four, was now at the height of mature beauty, carried herself with a nobility and grace and, above all, was an individualist. It was no secret that before she came to Jouarre, ten years earlier, she had wanted to be an actress, and though she was a devoted nun, she somehow managed to keep her gift for the dramatic very much alive behind the monastery walls. She was a presence, and she was never ignored.

Born in Paris on April 19, 1904, to high-society parents, she was given the name Marguerite Marie Jane Louise Trilles de Warren.

Mother Mary Aline's first glimpse of Soeur Benoît was in the church on a Sunday. She was sitting next to another nun, Mother Christine, who related well to her. The two of them were looking at the new novice and comparing observations. She and Mother Christine, knowing that Soeur Benoît was a doctor, considered that a good sign. "It meant she had a certain brain", Mother Mary Aline later reflected.

The Abbey had a custom that on Sunday afternoons in the common room, the novices would go down the aisle to greet each person. Because of the "actress" in her, Mother Mary Aline was always aware of appearances. After Soeur Benoît passed, she noted, with Mother Christine agreeing, "She's a very pretty lady."

Mother Mary Aline and Soeur Benoît didn't immediately get to know each other very well, since, as physician for the Community, the young doctor had to spend so much time in the infirmary. The Abbess had probably debated this assignment from the time Doctor Vera Duss entered, but the catalytic incident was when one of the Sisters had an accident.

"She was very old and had fallen. She couldn't walk and said she had to go to the hospital for an X ray. The Abbess told me to look after her. That was my introduction to 'monastic medicine'", Mother Benedict recalled.

After that, with about one hundred nuns under her medical charge, the novice and doctor, who also had to do regular monastic duties required of someone new to the religious life, found herself continually busy. It surprised her how many nuns came to see her in the infirmary with complaints, and she got to know all of them very well in a short time. "I couldn't understand why they talked so much, since the nuns at Jouarre were not supposed to be very talkative," she said, "but my being there had a magical effect. I was someone they could freely speak to."

To help their new physician, the nuns actually fixed up the infirmary by putting in cupboards so she could organize medications. Their doing that for someone in the initial phases of religious life, as was Soeur Benoît, was very unusual. The discipline of the enclosed life of those days literally required that deprivations and hardships be accepted daily fare for one in "training" for monastery life. The young doctor and novice soon saw that her coming must have been a breath of fresh air for the Community.

Before long, however, Soeur Benoît began to understand that the medical complaints and emotional problems pouring out of the Jouarre nuns were indications that the old style of monastic life for women was in crisis. Certain things had gradually been overemphasized, and some reform was needed to restore balance to the life, particularly in the area of individual, human development. Later, she was to find that even the chaplain, Canon Laffray, knew this, a knowledge that put him "on the edge of despair".

"He was a remarkable man, very learned. He understood the qualms the Community would have in changing times, and he wanted to make sure he responded in depth to the reality of these changes. We had two conferences a week with him, and he would talk about contemporary events. He gave us the world news", said Mother Benedict.

"And times were certainly changing, but religious life was still ruled with an older mentality, a me-and-God exclusiveness. It was no wonder that I was seeing so many emotional problems. The enclosure creates an isolation that can be a pressure cooker. A balance can be created with cordial relationships within a community. But if someone doesn't like you, the pressure of this containment is severe, and you can't succeed in trying to be indifferent to something like this. The rule was you couldn't seek to have friends, because you would fall into the temptation of taking care just of your own needs. No wonder the nuns began to look for help and sympathy from me, their doctor. A community atmosphere must allow for communication. That gives people the possibility of psychological and emotional wholeness and responds to the human need to be integrated in a network of inclusiveness. At Jouarre they had not yet reached this new birth of consciousness."

One of the nuns who came to consult frequently with the Abbey physician was Mother Mary Aline. It soon was clear to Soeur Benoît that Mother Mary Aline had her own private agenda for wanting to get close to her, and it had to do with the fact that the novice-doctor was an American. This vital French nun had always been attracted to America. She had never visited America, but she dreamed of going there.

She liked Americans, and when she saw Soeur Benoît at her Abbey, that whetted her appetite to pursue her dream to one day come and settle in America. She was always clear in what she was hoping for. She always believed the American novice was a God-given gift to her, and she paid no attention to Soeur Benoît's insistance, trying to make Mother Mary Aline understand that she had no intention of ever leaving Jouarre and going back to America.

The older nun never gave up, and steadily, a relationship grew between these two women, based on an honest and deep-felt mutual respect. Both were intelligent and well educated; both had superb diction, a great aptitude for language, a love for theater arts, a decided sense of humor and a certain pride in appearance, insisting that persons, including nuns, should always look their best. Both were offended when they found a lack of compassion in others, and they equally detested a spirituality, sometimes encountered, that would make a monastery an ugly, austere place.

Two personalities, however, could not have been more different. Soeur Benoît tended to be soft-spoken, quiet, never out to get attention, obedient, open to others, willing to listen to another's viewpoint, calm and well-balanced. Mother Mary Aline had a flair for the dramatic in everything she did. She had a stately walk, and she made a complete sweep of a room, like a ceremony, when she entered. She was absolute in her beliefs, and, when she spoke, this became the most important thing at that moment for anybody to hear. She also had a temper that would sometimes escalate into a tirade before she calmed down.

What these two women had most in common, though, was a genuine and profound vocation to the religious life. They had found themselves called to be available to God, for whatever purpose He wanted, and both had said yes. Their search for God had led them to a Benedictine monastery, where they could participate in community, in a continual discovery of God's love and in how to bring awareness of Divine love to others.

Just as Soeur Benoît could trace the seeds of this vocation to her childhood, so could Mother Mary Aline. In her youth, she had been very close to a Benedictine abbot who recognized she had a vocation, not to acting, but to the religious life. One day he told her, "You were born with a cowl" (a special Benedictine choir garment worn on certain occasions by professed members of the community).

In those days, arbitrary penances, hardships, deprivations, humiliations and other tough measures for transforming a young woman into a professed and total lover of God were certainly an established part of the formation process at Jouarre and other monasteries. But Mother Mary Aline and Mother Benedict later affirmed that these didn't make the nun downhearted or sad-looking. "No. There was certainly a great joy, and a great uplifting—spiritually speaking— doing those penances with the right spirit. And no one was afraid of doing them. You cannot say it's very enjoyable to be flat on the floor, eat your soup in the middle of the refectory or kiss the feet of the Sisters. But there was no sadness. I think in a way, on the contrary, you had a kind of realization of yourself, that by your willingness to cooperate with the love of God, you were doing something for Him, Who had suffered so much for us. I don't think our personalities were diminished. Not at all. I will say that we were stronger, in a way", Mother Mary Aline once told the Sisters at Regina Laudis.

To get some idea of the rigors of the life at Jouarre, one could consider the conditions under which the nuns had to do their work. In the summer Jouarre was very hot, and in winter the temperature was very cold. The only way the monastery was heated in the cold weather was by coal stoves, and to save money, the nuns had to buy their coal in July or August, when the price was very much cheaper. Also to save money, the nuns didn't buy bagged coal; they bought it by the truckful, but they still couldn't afford to have it unloaded. This meant they had to move the coal into the monastery themselves. The added complication was that the truck and the driver couldn't come inside the enclosure of this cloistered monastery. So the nuns had come up with their own system.

The truck would come right up to a little door outside the enclosure. The nuns would have big baskets piled up by that door. The strongest nuns would be recruited for this task, which began with the man in the truck filling the baskets one at a time, giving each one to two of the Lay Sisters.[1] These were members of the Community who were not strictly cloistered and had permission to be outside the enclosure; they did much of the garden work and were a liaison with people outside the monastery. The two Lay

Sisters then opened the door to the enclosure, passing the heavy, filled baskets of coal to the Sisters inside, who made a chain, moving the baskets along until all the coal got to the storage room. As Mother Mary Aline explained, "So you had to have two strong Sisters outside to take the thing from the man. Then fairly good strong people to make a chain. Then two very strong ones who were on top, who had to throw the contents of the basket as high as possible to make the pile of coal. I was one of those strong persons at the top of the thing."

This work would begin at ten in the morning and finish about late afternoon, and always, this would turn out to be a sweltering July or August day. To make matters more uncomfortable, the nuns had to work with their veil partly down, to cover their faces, should the man happen to get a glimpse of them. "I assure you," Mother Mary Aline said, "if really the love of God wouldn't have been rooted in our souls, we would never have done this. Never. This was really one of the hardest jobs we ever had to do."

If anything bothered her, Mother Mary Aline was not one to keep it inside herself. She loved to read and was a zealous note-taker. At Jouarre, the nuns never had writing pads, but she'd manage to find numerous sheets of paper and was always writing something down. She communicated by passing notes to the others. At the end of the cloister, there was a big stairway, and it was very drafty. Soeur Benoît would find notes on the corner of the railing, always some information Mother Mary Aline thought she should see, and always going back to the same subject—America. She never stopped talking about going to America.

Disturbing winds started to churn in France in the summer months of 1939. Word of Hitler's military activities had gotten around, making people nervous about what

Germany was really up to. On September 1, 1939, they knew. Germany had invaded Poland. Two days later Great Britain and France declared war on Germany. By May 1940, Germany began a lightning sweep across Belgium, crossing into France. France had constructed an elaborate defensive barrier in northeast France, called the Maginot Line, as a permanent defense against a German attack. Unfortunately, the line covered the French-German frontier, but not the French-Belgian border. The Germans came into France via Belgium, making the acclaimed Maginot Line defense useless and bringing great jeopardy to the French population.

With Germany at war with France, Soeur Benoît's mother Elizabeth Duss became even more of a liability at the Abbey at Jouarre, for she was an outspoken defender of Hitler, much to the embarrassment of her daughter. Soeur Benoît soon found herself in a very unusual position when Jouarre was made into a temporary French Army hospital, with herself as the twenty-nine-year-old nun and doctor in charge. It became well known that an American was a nun at Jouarre, a visibility that would put her in immense jeopardy later when the Americans joined the war. The Germans, then occupying France, considered all Americans in France to be enemies and ordered the Gestapo to smoke them out for an unknown fate.

In these first days of September 1939, World War II had begun and never again would life be the same for anyone, especially Sister Benoît of Jouarre.

⚜ ⚜ ⚜

When the Germans invaded France suddenly and unexpectedly, bypassing the Maginot Line, they descended upon the surprised French regiments near the Line and quickly took soldiers and officers alike as prisoners. The word spread quickly, and the French people had a feeling of having been betrayed, as fear permeated the inhabitants of the country, now so vulnerable to the destruction of another war. The nuns at Jouarre were especially conscious of the danger of their position because of the location of their monastery. Being situated southwest of the Marne, directly in the path historically taken by German invaders, the Abbey was said to be located on a battlefield.

Because of this, a long-ago pact had been made between Jouarre and the French state that in the event of war, half the Abbey would be taken to be made into an army hospital. Honoring this agreement, in late 1939 the Abbess marked off the novitiate, the refectory, the kitchen, the cellars, the pharmacy and a small chapel called Our Lady of the Seven Dolors for the making of the hospital. Soeur Benoît was chosen to head the hospital. Her staff included all the nuns who had degrees as nurses, and a contingent of medical people from the French Army, including a physician, five Army nurses and a number of male workers and attendants. The first French soldiers needing care totaled about thirty. The war was definitely heating up, and the times were looking ever more dangerous.

The nuns at Jouarre tried to keep up a semblance of normalcy, but many of them found it difficult to sleep. When it began to look as if the Germans might actually come to Jouarre and occupy their Abbey, the nuns began working at night, trying to find places to hide their most precious belongings—vestments, archives and books. Mother Mary Aline worked mostly in the kitchen in those first months of the war, and Soeur Benoît worked very long hours in the makeshift hospital. She was so efficient that the French

Army doctor assigned to the hospital actually left to work elsewhere, saying that because of the medical expertise of the young nun, he was not needed; she could take over completely.

On the night of June 9, 1940, Soeur Benoît was having difficulty sleeping. She saw a glow of lights and heard a lot of noise, seemingly coming at them all at once. Not knowing what was actually happening made her very uncomfortable. The next day they learned that the noise was coming from French Army tanks, passing through Jouarre as they hastened toward Paris. The word was that the Germans were about fifty miles behind them. A French Army major stationed in the town arrived unexpectedly at the Abbey and gave the hospital an order to move immediately, a sign that the situation was very serious and dangerous. And the nuns were told they, too, had to leave the monastery without delay.

It was impossible for one hundred nuns to leave all at once. The Abbess divided them into several small groups. They were all supposed to go to Normandy, where the Community could rent a big house and stay until it was safe to come back. She herself wanted to be the last to leave, and because she had a heart condition, she wanted Soeur Benoît to stay with her. Her plan was to try to reconnect with some of the other nuns in a day or two, probably in Paris. Meanwhile, on their last day at the Abbey, the Community opted for normalcy.

In the midst of the bombs, which they could now hear exploding regularly, the Community went on with plans to celebrate the Golden Jubilee of one of the nuns, Mother Dominique, and the consecration of another, Mother Telchilde. Soeur Benoît was happy to see the two priests who came to Jouarre for the celebration—Mother Dominique's brother, Father de Boissieu, and the Abbot of La Pierre-qui-Vire. Father de Boissieu had been her theology teacher when she was in early high school. He called her his "little theologian", which she had always found to be quite touching. This priest appeared to be unmoved by the dangers all around them, showing no anxiety and speaking of God and love from the heart.

The consecration was at eight in the morning. It was rapidly done by the Abbot, without any solemnity, but it had an impact on everyone there. At that moment, the Community was complete, but uncertainty lay ahead. By noon, some of the older nuns began to leave by car, and later, two or three more groups nervously and sadly left their Abbey. The visiting Abbot decided to take the young nuns from the novitiate back with him to La Pierre-qui-Vire, and they were excited over this invitation.

Now came an unexpected arrival of French soldiers. One of the men was unconscious. The hospital had already been dismantled, and Soeur Benoît quickly ordered the ill man placed in the chapel of Our Lady of Sorrows. She didn't know what had happened to him. He was in a state of shock, and his heart was completely erratic. There was no identification on him, and the other soldiers could tell her nothing. They said he had been running like crazy and collapsed when he reached them before he could say anything. She quickly began medical procedures to try to help him breathe more easily, but he was too far gone. Since the Abbot had not yet left, Soeur Benoît asked him to anoint the soldier, who was about to die. The soldier was buried right away in the Jouarre cemetery, with the assistance of the other soldiers. Years later his wife came to the Abbey. She had finally found out where his unit had been and was looking for information. "When I showed her the watch and the little articles I had found on him, she knew it was he", Mother Benedict related.

After the soldiers had buried the fallen man, Soeur Benoît asked them when they had eaten last and found out it had not been for days and days. They were literally starving. The healer in her then took over. She and another of the nuns, Sister Anne, made a kind of custard of eggs and milk, and Soeur Benoît ordered them to eat very slowly, a spoonful about every ten minutes or so, so that their starving bodies could accept the food. Meanwhile, knowing that she and the rest of the nuns were under orders to leave the Abbey, Soeur Benoît wanted to make sure these soldiers left before they did. These men were, in her words, "absolutely wild", perhaps from fright over what they had already gone through, and the nuns didn't want them left in their monastery without any supervision. Fortunately, the Abbey's telephone was still working, and so Soeur Benoît was able to call the nearby Army major, asking for help. He sent a truck, and the soldiers were taken away.

Before they left, Soeur Benoît asked them if they had fought the Germans. They answered that they had tried and then described how the Germans had started crossing the river, even though the bridge had been demolished. "It was no problem for them. In five minutes they had another bridge. And us? What could you do with a bare chest against a mechanized army? It's absolutely nothing you can describe, the impression it makes. Just this metal, and this fire, and this machine gun. So all you can do is survive, if you could", one of them said, pointing out that the French soldiers were just not in any way equipped to handle the Germans.

In relating this story, Mother Benedict said, "Jacques Maritain,[2] who had been in Paris when the war was declared, had used a very wonderful expression in a lament he later wrote from America after the fall of France. He said that there was an awesome beauty in the response of France. France knew it was in no way prepared, and could not meet this. And the Army as it left—in a sort of grim, desperate determination—was something awesome to witness. They just went, knowing what was going to happen. What could you do against an enemy that is armed up to the teeth, and you are not?"

That night, the few nuns who were left at Jouarre were surprised when two nurses and three officers suddenly came rushing right into the enclosure, expressing shock to find that some of the nuns were still here. They told them they had to leave that night. The Germans were coming in with their tanks, and anyone in the Abbey would be cannon fodder. Mother Mary Aline bargained for some more time so she and a couple of the other nuns could make sure the monastery was absolutely in order, and finally she was told they could stay, but only until five in the morning.

Soeur Benoît, meanwhile, had to leave because the Abbess, ailing from her heart condition, was set to go, and she was her physician. In the time she had left, she packed two suitcases, filled mainly with books, which she insisted she had to take with her, a Bible and volumes of Aristotle and Thomas Aquinas. Mother Mary Aline tried to lift one of the suitcases and put it down, complaining that it weighed a ton! She insisted Soeur Benoît couldn't carry them, but she did.

The plan was that Sister Domitille would drive the Abbess, Soeur Benoît, Mother Thérèse and Sister Gemma, a Lay Sister who was elderly and badly crippled with club feet, to the station at Coulommiers, where they would get the 8:00 P.M. train to Paris. When they arrived, however, the station was filled with people, but no train. They waited a while and then were told to try to find a place to spend the night. They knew a Catholic hospital was nearby because Soeur Benoît had met the Sisters who worked there. So Sister Domitille drove them there. The hospital, however, was already overcrowded with Army trucks and wounded people arriving. It was a pathetic scene of people walking without a destination, who had piled everything they could with their families in horse-drawn wagons, all of them looking like bedraggled refugees. It was utter confusion.

The Sisters at the hospital received the Jouarre nuns very kindly. They gave the four nuns one room with one bed, so at least the Abbess and Sister Gemma could lie down. Soeur Benoît and Mother Thérèse spent the night in chairs while trying to get some sleep. In the meantime Sister Domitille drove back to Jouarre to get Mother Mary Aline and the rest of the nuns. The plan was for her to drive them to Paris, where they would meet the others arriving by train. But since the nuns hadn't gotten on the train that night, they had decided that Sister Domitille would drive first to Coulommiers in the morning to find out what was happening with the train. On that drive back from Jouarre at five in the morning, the scene was alarming, with people walking away from the advancing Germans, refugees dragging belongings and their pigs, cows and ducks. One man, seeing the nuns in the car, called out, "Sister, there is no hope."

When the car arrived at the station at Coulommiers, the Abbess made a decision to have Sister Gemma trade places with Mother Mary Aline in the car. She didn't think Sister Gemma, who literally couldn't walk, would make it on the train. Whatever the delay, Mother Mary Aline found herself having to get to the train in a hurry, for it was about to leave. True to her dramatic bent, the nun saw a bicycle, grabbed it and got on, tearing a big hole in the bottom of her habit but reaching the train just as it started to move, jumping on to join her fellow Sisters. The only problem was that she had no luggage, since her suitcase, with her clean clothes and her fresh wimples, was still in the car. And for Mother Mary Aline, looking bandbox clean and fresh was a priority. But this was war, and she was philosophical. Besides, she had been thinking ahead, just in case something happened to the suitcase, and she had, for insurance, put a clean wimple in her pocket!

Mother Mary Aline had teased Soeur Benoît about her suitcases, and heavy as they were, amazingly, Soeur Benoît had gotten them on the train. "This was the last train that went from Jouarre to Paris. And then, while en route or upon arrival, the train was looted completely. You see, everybody's possessions were on that train, and some people knew that. In the panic of what was going on, those people seized and helped themselves to whatever they liked." Apparently, the looters weren't interested in the Bible, Aquinas and Aristotle, because three months later, a newspaper ad said that people who had lost luggage could come to a certain station and reclaim whatever of theirs was there, and Soeur Benoît recovered most of her books.

The arrival of the train in Paris was another entry into chaos. The nuns were, in effect, refugees, not knowing where they would find shelter. They hoped to be able to stay at the monastery of the Missionary Benedictines of Vanves, expecting they might be accepted because the foundress had made her novitiate at Jouarre. Everything was in a state of confusion, with crowds of people waiting in front of the station for a taxi. Finally, one taxi took the five nuns, with another group that had also piled into the cab, and it headed in the direction of Vanves. They didn't get very far when the driver stopped and let them out.

As coincidence would have it, at that moment, who was driving by but Sister Domitille in the monastery car, with Sister Gemma, several other nuns and a lay woman, Madame Mitre, Mother Thérèse's mother. They were on their way to Normandy, where the Community had rented a house. Mother Mary Aline was happy because now she could retrieve her luggage, but after some shuffling of suitcases, she came away with the wrong one. At least it was a lighter one, she would say later, keeping her sense of humor. Madame Mitre asked if she could join them so as to stay with her daughter, and the Abbess agreed. As Sister Domitille started to drive off, each group sadly said good-bye, and they expressed hopes of being back together again soon at Jouarre.

The nuns managed to get another taxi to Vanves, and by the time they got there, the Abbess was suffering terribly from car sickness, with Soeur Benoît not immediately able to help her. They were graciously received, but they were not welcomed because the nuns themselves were packing to leave. Everyone wanted to get out of the path of the advancing Germans. The group was invited to stay one night, and they gratefully accepted. They hoped to be able to get to the Sisters of Saint Joseph of Cluny the next day. Some of the Jouarre nuns had gone there. But the group couldn't make contact with them by phone, and they couldn't get transportation. The nuns still at Vanves said they had heard that all the nuns at the covenent in Cluny, including those from Jouarre, had gone to the south of France. The Abbess of Jouarre and her group decided to get to the station, where they could get a train and head south. The Abbess wanted desperately to get in touch with her own Community members.

That station was called La Gare d'Austerlitz, and they had to take the Metro to get there. Soeur Benoît, who knew

Paris well, suggested they get off the Metro before the station, knowing the station would be impossibly crowded, and this would be a better way to get through. They walked along the Seine, and then their hearts dropped. The station was filled with thousands of people, "just piles of them ... and the whole place was just packed with soldiers."

There was a large garden called Le Jardin des Plantes, which Soeur Benoît knew well, near that station. In her premed year, the school laboratory was contiguous to this garden, and the medical students used to go there often. This day, it all looked so different. She inquired of someone how they could get into the station to get a train. She was told to get in, one had to have a military permit. Now they were really stuck—that is, until Mother Mary Aline volunteered to go the Army headquarters and get a permit. The place to which she had to go was a huge, palatial structure called Les Invalides, built by Louis XIV and housing Napoleon's tomb under the cupola. The general who headed all the military operations was based in that building, and going there was a formidable venture for the usually cloistered nun.

Soeur Benoît would have gone with her, except for the Abbess, who kept her physician practically bound to her. Soeur Benoît couldn't leave her for a minute. If the Abbess didn't see her, she'd be asking, "Where is she? Where is she?" Her fear was understandable, for the Abbess had never traveled by herself.

So Mother Mary Aline went alone, running first to the subway, only to find no subway trains were running. She rushed on foot to Les Invalides. She found it to be well guarded, with two soldiers standing like sentinels on either side of the grille. In order to enter the small gate by the grille, one had to have the password. As Lady Abbess later recounted, Mother

Mary Aline didn't have the foggiest notion what the pass-word was, so, ever the actress, she just straightened up, looked at them as though she were at least a general and passed through, walking firmly, in a military way.

Her adventures within this huge place later became memories by which to entertain others. She first had to convince a young soldier, about twenty-five years of age, that she was most serious about her need to see a general. Finally, when she got to see a decent, old, typical white-haired general, he told her he had absolutely no power anymore and that the paper she wanted was useless. She said, "I'll take it anyway. It's a paper. It's something."

Before she left, she asked him, "Is Paris going to be an open city? Because if it is, there is no reason for us to leave." She never forgot his response. The general looked at her with his eyes completely open, big tears streaming down his face, and said he could not say anything, anything at all. She knew then they had to leave Paris.

When Mother Mary Aline arrived back at the garden with the permit, the nuns fought hostile crowds trying to move through the sea of people to get close to the station. A man was there saying, "The trains are filled. No one can get in." He saw the nuns with the paper and wouldn't even look at them. They had to take a different tack. They saw that the only doors that were clear were the exit doors and decided they had to find a way to enter through one of these exit doors, not an easy task. Leading the others, Soeur Benoît and Mother Mary Aline went to an exit door, which was being guarded by a reserve soldier. He wasn't going to let anybody get in a door that said "exit".

He had never before had to deal with a Mother Mary Aline, who wouldn't take no for an answer, not when she had a pass. She finally convinced him that she and her sister nuns absolutely had to be on a train, even if it was all filled. They started through the exit doors, but the officer got somewhat hysterical when he saw Madame Mitre going with them. The pass was only for nuns, he shouted. Mother Mary Aline shouted louder, "She's the mother of the Mother!" and the five of them got into the station through the exit door, leaving the baffled officer behind. Once inside, their path was blocked again by the sheer numbers of people. They had no choice but to wait for a later train and go to a different destination. At three in the morning, they were finally on a train bound for Tours.

Tours hadn't been hit yet by the Germans, and so it had the appearance of normalcy. When they arrived, they were able to take a bus to go to a place called Rochecorbon, about seven miles away. Since the age of fifteen, Sister Benoît had known a priest there, Canon Alexandre Le Goff, who was pastor in a village where she used to spend vacations. His housekeeper was Marguerite Legras, also a friend from her younger days. Madame Legras and her husband, Camille, who had died in 1931, had been something like surrogate parents to young Vera and her brother John, when they were children on vacation. Both Canon Le Goff and Madame Legras had come to Vera Duss' clothing at Jouarre and expressed how proud they were of her.

But on this day, when they saw four nuns and a laywoman standing there, they were concerned. The news was that the Germans were coming anytime now, and they felt this was not a safe place to stay. Yet their hospitality was great, and the visitors stayed two days, enough time to do their laundry and to get some decent food, after so many days of living mainly on dry bread. They were also able to participate in Mass, and that gave them great joy.

Later that Sunday, Canon Le Goff told them he had found a place for them to stay in Tours, a school where they would be well received and cared for. The nuns got their luggage together and put it on a borrowed bicycle. Then they began their long walk, with Soeur Benoît and Mother Mary Aline taking turns pushing the bicycle. Toward late afternoon, there was a sudden air raid. The women fell prostrate into the ditches. Then a man came out of his house, telling the Sisters he had a natural cave in his garden and calling to them to come and take shelter in the cave. When the danger from strafing was over, the nuns and Madame Mitre left and continued their long walk.

They crossed the bridge and arrived at the cathedral in Tours as it was getting late. They didn't know where to go for the night, and the Abbess was exhausted from the walk. It was a warm night, June 16, and they decided the Abbess, Mother Thérèse and her mother could sit on the luggage near the cathedral, while Mother Mary Aline and Soeur Benoît checked out the institution to which Canon Le Goff had sent them. They passed the shrine of Saint Martin and arrived at the school, where they were met by the two headmistresses. It was an experience. The two of them were prim and proper and were hardly friendly. They wanted identification papers, and they kept looking at the shoes the nuns were wearing, rather rough work boots. It turned out that these two women had heard that German parachutists often disguised themselves as priests or nuns, and they just wanted to make sure Soeur Benoît and Mother Mary Aline were really nuns!

They said the nuns could stay the night, but in the morning, they themselves were leaving. There was a sense of déjà vu. In the morning, the nuns were refugees again. Fortunately, Canon Le Goff had come into town to check on them. He had a key to a very picturesque house that belonged to friends who had left, and he gave it to the nuns. Then he said that the Archbishop told him the Jouarre Sisters could go to the Convent of the Purification nearby, should there be any trouble. That very day, the first explosion came just as the nuns were getting settled in the house—and Soeur Benoît was taking a much-anticipated bath. She hastily dried herself and dressed, and all of them rushed to the convent, leaving their belongings behind in the unlocked house.

It turned out the whole neighborhood was converging there because the convent had a safe area, an enormous Roman brick cellar connected to the convent by a long corridor. The room was massive, with very high, vaulted ceilings. It had the feel of an old basilica, and entering it was like going into a crypt. But once there, it was astounding. The nuns and about one hundred people, adults and children, settled there, with their mattresses and a few possessions. The nuns were each given a chair. The room also had an altar and relics and the Blessed Sacrament. Each morning the chaplain came to say Mass.

In the convent cellar, a radio was played constantly, and on June 17, 1940, they heard Marshal Pétain declare an armistice, and General Charles de Gaulle a call to arms. Pétain said, "It is with a heavy heart that I tell you we must halt the combat. Last night I asked the adversary whether he is ready to seek with us, in honor, some way to put an end to the hostilities." [3] De Gaulle countered, "This war is a world war. I invite all French officers and soldiers who are in Britain or who may find themselves there, with their arms or without, to get in touch with me. Whatever happens, the flame of French resistance must not die and will not die." [4]

Not all the French people were pleased with Pétain. As Mother Benedict explained, "Marshal Pétain agreed to an 'honorable' armistice. And as you know, with the Nazis there was no such thing as an honorable armistice. So it was a very morally degrading and humiliating kind of thing."

Yet the news of the armistice, which in effect was a surrender, allowing the Germans to occupy France, gave everybody the hope that the fighting had stopped. Indeed, Tours was now quiet; there was no more noise from firebombing; and so, after three days, people left their cellars and came back out into their world. Likewise the Sisters then left the shelter of the convent.

The group of four nuns and "the mother of the Mother"—as they kept referring to Mother Thérèse's mother—started back to the house owned by Canon Le Goff's friends, where they had stayed briefly before the attack. They wanted to collect their belongings, which fortunately were still there, and try to find a way to head back to Paris. After they packed, Mother Mary Aline and Soeur Benoît brought everything out of the house. The street was completely empty, but suddenly, seemingly out of nowhere, there stood a German soldier. Mother Mary Aline noticed he was wearing a little cross, and she thought perhaps he was a chaplain. He bowed to the two of them.

Later they would learn that the goal of the Germans when they arrived in France was to be extremely friendly to try to get France completely on their side and, of course, turn them against de Gaulle. That friendliness lasted only a few months.

The German soldier said "*Bonjour*" to the two nuns, who remained silent. The others had now joined them, and they had planned to walk back to the shrine at Saint Martin's. They had learned that some Benedictine nuns from La Rue Monsieur, a large monastery in Paris, had been put up in a building near Saint Martin's, and they wanted to see them.

No sooner were they on their way than they saw the German Army entering on the main street in Tours. The soldiers marched about ten abreast, and they were singing, tauntingly, over and over, "France was not defeated; it was sold."

"It was obviously a sort of display. You couldn't cross that street. First the Army went by and then after that the trucks, one after another. It was really to impress the people—who had just really lost any kind of hope", reflected Mother Benedict later. When the group was finally able to move on, they saw much destruction, houses and businesses destroyed, some still burning. To their surprise, they saw that the shrine of Saint Martin's and the convent had been completely spared from the fire, even though it was right in the middle of the destroyed and burning area.

At the convent, the nuns were taken to see the Sisters they were seeking. These nuns had been put in the attic, which was very large and neat. Six of them were lying in bed, obviously not in good physical shape. The place looked almost like a hospital ward. Their story was sad. When the news came that they had to leave Paris, with almost no warning, the group started out on foot and walked south. These women were not accustomed to that kind of exercise. They got as far as Orléans on foot, a distance of about eighty miles, before it became evident that some of them could not go on because of the condition of their legs and feet, which were swollen and bleeding. They had reached the train station, however, and a stationmaster took pity on them and put them on a freight car, which brought them into Tours. Somehow they made it to the convent near Saint Martin's.

Imagine their surprise and joy when they saw a physician! Mother Benedict would say in later years that she could not remember exactly what she did for them, but it must have been the best medical care possible given the circumstances. In 1964, she returned to visit them at their monastery in Paris. A few of them came up to her and thanked her for "helping me so much in Tours".

On July 12, 1940, after more than three weeks in Tours, the task ahead for the Jouarre group was to find a truck that could get them back to Paris. They were not at all sure whether they could go back to Jouarre because the rumors were flying now that the monastery had been bombed and burned and that the town there was suffering from the black plague. But if they could get to Paris, that was in the general direction of their Abbey, and that was where they intended to head. They had to go to German headquarters to get some help and were told that a man with a big, open truck was going to Paris, but he already had maybe twenty-five nuns ready to go with him.

At this point, the Jouarre group was now just four, all nuns, because Mother Thérèse's mother was no longer with them. A day or so earlier, her son, a priest, l'Abbé Raymond Mitre, having heard that his mother was in Tours, had traveled there on a bicycle from Paris, facing the German armies and other troubles, so as to join his mother and get her more comfortably back to Paris. The four nuns had a great visit with this buoyant young priest, especially Mother Thérèse, who didn't get to see her brother very often, and they were happy and relieved to hand over the responsibility of caring for Madame Mitre to her son. Without hesitation, they joined the other twenty-five nuns and got on the truck heading for Paris, sitting on some of the boxes packed with their belongings. It was far from a comfortable ride, with bundles and boxes rolling back and forth. But a joyful moment came when they passed Chartres, for they could see the great cathedral. It had not been destroyed, as the rumors had indicated. It was standing!

They arrived in Meudon and were courteously driven by the truck driver directly to the cloistered monastery, which had once been a large, old seminary and was located to the northwest of Paris. They were greeted warmly and lovingly by the Abbess, who invited them to stay as long as they wanted. She had heard the terrible rumors about Jouarre and didn't think it was safe for them to return. "We stayed only two days at Meudon because everybody was anxious to get back to see if there was anything left of Jouarre", said Mother Benedict. They were delighted to hear that Paris had not been destroyed in any way.

The Jouarre group got to the city of Paris on July 14 and stayed at the apartment of some Oblates, lay people who work in the secular community but live according to the Rule of Saint Benedict, founder of the Benedictines. As a special treat, the nuns walked to attend Mass at the Cathedral of Notre Dame. Two days later, on Tuesday, July 16, 1940, the four nuns decided they would go back to Jouarre the same way they left, via Coulommiers. They took a train from Paris to that station, filled with people who had come back from the exodus. When they arrived at Coulommiers, the station was crowded with people who had stayed there during the invasion, coming to meet the train to see if any of their relatives were coming back. No one was there to meet the Jouarre nuns because no one knew they were coming back. They looked around and found a man with a car, who said he would drive them halfway. Jouarre was about eighteen miles from the station, but halfway was better than being stranded in Coulommiers. Mother Thérèse got the man to call Jouarre to see if someone was there who could bring a car to meet them where he would leave them off. To their joy and surprise, someone at the Abbey answered and sent a car to meet the Abbess and the other three nuns.

As the four of them rode toward their beloved Abbey at Jouarre, they could hear the ringing of the Angelus. Mother Benedict often spoke of the beauty of that evening, looking at the wheat growing, just at its peak, the combination of flowers in bloom and the sight of the impressive Abbey tower. But most moving was to hear the bells and know that some of the nuns were there. The reunion was incredibly emotional. Only four nuns were there, Mother Mechtilde, Mother Gudule, Mother Bénédicte and Mother Jeanne, but the happiness the eight of them felt at being together again and at "home" brought a prayer of thanksgiving to their hearts.

The nuns, however, weren't the only ones at the monastery. Jouarre was now occupied by the Germans, and the nuns, whose lives had been disrupted for thirty-six days by their forced evacuation from their enclosure and the ensuing radical change in the pattern of their religious life, had now to face new adjustments. German soldiers now inhabited their sacred space, and they had to learn how to live with this intrusion.

But the worst was yet to come a year later, when the Americans joined the Allies in fighting the German Nazis, who occupied France. This initiated a long period where it was dangerous to be an American in France—as Soeur Benoît, the American nun at Jouarre, was to find out.

Chapter 5

GERMAN OCCUPATION

— Life at Jouarre under German Occupation
— Village Doctor
— Mother and Daughter
— Opening a School

The nuns arriving back at their Abbey had heard the bells ringing and the birds singing and had felt a momentary surge of peace and sense of well-being, for they were home again. But their relief was fleeting. As the Abbess, all smiles, began to walk toward her monastery, Mother Mechtilde quickly stopped her, telling her they could not go into the Abbey because the Germans were living there and had not given them permission to return. The nuns could go in to clean, but not to take up residence or sleep there.

Mother Mechtilde began to cry as she told them about the garden, full of holes from the bombings. She had counted them and found eighteen craters from the bombs. Everything in this July garden had been destroyed. They would have nothing left to harvest or preserve for the coming winter.

The nuns had only one place to stay, the chaplain's house across the street from the monastery. They went there, trying to assess what their life would be like under the German occupation. Having supper together for the first time in five weeks, even for so small a number of them, gave them great happiness.

The next morning they went into their Abbey to see what had happened to their home since they had been forced to leave. What they saw both shocked and dismayed them. Their monastery had been trashed by the German soldiers and the people the soldiers had brought into the monastery for their amusement. Every personal belonging in each nun's individual cell had been pulled out, thrown around and handled. Bullet holes and shells were everywhere, indicating that if the nuns had stayed and not obeyed the order to evacuate, many of them probably would have been killed. The nuns later learned that after the second group left on June 11, French soldiers had taken over the Abbey. When the Germans from La Ferté came up the hill to the monastery, they began the bombing and the shelling. The French retreated, and the Germans came in. Fortunately, the bombing had been confined to the garden, and so there was no permanent destruction of the building.

The nuns found that the monastery had also been looted, and everything of value stolen, down to their supplies of candles, soap and even thread. But worst of all was the mess of dirty clothing, piles of shirts, stockings, jackets, underwear, sheets, towels and such, along with garbage filling the rooms and the corridors. From the soil on the napkins and tablecloths, and the undergarments thrown around, it was evident that sexual orgies had gone on here in this sacred place, and the nuns felt sickened. They began the arduous tasks of cleaning, throwing out the filthy trash and laundering the clothes and dirty linen. Laundering was the hardest task because, with their soap stolen, what they had to use in its place was a kind of pumice, or rough lava, a white powder they had found in barrels that was used by the soldiers for cleaning their machines.

After the first three days of cleaning, the nuns decided they should move back into their Abbey, and, without consulting the German soldiers, they did just that. At this time about thirty soldiers were occupying the Abbey. They had taken over the rooms in the novitiate—the quarters for the still-unprofessed Sisters—and so the nuns felt free to go back to the part of the monastery that was empty. Little by little, the rest of the nuns were returning to Jouarre, but it was clear that life would be far from normal with a war going on. Even to go into the garden required courage, since one could look up toward the novitiate and see the machine guns pointed toward them. The kitchen had to be shared with the Germans, who did their own cooking for fear of being poisoned. And then there were other reminders of the godlessness that had entered there. For instance, the nuns found one of the big, leather-bound breviaries on the Abbess' prie-dieu in the choir, purposely put there and opened to the first page. Written on it in German were the words: "It's better to have a good army than to say a lot of prayers."

Especially difficult for women who had chosen the cloistered life was to know that at any moment an uninvited man could enter their space. The nuns would be doing the laundry or cooking or cleaning, and suddenly behind them would appear two or three German soldiers. On one occasion, Mother Mary Aline and some of the older nuns were going up the staircase to go to the refectory when one of the Germans came down the corridor, completely naked. Without blinking an eyelash, they continued on as if he were invisible. But they didn't take this lightly. Mother Thérèse went to the commandant in charge of the soldiers at Jouarre and insisted the Germans couldn't do such a thing as walk around naked in a monastery. The commandant agreed. The soldier was punished, severely whipped with a whip having lead weights at its end. When the nuns found out, they were appalled. Never would they have reported this misdeed if they had known that the soldier would have been given so severe a punishment, one that could actually have killed him.

Soeur Benoît had been back at Jouarre only a month when she received a letter that shook her. It came from the American hospital in Paris telling her that her mother was very sick and that she had to come to the hospital right away to make decisions regarding her care. Elizabeth Duss had apparently been staying in Paris. Her daughter had seen her only once, in 1938, when Mrs. Duss arrived unannounced at Jouarre and demanded that her daughter leave and end the nonsense of becoming a cloistered nun. Angry and perhaps upset, Mrs. Duss had gone away from Jouarre after Soeur Benoît made it clear that this was her choice and her vocation, and nothing her mother could say or do would change her decision. Mrs. Duss had not stayed in touch with her daughter, but apparently she had stayed in Paris, and now, two years later, she was in serious trouble and had turned to her daughter for help.

Soeur Benoît hastened to Paris and was devastated when she saw how ill her mother was. It was even doubtful that she would survive. The American hospital referred her to another hospital, and Mrs. Duss remained there for the next five months, visited by her daughter whenever she could travel to Paris.

At the monastery as the summer wore on, the soldiers were continually something of an enigma to the nuns, as Mother Mary Aline later reflected in one of her memories of this time. She especially recalled one very hot, Indian summer October day. She and Mother Gudule were doing the laundry on that oppressive day. The laundry room had four little windows, and just outside these were two old benches. Two very young Germans, maybe eighteen or nineteen years old, came to sit there. They looked so innocent that the nuns left their work and went out to talk to them. Mother Gudule could speak German, and she asked them about their families. One of them pulled out some pictures, including one of a pretty, blonde girl who he said was his fiancée.

Spontaneously, Mother Gudule challenged him, asking since he loved this girl and wouldn't want her to be killed, why would he be willing to kill fiancées of French men? Suddenly his boyish face turned hard as a rock; looking at her icily and indicating the picture, he said, "If Hitler tells me to kill her, I will kill her."

Mother Gudule went on, "And would you kill your mother if Hitler said so?"

"My mother also", he answered.

Mother Mary Aline later commented, "He became stiff like an iron bar, and his face was like someone else. And really, Mother Gudule and I were terrified. Because we felt, really, that the devil had come into that boy. It was absolutely another person."

In the late fall of 1940, a great offensive was being planned by the British, and some of the German soldiers knew they would be sent to fight against this attack. One evening, Soeur Benoît was out by the farm where the chickens were kept when another German, this one also very young, came out to get a couple of eggs. Something about him touched her, maybe because he was crying. Mother Gudule was also there, and Soeur Benoît asked her to find out why the soldier was crying. She asked him in German what was the matter, and he answered, "We're going to England, and I know we won't get there. But we have to go. I know we're going to be killed." He was right. The nuns were to learn that no one came back alive from that offensive.

The exodus that forced people to leave their homes that June had severely altered not only life at the monastery, but life in the nearby town of Jouarre as well. Jouarre's major catastrophe was that all the doctors in and near the town had gone. Not one was left to care for the people there. The mayor himself was incapacitated, having lost a leg in the fierce battle that had taken place in Jouarre after the called-for evacuation. Like him, many people had chosen to remain in their homes rather than become refugees and had been in great danger when the Germans came with their bombs and guns.

One evening at about six o'clock, the acting mayor of Jouarre, accompanied by a woman, came to the Abbey and asked for Soeur Benoît. He said, "We know you're a doctor, and since there is not another one around, is there any way you can be permitted to come out? We have real problems on our hands, and we just can't do anything." They didn't want to interfere with her obligations to the Abbey, so he suggested they could come every evening at six o'clock to accompany her to town. A lady would always be present so she would never be alone. He asked, "Is this possible?"

Soeur Benoît responded that she would ask the Abbess, who, in turn, said that since the enclosure had not yet been reestablished, she thought Soeur Benoît could do this, if she got the Bishop's permission. She did, and Soeur Benoît began her daily work of being the town's physician now, in addition to being the Abbey's doctor.

Her main work was in the hospital, with visits to a leprosarium and a nursing home, both nearby. She established a dispensary where people could come for shots, made home visits and handled emergency calls as well as more routine medical care. Because she cared for so many people, she became very well known in the town, and later even beyond this area, as word got around about the beautiful young American who was a nun and a doctor at Jouarre.

Some cases required immediate action—like the woman who sought her out because she was hemorrhaging so badly. Soeur Benoît could see that she had an early case of cancer of the cervix and immediately got her transferred to a hospital in Paris where she could get proper treatment. The woman survived and many times in the coming years would go to the Abbey to see Soeur Benoît and thank her again for saving her life. "That became a real problem for me later when the Abbey was trying to hide me from the Gestapo, who were trying to find the American who was a nun and a doctor. She kept the memory of my presence alive in ways the monastery didn't particularly care for", said Mother Benedict.

Soeur Benoît wrote many a death certificate, too, in this period of being a village doctor, and these situations, where she felt the pain of families, taught her much about the endurance and faith of these people. In one case, she was called to the bedside of a man, the tavern keeper of Jouarre, who was deathly ill with cirrhosis of the liver. She had rarely seen a case so typical, and it was evident that he was going to die, probably that same night. She found the desolation of his wife and family and friends to be absolutely poignant. In the morning, Soeur Benoît returned and was taken to the bedroom where the man, indeed dead, was reverently laid out in the double bed shared by his wife. It was evident that his wife had slept beside him that night, and when Soeur Benoît arrived, the wife jumped up to receive her.

As Soeur Benoît made out the death certificate, she could not help but notice how composed the wife was. Somehow, in preparing her husband for his otherworld journey, and spending the night at his side, this woman had found a great source of strength, which gave her the ability to cope with her husband's death with an extraordinary matter-of-factness. Soeur Benoît sensed this was how these people had dealt with the death of a spouse for generations, so humanly, so simply. It touched her deeply.

After the regular doctor returned to Jouarre, Soeur Benoît's workload was scaled down, and she continued working mainly in the dispensary. Meanwhile, things were changing at the Abbey, especially after the British offensive in the late fall of 1940. The German soldiers were given orders to leave Jouarre, probably because they were being assigned to active duty rather than merely occupying a monastery, and so, by the end of the year, all of them were gone. The Abbey now belonged to the nuns once more.

The new year of 1941 began with a great sense of happiness for Soeur Benoît, for that month, with the Abbess' blessing, she was to take her final vows, making her permanently and fully professed as a Benedictine nun, who would from then on be called Mère Benoît. On the morning of January 21, all was ready for the ceremony. People from the village began arriving to attend the event. The gentle, quiet nun had been their physician, and they loved and respected her for the care she had given them. They wanted to be here for the great moment of her consecration. Because this was wartime, it would have been impossible for anyone from her American family to attend, and Soeur Benoît was saddened that her mother, still deathly ill in a Paris hospital, was also unable to be there. But one relative did come, her second cousin Yvonne Densmore,

Aunt Alice's daughter, and Yvonne's husband, Abel Luthy, who lived in Paris.

Within two weeks of her profession and consecration, the nun, who could now wear a cowl and a black veil and would be called Mère Benoît (later Mother Benedict), received another surprise, a call from the hospital in Paris saying that her mother had made a complete recovery and that she was to come and take her away. Mère Benoît put her problem right at the feet of the Abbess, who said, "Well, we'll take her in the monastery." They brought Elizabeth Duss, reduced by her illness to skin and bones, to Jouarre in February 1941. She was literally homeless and too weak to care for herself. The Abbess created a small apartment for her, and so Elizabeth Duss became a resident of the monastery for the next five years.

As her health improved, Elizabeth Duss settled into her new "home" at Jouarre. By late spring, the Abbess also gave Mrs. Duss a piece of land in the garden so she could plant flowers. Because she was out there so much, the Lay Sisters who worked in the garden got to know Mrs. Duss very well. She was very entertaining. Sometimes she would get food packages from friends with treats that she would share with them. One thing everybody agreed upon was that Elizabeth Duss brought her own energy to the monastery, and that in itself demanded attention. At times she made life very uncomfortable for her daughter, because Mrs. Duss was an outspoken defender of Hitler, a position that didn't sit well with those in the monastery who detested the official Vichy state under Pétain (which put half of France under German occupation) and who were solidly in the de Gaulle French nationalist camp.

With the nuns trying to get the monastery and their lives back on track in that late winter of 1941, now came another order, this time from the Bishop, telling the Abbess that she was to open a high school. Obediently obliging the Bishop, the Abbess started the school. The Community was in an uproar over this, believing that they had chosen the contemplative life and now were being forced to live the active life. For a few days, all of them would be in tears at the drop of a hat, but finally, bowing to obedience, they submitted to becoming teachers. Mère Benoît, who had asked to be assigned to teach philosophy, was instead, under protest, told she would have to teach science and math—this in addition to her duties as doctor.

Unknown to anyone at the time, having Mère Benoît in the school with children was to put her in a further position of jeopardy when, in December 1941, the Americans entered the war. All Americans in France were then declared "the enemy", forced to go into hiding, hoping no one would recognize them and betray them to the Gestapo. Now Mother Benedict was even more widely known, not only by the villagers she had cared for, but also by the children and parents who had seen her in the school. Frightening times were ahead of her as World War II continued to sear France with new wounds, and she, because of her American birth, would be a wanted fugitive.

Chapter 6

FACING DANGER AS AN AMERICAN
IN WAR-TORN FRANCE

— In Hiding
— Visiting Paris . . . and the Gestapo
— The Doctor Falls Ill

As soon as the declaration of war against the Germans had been made by the Americans in mid-December 1941, the Germans had posted huge signs throughout the country saying "All American Citizens in France Should Declare Themselves". This meant that Mère Benoît and her mother, as American citizens, were now automatically enemies of the Germans occupying most of France and, by their presence, were a threat to the Community. No one knew what would happen to Americans showing up to "declare themselves", but rumors were that many might be arrested. No one believed that the Germans, under threat by America, would respect any Americans who were in France and therefore under their control.

The nuns were unsure of how to deal with this very serious problem of having Americans inside their walls. Many of them were afraid for their own safety, and this made for a very uncomfortable environment for Mère Benoît. The Abbess, with the support of the Bishop of Meaux, Georges Louis-Camille Debray, decided that the two American women could stay at the Abbey, but they had to be in hiding. The Bishop also insisted Mère Benoît had to get a false identity card.

One of the nuns, Mother Jean Marie, had two brothers who were in the French underground. This nun was the grand-niece of a man who had been canonized in 1925, Saint Jean-Baptiste Marie Vianney, also known as the Curé d'Ars.[1] One of her brothers, Monsieur Vianney, worked at a boys' school in Paris and was an expert in getting false identification cards made. Mother Mary Aline took on the responsibility of getting the card made. She managed to get photos taken of Mère Benoît and went to Paris. There she was picked up by Monsieur Vianney, who had received a message from his sister that Mother Mary Aline would be arriving. When the false card was completed, Mère Benoît had a new official name, becoming "Mère Marie d'Assomption Trilles". It was Mother Mary Aline Trilles de Warren's idea to share her name, because, she said, there could be no doubt that Trilles was French.

Now days of torment had really begun for Mère Benoît. To be suddenly put in a position where no one really wanted her around, because they feared for their own safety, gave great pain to the thirty-two-year-old nun, who still had to carry out her duties as the Abbey physician and a fully professed nun. She had to watch constantly that no one other than the nuns would see her. Having been a doctor in the town and a teacher of the children, she was indeed very well known, and the nuns couldn't risk having word get out that she was still in the Abbey. To add to her pain, she was also told she could not sing with the Community. Lay people were always welcome to come to the church for certain prayers sung by the nuns in the choir. Mère Benoît had a very distinctive voice, and the other nuns feared she would be heard by someone who would recognize her voice and report to the German authorities that the American nun was still at Jouarre. This was an extraordinarily difficult penance for Mother Benedict, who loved to sing, believing that singing was the backbone of their communal life, the expression of what their work was about.

An added problem was Elizabeth Duss. Mère Benoît knew it was the height of imprudence to have her mother at the Abbey, especially since she was not one to be told how to act or behave. Both she and Mother Mary Aline, who remained her faithful friend, believed that the best strategy in dealing with Mrs. Duss was not to tell her that the Americans had entered the war. They knew she was a loose cannon and that if she found out the Americans were at war with the Germans, she would have "raised Cain to get to Hitler. She really would have. And it would have involved the monastery", Mother Benedict said. As an added protection for the Community, the nun-doctor-daughter made up a medical chart saying that Mrs. Duss had tuberculosis, a very serious, contagious disease at the time, and that she was in quarantine. The strategy was that should the Germans come to the Abbey looking for Mrs. Duss, they would not want to risk getting that disease and so would leave her alone.

The gossip in the town was that the American nun was really still at Jouarre, in hiding, and it made life a little more interesting for the people to speculate on whether she was or wasn't there. This meant that Mère Benoît had to be careful of her every move. She couldn't even be free to walk in the garden, she said, commenting, "I couldn't be here, and I couldn't go there. And if there was a workman in the house, I had to stay in my cell."

In spite of her strained position at the Abbey and her own health, which was deteriorating, Mère Benoît still carried out her duties of caring for the nuns, who came to her with ailments of one sort or another. One real problem was the matter of writing prescriptions for medications. She couldn't have her name on them, since the Abbey's position was that the American nun was no longer at Jouarre, so she developed her own system. She had gotten one of her doctor friends in Paris to sign a number of blank prescriptions, and then she would fill them in as needed.

Things got worse for Mère Benoît. Now the Abbess decided she had to change her name again and said she would be called Mère Hildegarde. Besides having to hide all day, every day, she had to wonder what identity to take on periodically. And she had to deal with the psychological problems being laid at the feet of the Abbey physician as everybody's nerves were getting more and more frazzled. It was a legitimate fear they were feeling because the enemy was in their own country; they knew they were not safe should the Allies begin to attack on French soil. It was hard for them to live every day with this constant threat of death, and their doctor understood.

Mère Benoît had little contact with her mother at this time, even though they both lived in the monastery. Because she had been ordered to stay in hiding, she would rarely go to her mother's apartment. She was virtually a prisoner in her own monastery. She was worried about her brother, too. She knew he had joined the U.S. Marines, but neither she nor her mother had heard from him. She prayed constantly that he would be safe on these turbulent seas of war.

Later they were to find out that Mother Benedict's brother had been on an escort aircraft carrier, the Bismarck Sea, *in the Pacific. It was sunk by suicide bombers in 1945. Most of his fellow crewmen died in the explosion that destroyed their ship or lost their lives because they panicked in the water. John Duss and about ten others managed to stay afloat by hanging onto debris and swimming. He would later say he worked to save his life. "He swam ten hours. How he ever did it, I'll never know. Finally an American ship spotted them in the water in the night. When they picked him up, the captain called his survival extraordinary. John Duss told him, 'Someone was praying for me.' Of course. You just don't survive that long under those conditions"*, Mother Benedict said.

In all the time that Mère Benoît had to remain in hiding at Jouarre, Mother Mary Aline kept up her agenda, which was consistent and insistent. She greatly admired America, and she kept telling Mère Benoît that she should go to America. Mother Mary Aline was really worried about her friend, especially as the war went on and the danger to Americans in France heated up. The whispering in the monastery was getting serious as the nuns became more fearful about possible repercussions should the Germans discover the American nun had never left Jouarre. Being an exile in her own home was taking a heavy toll on Mère Benoît, and she began to experience recurring illnesses. At times she couldn't work, so the Abbess had to bring in doctors from outside.

A crisis occurred in 1943 when Mère Benoît developed a terrible tooth condition, an impacted wisdom tooth, that gave her such excruciating pain that she paced her cell every night in agony, unable to sleep. The Abbess said there was nothing they could do about it. She couldn't send her out of the Abbey to a dentist. But after three weeks, Mère Benoît knew this had to be taken care of. Finally, the Abbess gave her permission to go by train alone to Paris to find a dentist. She was to stay with some Benedictine nuns who didn't know her. They were supposed to find a dentist, but Mère Benoît instead called on her friend, Doctor Françoise

Bonnenfant, to find one for her. Doctor Bonnenfant brought her to a young man who had left medical school to go into dentistry, and while he was very friendly and competent, he didn't know exactly how to fix her problem. Not knowing the nun was a doctor, he kept explaining to Doctor Bonnenfant what was going on. In the process, Mère Benoît would never forget how he broke all his American tools and left her too sick to go back to the Benedictine Sisters. Françoise took her back to her own apartment and cared for her. Ironically, this put Mère Benoît in the same building where some of the Gestapo were quartered, for Doctor Bonnenfant lived on the third floor of a four-story building where the Gestapo occupied the first, second and fourth floors. The two women stayed calm and cautious, and after a few days, Mère Benoît left her friend's place and took a subway to the train station. With a muffler covering most of her face, she boarded a train and returned alone to Jouarre.

In the midst of this new wave of worry about having an American nun at Jouarre, the Abbey received a canonical visit from Bishop Georges Debray of Meaux. Unexpectedly, he became deathly ill with fever from an acute inflammatory infection, something that had never happened to him before. Greatly agitated, the Abbess asked Mère Benoît to care for him. The latter had managed to get some medications delivered to the Abbey, among them some sulfa drugs. She knew these would cure the Bishop's illness. A day later he was feeling so much better, he began to express his immense gratitude and wanted to know more about this nun who was American and a doctor. When he heard of her painful position, to be the Abbey physician to her sister nuns while having to remain in hiding, he told her empathetically that this could not go on. In his few days of recuperation, Bishop Debray got to know and respect Mère

Benoît and became convinced that she had to try to find a way out of her impossible situation. Later, Bishop Debray became a "providential link" in helping Mère Benoît with her mission of starting a Foundation in America. She would credit his support as the crucial trust she needed for making the Foundation possible.

From her work of listening to the nuns as their physician, Mère Benoît was learning that the sense of vocation at Jouarre was not in harmony with the present state of society. Each nun was a person of unquestionable faith, according to her social milieu and background. She would never question what she had to do, and each believed that God, and not personal fulfillment, came first. But many were in turmoil, and Mère Benoît suspected this was because they were holding to values from a different world. All that God-emphasis didn't take care of needs on a different level. Those in authority had a lack of recognition of normal human needs, and absolutely no understanding of the importance of relationships, and "the Bishop was very aware of that", said Mère Benoît.

"As one example, all were told they had to love everybody in exactly the same way, which is impossible. You cannot love everybody the same way. I fought like mad against that—but I paid for it. I heard all the emotional disturbances the nuns were feeling from talking to them, but I had to keep all this to myself. When we entered Jouarre, the life was austere. We were the toughest monastery at the time. At Jouarre, we were only to obey. It was forbidden for anyone to stand up and say, 'I have an idea.' I was in a really difficult position. For a young, professional woman to stand against that aura was a burden." And Bishop Debray understood. He counseled her that this was an unfair assignment and compassionately encouraged her to seek a change.

Toward the end of 1943, Mère Benoît, realizing that the Abbess and all the nuns at the Abbey were becoming ever more fearful about harboring Americans because it put them in such a dangerous situation with the Germans, decided it would be a good idea if the Abbey could say she had left France. The strategy she came up with was to write a postcard to the Abbey saying she had passed through the line and was going to Spain, leaving from there by boat to get back to the United States and to her family in Florida. She wrote the card, saying, "I am safe. I am going to Florida." She had friends at Tain l'Hermitage in the Rhône Valley and knew that at her request they would mail the postcard from there back to the Abbey. She gave the postcard to a trusted Abbey guest to mail for her.

That turned out to be a wise strategy, because on April 21, 1944, "Miss Vera Duss" received a summons from the Gestapo that she was to appear in person at Rue de Saussaies, their infamous headquarters in Paris, on such and such a day, at such and such a time. At the Abbey they couldn't come up with a definitive explanation for how the Gestapo had found out about a Vera Duss being at Jouarre. They knew the Gestapo had taken possession of the American Embassy; possibly they had found her name in the file. There was also a worry that a man in town had informed the Nazis that an American nun was at Jouarre. The nuns had received this information from their gardener, Monsieur Naville, who was with the French underground. He reported to the Abbey that one man in the village had said, "Vera Duss is in the Abbey. I'm sure she is. *J'aurais sa peau*", which means in English, "I will have her skin."

The Community was in shock. The Abbess was flustered and sent for Mère Benoît, saying over and over, in consternation, "What are we going to do?" One thing they knew.

She could not stay at the Abbey because the Gestapo letter said if she did not appear at the appointed time, they would come to the Abbey to get her. This was a time of panic for everybody at the monastery.

A plan started to be worked out by Mother Mary Aline and Mère Benoît. They decided they should leave the Abbey together. Mother Mary Aline insisted she would be the one to go to the Gestapo, and she would show them the card written by Mère Benoît, saying she was going to Florida. She would make a strong case trying to convince them that Doctor Vera Duss had returned to America. The Abbess was concerned. She said she couldn't ask anyone to put herself in danger like that. She was sure Mother Mary Aline was going to be arrested if she went to the Gestapo. Ever the actress, the latter insisted she would be up to this, that she would tell the Gestapo she was superior in the Abbey, and they would listen.

They then had to figure out how to get to Paris. They couldn't take the closest train at La Ferté-sous-Jouarre because someone might see and recognize Mère Benoît. The only place with less risk was Meaux, which was to the west of Jouarre and considerably farther away. Their plan was to say Mère Benoît had a very serious sinus infection. That would let her get away with wrapping a big cloth around her face. Again there was a suitcase problem, since Mère Benoît, not knowing how long she'd be away, had to take her books with her—Thomas Aquinas, the Bible, the Desert Fathers, the Fathers of the Church. Mother Mary Aline shook her head, grateful that she was strong in those days, figuring she would have to help carry those bags.

While Mother Mary Aline was frantic, making arrangements to get them both to the train, Mère Benoît had a sick nun to take care of, and that was the most important thing at the moment for her. Sister Solange[2] had come down with an illness that was difficult to diagnose, and Mère Benoît knew she had to be hospitalized in Paris. Her concern for her patient was her primary problem at that moment, putting her own problems on hold. Getting Sister Solange into Paris was a complicated process, but Mère Benoît arranged this, giving her a prescription to be filled on arrival.

When Sister Solange arrived and gave the prescription to her doctor, the doctor said something like, "Oh—paper signed by Doctor So and So and written by Doctor So and So." She panicked, knowing that Mère Benoît's plan for getting the prescriptions needed by her patients was no longer a secret. All the while she was hospitalized, she was tormented, believing that Mère Benoît had probably been found and arrested. When she returned to Jouarre and discovered Mère Benoît wasn't there, she later said she was in agony until she found out that her beloved friend was in Paris.

A year after Mother Benedict came to America to start her monastery, six French nuns from Jouarre came to join her in Bethlehem; Sister Solange was among them, taking the name Sister Genevieve.

Meanwhile, Mother Mary Aline had managed to find a man from the village who had a car and said he would take them to the train station if they provided the gas, which was very scarce. He was one of the few people who didn't know Mère Benoît, for he had only recently moved to Jouarre. Fortunately, Mother Beatrix had a permit for gasoline for the Abbey car, and so they could give the man the required gasoline.

By about four in the afternoon, Mother Mary Aline, who had been excitedly telling Mère Benoît that the car was waiting, managed to get her friend and the suitcases into the car, and she and Mère Benoît headed to the station at Meaux. They were supposed to get a train at seven o'clock, but there was no train until around nine that evening. They got on but then waited and waited. The train didn't move. Finally they heard what had happened. There had been a terrible bombardment in Noisy-le-Sec near Paris. It had blown a hole near the train tracks and damaged buildings around them. The falling debris had completely obstructed the track. The engineer finally decided to take a detour. When the nuns realized that they were on an unfamiliar course, they could do nothing about it. They were on this train, and as it started to move, they knew they would get off when it stopped, wherever that was, and at whatever time it would be.

Eventually the train slowed, finally stopping at a deserted freight station. Fortunately Mère Benoît, who knew Paris like the back of her hand, recognized where they were. She had taken the small train that normally went to this freight station once in her life to go to a little town near Paris. It was now about two in the morning, and when they left the train with the other passengers, they knew they could not remain in the station. They would be vulnerable should the Gestapo come by and ask for identification. Mère Benoît had changed her identity twice and was carrying her second set of papers. It would be very easy for the police to check and discover that the papers were forged. The two nuns felt it was better to be outside, even on the street, rather than be locked into a place.

They convinced the stationmaster that they had to leave and he had to give them a pass. He nodded his head, warning them that it was very dangerous to be roaming the outskirts of Paris in the middle of the night. They thanked him, picked up the heavy suitcases and left. Mère Benoît felt she would not get lost and that they could walk to the home of her cousin Yvonne and Yvonne's husband, Abel Luthy. They lived in a building in the tiny square that had housed the Benedictine Abbey of Saint-Germain-des-Prés in the Latin Quarter. Their apartment had been carved out of the stables of the Abbey when the Abbey had been dismantled and sold during the French Revolution. Only the church remained. The stables-turned-residences had status because the great French Romantic painter Eugène Delacroix had had his studio in that building. Mère Benoît's cousins occupied the famed painter's former studio.

The two nuns, lugging their suitcases, left the station. Mère Benoît assured Mother Mary Aline that she knew the way extremely well. She estimated it was about a three-mile walk. They began their trek, grateful that it was a moonless night, making them less visible in the pitch-black night, but this also meant they had to be extra cautious that they did not trip on the uneven pavement. The night was cool for mid-April, and they found they had to walk slowly, feeling their way with their feet. They had to switch the suitcases frequently from arm to arm because of their weight. To add to their discomfort, they knew they were in a very dangerous situation, two women alone, on foot, in the middle of the night, approaching Paris, a city continually patrolled by the Gestapo.

They followed the Left Bank of the Seine, walking along the river, coming to the back of the Cathedral of Notre Dame. That took about an hour and a half, and in that time they hadn't met a soul. After they had passed Notre Dame, they were on a portion of the bank where the river was flanked by a high wall when suddenly they saw the big floodlights of a patrol car coming in their direction. They both realized at the same time that while they were in black habits and veils, they had white bandeaux and wimples, which would really stand out. Careful not to make any sudden movements, they turned against the wall, hoping their black habits would blend with the darkness of the wall, making them invisible.

They could hear the car slowing down, and they were conscious of the floodlights sweeping the area. They hugged the wall, staying absolutely still, praying intensely and silently. Miraculously, the lights of the officers' car, flashing all along the wall, stayed just above the nuns' heads. If the lights had swept the wall just two inches lower, the nuns would have been seen and arrested!

When they felt it was safe to venture forth, Mère Benoît and Mother Mary Aline continued on their way, turning left at the next bridge to get to the street that would take them to the area of Saint-Germain-des-Prés, about a twenty-minute walk. Mère Benoît knew these streets perfectly, since she once had lived in this area herself. It was four in the morning when they got to her cousins' building. The two nuns knew a curfew was on. They wondered if the concierge would answer if they rang the bell and would open the automatic gate for them. They had no choice but to try, and to their surprise, the gate opened.

They had to cross a courtyard and go up a very straight staircase, still lugging their baggage. Once inside the staircase, Mother Mary Aline, who had had the presence of mind to put some candles and a cigarette lighter into her pockets, lit a candle so they could be seen right away should someone answer the door. Mère Benoît rang the bell, and they heard a noise, then silence. They began to pray. After some tense moments, they rang again, and finally her cousin's husband came and opened the door. When he saw those two faces, visible by candlelight, he caught his breath in astonishment. They then noticed his intense relief.

He brought them quickly into the apartment and locked the door, telling them he had been afraid it was the Gestapo at his door. The evening before, he and his wife had taken in a Jewish couple. They were caring for them until the couple could get to another place where they were expected and could be safe from the Nazis. When he heard the bell ring at four in the morning, Abel said he expected it would be the police.

The Luthys didn't have extra beds. The Jewish couple were in fact sleeping on chairs. Abel brought out two comfortable armchairs and blankets for the nuns, but by this time all were awake, telling their stories. The Jewish couple, named Girard, had been separated from their parents, industrialists, and hoped to leave the next day and get away from the Nazis. Mère Benoît's cousin Marianne Densmore, Yvonne Luthy's sister, was there, too, sitting quietly but so happy to see her cousin. Eventually, they decided to get some rest, and everybody settled in for a few hours of sleep.

The two nuns got up early, anxious to go to morning Mass at Saint-Germain-des Prés. When they returned, there was a welcome surprise waiting. Her cousins had a big dining room that opened onto a beautiful garden, and the table was all set for breakfast. They sat together, the seven of them—the Luthys, the Girards, the two nuns and Marianne—enjoying a wonderful breakfast, thanks to the fact that the Luthys knew people in the black market and could get good food. It was a momentary contrast to the misery and danger all around them. Everybody was peaceful, savoring the beautiful spring morning, with the sun on the trees, enjoying the fine food and conversation, and above all, the graciousness of their hosts.

Mère Benoît and Mother Mary Aline found another surprise in the apartment. The Luthys had a printing press, and blank paper for posters and postcards, all in readiness for the liberation they expected would come. Everything was in readiness for what would have to be written and posted the moment the liberating army would enter Paris. They were very conscious of how serious this was, knowing that if it had been the Gestapo ringing the bell at 4:00 A.M. instead of the nuns, everyone in the apartment would no doubt have been shot.

The nuns had been told by their Abbess that they were to go to the monastery of the Benedictines of the Blessed Sacrament in Paris. She was sure they would be welcome there. By late morning, they had said good-bye to the Luthys and were on their way, not expecting to run into any problems at this monastery. The warm welcome they received upon their arrival made them feel relaxed. They had finished lunch and were unpacking when the welcome suddenly changed to coldness. The Mother Prioress called for them and, looking at Mère Benoît, said, "I think I remember that you are—American." She went on to say that she was responsible for her community, and so she had consulted with their ecclesiastical superior about taking in the American nun. She would let them know what his decision was in the morning, after he got back to her.

The two nuns had never felt so humiliated. This was a Saturday, and despite wanting to get up and get out of there immediately, they stayed, uncomfortably, that night, planning on attending Mass in the morning. As they went into the choir for Mass, the Prioress came up to them and said that much to her regret, her ecclesiastical superior said they could let Mother Mary Aline stay, but Mère Benoît had to go. Later, in her office, the Prioress related that the Reverend Father literally said: get rid of her; tell her she can do whatever she wants. And he suggested that she take off her habit and dress as a laywoman.

Now the two nuns were furious. That anyone should recommend that Mère Benoît try to escape from Paris by exchanging her habit for civilian clothes was shocking to them. If wearing her habit meant she would be recognized and punished, then so be it, Mère Benoît felt. Better to die than to betray who you are. Mère Benoît asked the Prioress if she could use the phone. She called her friend Doctor Françoise Bonnenfant, asking if she could come and stay awhile with her. Françoise asked where she was and said she would come by subway to pick her up immediately.

Mother Mary Aline was frantic. She insisted that she would go with Mère Benoît and stay at Doctor Bonnenfant's apartment, too. Mère Benoît insisted Mother Mary Aline had to stay at the monastery, in obedience to her Abbess at Jouarre. When Doctor Bonnenfant arrived, helped Mère Benoît with her suitcase, and both of them said good-bye, it was a bleak time for Mother Mary Aline, who knew she wouldn't be able to stand being in that monastery. Luck was on her side, because two days later, the Prioress told her that "Monsieur le Superieur" said she, too, had to leave. The Reverend Father had concluded Mother Mary Aline was more dangerous than Mère Benoît. Elated, she wanted to leave that night, but the Prioress wouldn't hear of it. Mother Mary Aline left in the morning and got the subway to Rue Freycinet, the street where Doctor Bonnenfant lived.

Mother Mary Aline was nervous, to say the least, when she rang the apartment bell and didn't get an answer. Because it was early morning, she could assume that Mère Benoît and Françoise had probably gone to Mass, but it was also possible that they had been taken in by the Gestapo. All she could do was sit on the steps and wait, all the while observing that there were members of the Gestapo on almost every floor of this house and that the doorwoman was a great friend of the Gestapo. It hit her that in two days, she would be keeping Vera Duss' appointment at the Gestapo headquarters at La Rue des Saussaies. She got even more nervous.

After about a half hour, she saw her friend and the doctor returning. Françoise said something like, "Don't tell me—you, too?" She was smiling. They all went upstairs, and Mère Benoît told her fellow nun how she had been spending her time here, with two outings a day, one in the morning for Mass and one in the evening to cross the Champs-Élysées and visit the Dominican church. She was never to go out during the day or be seen without Françoise. They were both comfortable with this arrangement.

Time was getting close now when Mother Mary Aline would have to go to the Gestapo to try to convince them that Mère Benoît had returned to America, and she did not want to go alone. She called on a friend, Madame Baggot, who was absolutely ignorant about why she was going to the Gestapo, and she agreed to accompany her. They went to the building taken over by the Germans for their Gestapo headquarters. Mother Mary Aline had heard there was a torture room in the basement and that people very often did not reemerge from that building. She was nervous, but, thanks to her acting ability, she didn't show it. At the entrance, she and Madame Baggot were met by a German who spoke very little French. He asked Mother Mary Aline for her papers and everything she had in her pockets. She had some clean pieces of paper, a Rosary and her little knife, which she always carried with her. He pored over these, and then he asked for her identity card. Her performance at that point probably rated applause, because she scolded him for thinking she should have such a card. "I am a nun", she said emphatically, raising her voice. Rather confused, the officer let her through, telling her the room number where she was expected.

Mother Mary Aline and Madame Baggot knocked, and in perfect French, they heard, *"Entrez."* They entered and found themselves face-to-face with a woman. She was very beautiful, with extraordinary green eyes, but Mother Mary Aline was stunned by the coldness and harshness that made her a terrifying presence. Immediately, the uniformed woman was sizing up the incredibly attractive nun who was facing her. With no accent at all and in a very distinguished voice, this German officer invited her and her companion to sit down and then asked, "Are you Mère Duss?"

Mother Mary Aline said no and began her spiel, saying the monastery couldn't understand what was going on and that Vera Duss, Mère Benoît, had left France and gone to the United States. She said this card proved it, showing her the card Mère Benoît had written. She also said the Abbey had no further news of her since it was impossible to communicate with the United States at this time.

The German woman took the card and looked at it. Then she looked at Mother Mary Aline, saying that the Gestapo had sent the letter to them at Jouarre because "they think she is in your convent." Staring at the card again, she said, "This is very strange." With a very stern look, she left the room. The two women were frightened and didn't say a word. When the German woman came back, she had two SS officers with her. This was a tragic moment for Mother Mary Aline, who was very conscious of the fact that, while the woman was very calm, she really was an icy enemy trying to catch her in a lie.

Mother Mary Aline had been counseled by Abel Luthy not to talk too much, so she decided to say only that "Vera Duss is not at the monastery. She left for Florida.

That's all we know." But she did add, "We are cloistered. I cannot go out except for the business of the monastery. If you send us another letter, I cannot come every time to see you. We are cloistered! And besides, it costs a lot of money to come."

The German woman told her that maybe they found Vera Duss' name in a file that had not been destroyed, and that may have accounted for why the Abbey got the letter. She said they would tear up the letter and shook hands with Mother Mary Aline. They smiled at each other, and the nun, walking very slowly and with dignity, left with her friend. She stopped by an officer at the door, asked for her belongings and got them back. It was a bright, sunny April 26, and she felt happy that her mission had been accomplished. More than that, she felt a physical relief, as someone does who has been saved from a frightening fate. She did not doubt for a moment that she had been dealing with a dangerous woman, one whose beauty could not really mask the cold evil within. Ever cautious, when Mother Mary Aline and Madame Baggot parted, the nun didn't go straight back to Doctor Bonnenfant's. Thinking she might be followed by the Gestapo, she took a number of different subways, finally arriving at Rue Freycinet to bring the good news to Mère Benoît and Françoise. The three women rejoiced that night.

The next day Mother Mary Aline returned alone to Jouarre. Mère Benoît stayed a few weeks with Françoise, confined to the apartment except for morning Mass, and Rosary and Benediction in the evening at the Church of the Blessed Sacrament. It was a contemplative time for her. During the day, she listened for hours to a record of Gregorian chant from the Abbey at Solesmes—a Benedictine monastery in France famous for its emphasis on the celebration of the liturgy. The record had been given to her by her cousins, and she studied this musical form intently, learning to understand and discern the unique quality of Gregorian rhythm. It also was a form of prayer for her. She had to keep a low profile because Françoise's apartment was in the midst of Gestapo activity, and her friend was bravely involved with the underground. Both Françoise and Mère Benoît felt that it was safer to be in the heart of danger if one is really trying to skirt something. Françoise was making medical certificates for people, helping many of them get to Spain, and she had counterfeit cards in her books. In the elevator, under the mat, she hid the code of the underground. It was crucial that this never got into the hands of the Germans, who would then decipher the code and learn the names of all who were in the Resistance. The Gestapo were walking on that code every day. Yet Françoise's belief was that the more open she was, the less she would be suspected.

Abel Luthy apparently had received some information that the time of the Allied invasion was getting close. This could put Mère Benoît in even more danger should she be discovered, so Abel advised her to return at the end of May to hide again in her Abbey. Mère Benoît decided to do this. She relayed the message that she was coming back to Jouarre to the Abbess on a phone in the guest house. The Abbess, evidently agitated and unhappy with this news, told Mère Benoît to get off the train one stop before the one she would normally take, and someone would be there to meet her. The Abbess was still terrified that when Mère Benoît got close to Jouarre, she would be recognized and reported to the Germans. Mère Benoît obeyed and was met at the distant train station by the gardener Monsieur Naville, who was driving a horse and wagon, and Mother Imelda, who had brought a sandwich for her. Mère Benoît didn't know then that the decision to give her something to eat was not pure kindness. The Abbess wanted to make sure that Mère Benoît did not go to the kitchen when she got to the Abbey. She wanted her immediately out of sight. The ride was silent, with no one talking.

When Mère Benoît arrived at the monastery, she was literally whisked up to her room. Mother Mary Aline started to inform her about what was happening, saying, "You are glued to your—" but she was stopped, not permitted to follow her friend. Mère Benoît was left in complete silence. She was devastated at this lack of welcome. In the days to follow, she was allowed to work in the infirmary, but she had few medicines and practically no way to treat the few Sisters who came to her other than listen to them. It was very clear that almost everyone at Jouarre just didn't want her around. It was a time of tremendous suffering for her.

Then, on July 11, Mère Benoît began to feel very sick one afternoon at Vespers. She was wretched enough to go to bed early. She began running a very high temperature and vomiting. For eleven days, the temperature stayed high, and she couldn't retain anything, but still the Abbess would not call a doctor. Mère Benoît thought she was going to die, and this made her happy. She had never been in such a depth of misery, being unwanted, a threat to her monastery. She felt she had nothing to live for and was spiritually dry. It was truly her dark night of the soul.

The Abbess finally knew she had to call a doctor, who confirmed what Mère Benoît had suspected. She had a bad case of hepatitis. He prescribed a medication that stopped the terrible, violent nausea, and Mère Benoît then realized, unhappily, that she was not going to die. She was too weak to be moved to the infirmary for nearly a week, and then, when two of the nuns lifted her to carry her down, they were amazed at how light she was; she had lost so much weight. The Abbess came to see her the first evening she was installed in the infirmary. She didn't come back for another three weeks.

To insure that she remain a hidden person, the Abbess had absolutely forbidden Mère Benoît to have any visitors. She was in a kind of hell, sick, suffering and alone. Fortunately, she had strength of spirit and her books to help her survive this strange imprisonment. She had been alone in this dreary place, reading the *Gifts of the Holy Spirit*, by John of St. Thomas, and hoping to find some spiritual understanding and joy. Instead, she felt only spiritual dryness and emptiness. "I don't think I've known a greater moment of despair— when you see this order of things that you are desiring absolutely, strenuously and piercingly, and absolutely no way to relate to them. I didn't know where to turn, except to continue ... but all I felt was an absolute blank ... void...."

She said of this time: "The dominant feature of my feelings was that I had nothing to live for. You see, I had just seen those terrible principles of the spiritual life, and I had absolutely no way of putting them into practice ... and obviously the Community didn't want me, so I had nothing to live for.... I didn't feel there was any real purpose. There was nothing I could see that was meaningful....

"Obviously the meaning of life is within itself. But we sometimes have to face the experience of not having any concrete way of seeing this. I'm just saying that this is what happened to me, and I'm glad it did, because I'm glad I know how it feels, so I can be sympathetic to people who feel the same thing."

When she was able to get up and around, she could hear rumors of the coming liberation. What she didn't know was that the Liberation would radically and permanently change her life.

Chapter 7

GOD CALLS FOR A NEW MONASTERY
IN AMERICA

— A Time of Torment
— Liberation of Jouarre, August 27, 1944
— The Decision to Return to America
— Garnering Support to Found a Benedictine Monastery

Before the month of June 1944 was over, word had filtered back to Jouarre that the Allies had invaded Normandy. Everyone talked about how the Germans were being routed and that they would soon be defeated. Yet the days were heavy, even as people lived with hope. They had been under German control for too many years, and they knew no one was yet safe from harm at the hands of these invaders of their country. As the summer rolled on, Mère Benoît remained in solitude most of the time. Her books gave her some comfort, as did music. To add to the insult of how she was being treated, she was now given a new official assignment—making the little napkins given to each individual nun to use at mealtimes. She was still the Abbey physician, but being in hiding, and unable to get medications or write prescriptions, about all she could do was talk to the nuns who came to the infirmary, hardly the kind of medical care she really wanted to give. The little napkins the Abbey used at meals were falling apart, so she had to spend hours mending the repairable ones and making new ones. It was tedious, unfulfilling work, truly a form of punishment for her.

The Abbey had a three-level tower that was virtually abandoned space, and on days that she felt stronger, Mère Benoît would put the mending down and climb the very high, narrow steps to the first level, which had a low-ceilinged room they called Saint Gregory's. This was a room mainly for storage of trunks belonging to the Community, but a little organ was also stored there. Mère Benoît would go by herself to that deserted spot and practice the organ for hours in Saint Gregory's.

On the night of August 26, 1944, she was in the infirmary by herself as usual when she could hear and sense chaos around the Abbey. She had heard that the Germans had put up a proclamation in the village announcing very severe constrictions on the people. Everyone knew this was obviously a sign that the Allies were close on the Germans' heels, and the Germans would have to leave. The word had gotten around that wherever the invasion by the Allies was successful, the Germans, knowing they would be in retreat, did as much damage as they could to the place they were leaving.

The noise indicating that the Germans were spottily bombing around Jouarre as they readied themselves to leave was disquieting to the nun, alone in the infirmary, a big, comfortless room. She began to have all sorts of visions of what could happen if the Germans decided to force their way into the monastery, then searched and found her. She would be the enemy American if they found her, and she knew her life would be in danger. She felt fear, and this was new to her, for this was the only time she had ever been afraid in so disturbing a way, either in the monastery or in any other place. But then, putting her trust in the Lord, she decided she just had to quiet down, because nothing would happen that was not supposed to happen. Eventually she fell asleep sometime late in the night.

The next day was a Sunday, a gorgeous, colorful, flower-filled August day. The Community was at recreation in the Our Lady of Lourdes garden. Mère Benoît was alone at the far end of the garden, which they called the Infirmary Garden because of its location outside the infirmary. She was drawing, copying, in red and green, the symbol of Saint Athanasius, which was in the Infirmary Garden, when she very suddenly heard air raid sirens and machine gun blasts to the southwest, in the direction of Coulommiers. Soon someone started ringing bells in the parish church, and before long, one of the students at the Abbey's school, Olga Afa-nacieff,[1] a young Russian girl living with her mother in the town, arrived at the Abbey. She had been sent by the parish church to ask the nuns to join in the ringing of the bells. Mother Mary Aline excitedly asked the Abbess to let them ring the bell, but the Abbess said no. Somehow Mother Mary Aline got her to change her mind, and Mother Mary Aline then ran and took over the ringing of the majestic Abbey bell, believing the Germans had left.

Because of the noise of the shelling, the sirens, the vehicles and the excitedly shouting people, Mère Benoît, who had gone back to her infirmary quarters, did not hear the bells. At three o'clock, she went to her choir stall for Vespers. During Benediction, the nuns heard the rumbling of very heavy rolling equipment driving in the street that bordered their monastery. The rolling noise continued, causing most of them to feel a combination of curiosity and excitement, though some were fearful. When they came out of the choir, they gathered near the door of the church. One of the

younger nuns had popped her head out the door, then suddenly she pulled back, turning to inform the others, "One
of the Lay Sisters said that the British are here!" Then someone shouted, "Let's go to the Tower and watch!"

Mère Benoît hesitated because she didn't feel physically
up to it. Just getting to Vespers had drained her of energy.
But almost immediately, she reconsidered and went with
the crowd of them to the base of the Tower. She was the
first to climb the narrow stairway, called a "snail" stairway
by the nuns because only one could climb at a time. Somehow she managed to climb past Saint Gregory's on the first
level and past the second level, reaching the third level, an
attic, where no one ever went. All that was here was a window with the glass blown out. Mère Benoît was amazed to
find that, while she was a bit out of breath after her climb,
she suddenly felt much better. Since she was the first there,
she went right to the window, stuck her head out and saw
the street packed with tanks, one after the other, and a few
jeeps. The vehicles were a dark yellow-brownish green, and
each had a white star painted on the green. She just stared
at the white stars, which took on a tremendous significance
for her. They told her immediately that the liberators of
Jouarre were Americans.

From that height, she could also see a section of the valley of the Marne with the town of La Ferté-sous-Jouarre at
the foot of the cliff. Every minute or so she'd see smoke
coming in the direction of the train station, and she could
hear the artillery shells. The Germans were still trying to
destroy as they made their retreat, but they were obviously
not stopping to place bombs. Later she would find out that
both the station and the bridge had been spared destruction from bombings because of an error on the part of the
monastery in the timing of the ringing of their bell. Mother

Mary Aline had actually rung the bell too early, before the Americans were in sight. But the Germans, hearing the bell, thought this meant the tanks had arrived, and so they moved on sooner, not waiting to bomb La Ferté-sous-Jouarre.

With the American soldiers coming through as their liberators, everyone in Jouarre was wild with joy and relief that their occupation by the Germans was at an end. The noise was deafening, but it was a happy sound. In the Tower, Mother Jean Marie came up behind Mère Benoît and looked down, over her shoulder. Mother Jean Marie, probably thinking of her two brothers in the Resistance, said, "This is the French underground!"

Mère Benoît said in French what would be "My eye!" in English. "Those", she proclaimed loudly, "are the Americans."

As Mère Benoît stared at the soldiers, she was taken by the condition of the young men driving those tanks. "They were naked to the waist, dark brown from head to foot. They were just so sunburned, and so exhausted, and their khaki uniforms were so dust covered. It was just terribly moving to see them. That really hit me hard", she later said.

Now the little attic space was getting crowded. Mother Véronique was behind Mère Benoît, holding her by her scapular, the sleeveless garment part of the nuns' habit that hung loose over the shoulders. Somehow the Abbess had made it up those stairs, and she was saying, "Hold her by her scapular so she doesn't fall out the window!" She was probably genuinely concerned because at the moment, Mère Benoît was really hanging out the window. She suddenly had seen a huge American flag, and it was an incredibly exhilarating moment for her, she said. "It was a special grace for me at that moment when I saw the American flag." She felt a radical change within herself, as she was drawn like a magnet to her countrymen.

She left the window, surrendering her place to whomever wanted it. She turned and saw the Abbess. "I really
looked at her, and she really looked at me. And it is after I
looked at her that this incredible experience that I can't
describe happened. Because I was so drawn to these American men, I had to do something. They had been willing
to give their lives, and I could feel for the others, the ones
who had given their lives so that these men could be here
this day. And it was right after I looked at the Abbess—
like, who was she?—that I had this image of monastic life
planted in America and the knowledge that it would involve
me in a very special way. It was so totally unexpected and
yet so absolutely evident and clear that I didn't question it.

"So anyway, I went down from the Tower. I was so
exhausted that I realized I should go back to the infirmary.
After the shock of the insight I had just been given, naturally I started to question what had happened. The first
thing I tried to say was that I was just tired, that's all. So I
went to the infirmary and just plopped into an armchair. I
was there all alone. I was content to be there quietly. And
then, for the first time, I saw Jouarre in a detached way. Up
to then I was identified with it completely, very, very strongly.
And the slightest mention of not being there or leaving for
any reason whatsoever was absolutely unthinkable. I couldn't
bear the idea of leaving that place. But now that had suddenly changed.

"Then Sister Étienne came into the infirmary. She was
carrying a roll of Lifesavers. She told me she had been looking all over for me because some soldiers had given this to
her, and she wanted me to have the first one. And she asked
me if I could give her a message to take back to them.

"I looked around, and there were two roses in a vase,
one already drooping, but one still beautiful, a very pale

pinkish yellow. I took the rose, gave it to her, and I told her this was my message. Go and take it back to them.

"She came back later to tell me she gave a soldier the rose, saying, 'This is from an American nun.' And she told me he burst into tears.

"I went to Compline that evening. I went to my stall, and I had this feeling of strangeness, of all of a sudden being in a strange place where I wouldn't stay. It was such a strained experience, because now I was seeing the reality of what Jouarre had become for me from a completely different angle."

Mother Benedict, looking back at this experience, related that she had gone to Europe to be in Europe. She hadn't wanted to live in America. But the war made a radical change in her, generating a very great love for her country in a very new way. Seeing the Americans—she later found out this was the Third Army—passing through Jouarre was "an absolutely astounding experience for me. It shook my foundations, if you will. I realized how much blood had been shed for this Liberation, and I had to ask myself, how was I going to match this gift? The only thing I could do was start a Foundation of monastic life in America, to extend the life-giving work of these men in this country." Mother Benedict also began a long search to learn about these first American soldiers she had seen. "I spent twenty years trying to find out what army had freed Jouarre. At first I thought it was Eisenhower, but he never put a foot on the boundary of that town. In the early '60s, I heard it was the army of General S. Patton, Jr. Then in the summer of '64 in France, there were many publications on the anniversary of the Liberation that documented it was General Patton who had liberated us. I'm not sure what would have happened if he hadn't been around."

Mère Benoît was in for another surprise when she realized the Abbess was still going to keep her in seclusion in spite of the fact that the Germans were gone. As the authority at Jouarre, the Abbess had no intention of declaring the presence of the American nun. But one day the gardener, Monsieur Naville, saw Mère Benoît in the garden and asked her if she'd like to meet an American soldier. Mère Benoît wanted very much to meet an American because she wanted to get word to her paternal grandmother in Florida that she was fine, and she believed an American soldier could get a letter through for her. Susanna Duss was now in her eighties, and Mère Benoît knew she would be wanting to hear from her granddaughter after these war years. But the Abbess refused to let her go to town with Monsieur Naville, still not wanting anyone in town to know Mère Benoît was at the Abbey.

That didn't faze the gardener. Soon after, he brought a nineteen-year-old soldier to the Abbey to meet Mère Benoît. The soldier was a matter-of-fact sort of fellow, very precise and polite, who said he would personally write to Mrs. Duss to give her the information about her granddaughter. Mother Benedict never remembered his name, but she remembered his deed. The soldier kept his word and sent a letter to the Dusses in Florida. Her relatives were so happy to hear news of her that they had a story printed about her in the local newspaper.

The months following were difficult for Mère Benoît, who knew now that her sights were definitely set on the United States. She was more than supported in this quiet plan by Mother Mary Aline and Mother Mary Dorothy, who both wanted to be part of this new venture. In a Community where people live so closely together, it is difficult to keep secrets, and some of the other nuns got wind of the fact that something was going on with Mère Benoît and a few others. They sensed a betrayal and made their disapproval felt sometimes in words, sometimes in body language. On May 7, 1945, the Abbey, like the rest of France, got word that the war in Europe had ended, and again there was rejoicing. Mère Benoît felt relieved, believing her time had come to begin making plans to get permission for her proposal to start a Foundation in America.

The problems that had been building up for Mère Benoît among her peers in the Community escalated, and as New Year's Day 1946 dawned, she heard that some nuns had written to Bishop Debray to complain about her and what they felt was an underlying betrayal of Jouarre, since they were aware that the Abbess didn't know about what Mother Benedict and a few of the nuns were quietly planning. The nuns who had remained her friends throughout the years of her mistreatment because of the war—like Sister Solange, Sister Louise, Sister Frances and, of course, Mother Mary Aline—told her about the letter and said she, too, should write to the Bishop. She sent the letter on January 2, explaining her position and asking if she could meet with him in person. She wanted to seek his permission to pursue the idea that now never left her, the dream of starting a Foundation in the United States.

To her surprise, Bishop Debray showed up at the Abbey on January 4, two days after she had written to him. He clearly liked and respected this American nun. He had great compassion for her, knowing all she had been put through, and agreed with her position that rules are made to protect religious life and not vice versa. He told her he supported her and was more than open to her desire to leave Jouarre and go to America. In fact, he informed her that he had heard from American authorities that any person who was not American-born but was an American citizen had until September to get back to America, otherwise such a person would lose his citizenship. That applied to Mrs. Duss, who had been born in Geneva and had become an American citizen after her mother brought her to America. Mère Benoît knew her mother was not in any condition, physically or psychologically, to go to America alone. She would have to bring her mother back to America herself.

This became the perfect moment to ask the Bishop if he thought that while she was in America, she could start a monastic Foundation. He answered, "It seems to me it is an excellent idea. Have you spoken to the Abbess?"

She answered no, that she didn't want to do that until she had spoken to him to know what he thought about the idea. The Bishop advised her to tell the Abbess what she was hoping to do and that if the Abbess wouldn't support her in this, then he would speak to her. He also told Mère Benoît to write right away about what she had in mind to the Sacred Congregation for Religious in Rome.

Mère Benoît followed Bishop Debray's advice, going soon to talk to the Abbess. When Mère Benoît told her that she had been thinking about this for nearly a year and a half, the Abbess was completely floored. She couldn't believe this idea had been afoot, yet she hadn't heard anything about it. "Well, really, you keep your secrets well, don't you?" she said. The Abbess had a hard time grasping the facts that Elizabeth Duss had to be brought back to America to save her citizenship and that Mère Benoît was serious about starting a Benedictine Foundation in the United States. Then, almost resigned, the Abbess said, "I will never stand in the path of God's will. You may write the letter to the Sacred Congregation, and I give you every permission to do whatever you think you can do. But I will not help you in any way, either materially or spiritually—except that I will certainly pray for you."

As Mère Benoît was preparing to put down her thoughts on what information should be put into the letter that would be sent to Rome, she suddenly developed symptoms of appendicitis. Though she was trying to ignore her pain, Mother Mary Aline, insisting that Mère Benoît had to see a doctor, called their friend, Doctor Françoise Bonnenfant, who immediately came to the Abbey. Françoise took one look at Mère Benoît, examined her and immediately ordered her to go to Paris for an operation. The doctor in Mère Benoît, knowing she had a severe personal medical emergency to deal with, reluctantly agreed to go. But if she was going to Paris, she wanted to use this also as an opportunity to make contact with Jacques Maritain, who had recently been made France's Ambassador to the Holy See and who could probably advise her on how to proceed in approaching Rome. She had been told by a friend that the noted Catholic writer and Ambassador was in Paris, and the friend had even given her his address, a hotel on the Champs-Élysées. Mère Benoît decided to write him a letter, seeking his advice on her plans to start a Foundation in America. It took her fully a day to write the letter, since she wanted it to be precise but compelling, and when she arrived in Paris, on the way to the nursing home hospital, the first thing she did was deliver it in person to the hotel where Maritain was living. From there she went right to the nursing home hospital, where the surgery was going to be done the next morning.

Before the evening was over, Mère Benoît had a special delivery from Jacques Maritain brought to her by Françoise. This eminent man had brought his response in person to the nursing home, but because of the nursing home rules, he wasn't allowed to see Mère Benoît. His note said he was very interested in her plan and asked whether she would come to see him in the morning. The time he requested was the very same time she would be in surgery. She knew that her mother, Mrs. Duss, as well as Mother Mary Aline and Mother Mary Dorothy, who also supported her plan and wanted to go with her to America, were coming to see her in the morning. She urged Françoise to get in touch with them and gave her a complicated message about how they were to see Jacques Maritain in her place and explain to him why she couldn't be there because she would be in surgery.

Mother Mary Dorothy, a slender, aristocratic woman, was selected to carry out this task. After she had seen the Vatican Ambassador, the message she carried back to Mère Benoît was that Jacques Maritain, well acquainted with the Vatican, said this idea of a Benedictine Foundation in the States was absolutely needed. His advice was that Mère Benoît should go to Rome as soon as possible, that her proposal had to be brought to the attention of the Holy Father, Pope Pius XII.

That response was an encouraging one for Mère Benoît. As soon as she felt well enough after the surgery, she wrote a letter to her Abbess, putting everything she had proposed to do in writing so that the Abbess could share this with the Community. Much to Mère Benoît's surprise, she was told that the Abbess said to the nuns that if any of them were interested in following Mère Benoît, they had her permission to do so. Sister Solange, the future Sister Genevieve, stood up immediately, saying, *"Je vais avec Mère Benoît!"* ("I am going with Mother Benedict!") The Abbess later wrote a letter for Mère Benoît to bring to Rome, saying she gave permission for her to go to America and start a Foundation.

Her dear friend Father de Monléon was another priest Mère Benoît wanted to consult about her plan to start a

Foundation in America. He came to visit her, and after hearing her, said he would do what he could to help. When she was ready to leave the nursing home hospital, Father de Monléon brought a duchess in to meet her. This woman had many American contacts and knew all the American Army chaplains still in Paris. She introduced Mère Benoît to two of the chaplains. One of them was a handsome, friendly priest named Father Maurice Sullivan, who came from Waterbury, Connecticut.

Mother Benedict could not have guessed at that time that her future Foundation would be in Bethlehem, Connecticut, a mere 25 miles from Father Sullivan's hometown.

Bishop Debray came to see Mère Benoît at the nursing home after her operation, and she asked him if he would give her permission to go to Choisy and stay awhile at the Dominican monastery for nuns that was near the Saulchoir, a great school of studies for Dominican theologians. Doctor Françoise Bonnenfant's best friend was Prioress there, and Mère Benoît thought she would get a better chance to rest there than in the infirmary at Jouarre, where nuns would be constantly calling on her for consultations. The Bishop agreed, and this became another astounding experience for her. She discovered that these Dominican nuns had absolutely no intellectual interests or pursuits, precisely so that the Friars—the men at the famed Dominican theology school—could always be seen as their superiors, more knowledgeable and wiser than the women. "They were playing the stupid, dumb creatures; there was something so out of whack there!" said Mother Benedict.

In contrast, next door to this monastery was another one, where a different group of Dominican nuns lived. These women tried actively to take part in intellectual work. They were called the Dominicans of Epiphany, and their very name indicated they were trying to develop their own way of manifesting their relationship to God. Mère Benoît found it astounding that the two contemplative houses of women, so different, stood side by side. As someone who hoped personally to start a monastery, she knew she would seek women with the intelligence and spirit of the Dominicans of Epiphany, and not the others.

While she was with the Dominicans, Mère Benoît wrote to Bishop Debray, telling him that Maritain said she should go to Rome. The Bishop wrote back saying that Maritain was a fine man but that he himself knew better what she should do, and that was to write the letter to the Sacred Congregation that he had told her to write. Period. She was not to go to Rome. Mère Benoît returned to Jouarre and told the handful of nuns who were enthusiastically support-ing her plan what was happening. Mother Mary Dorothy spoke up. She had a friend in Rome, Father Abbot Philip Langdon, a Consultor for the British Congregation, and she suggested Mère Benoît write to him. This was in February.

Around this same time, however, a strong sign came from a completely unexpected direction, a sign that seemed to indicate that Mère Benoît should not despair of eventually presenting her request in the Eternal City. In the aftermath of the war, Jouarre had no funds to spare, and the Abbess had made it clear she was not going to finance a trip to Rome. While Mère Benoît was in Paris, however, an unexpected letter arrived for her at Jouarre. This letter looked so businesslike and important that Mother Mary Aline called Mère Benoît in Paris to tell her about it. When Mère Benoît got back to Jouarre and opened the letter, she was in total amazement. It was from one of her childhood friends, Max-imilienne, daughter of the prince and princess of Croy. Her friend, whom she always called "Max", wrote, "Finally, Vera, I am able to give you the present I wanted to give you on your clothing day." She had included in the letter twenty-five thousand francs, more than enough to pay for Mère Benoît and a companion to get to Rome. The nuns found this unexpected gift of money, so perfectly timed to their need, to be an unmistakable sign from the Lord. Moreover, the Abbess graciously agreed the money could be used for this purpose when the time came.

Two months later, it was Easter, and Mère Benoît still did not have a reply to the letter she had written to the Congregation. She notified Bishop Debray that she was still waiting. Not one to mince words, he exclaimed, "This is ridiculous! Well then, you're going to Rome." Mère Benoît knew she would need a letter from him, or she wouldn't get past any Vatican doors. The Bishop said no, he wouldn't write one. She was to go to the Nuncio, the Vatican's representative in Paris, and get a letter from him, and Bishop Debray advised her to write and ask for an appointment. Again, no response was forthcoming. But time wasn't standing still, and, facing the September deadline for saving her mother's citizenship, Mère Benoît knew she had to get her proposal in motion.

She decided to go in person to Paris and knock on the door of the Nuncio, whose name was Archbishop Angelo Roncalli. She needed a companion, and the one she "hand-picked for the mission" was Mother Ethelburga, a dignified woman who looked exactly like a British governess, with gold-rimmed glasses and mannerisms to match. "She was very gentle, a perfect angel really, but her principles were iron. So I was sure not to go astray with her!" Mother Benedict said.

Good luck came her way when, as the two nuns were packing to leave, American Army chaplain Father Sullivan called and then offered to transport them to Paris. The two nuns were going to stay with Mère Benoît's cousins, the Luthys, and the offer of door-to-door transportation was a godsend. When Father Sullivan arrived at Jouarre to pick them up, Mère Benoît wanted him to meet the Abbess. Since he knew little French, and the Abbess knew little English, Mère Benoît acted as interpreter. When the American priest left to put the luggage into the Army vehicle he was driving, the Abbess turned to Mère Benoît and in great dismay said, "Oh, he's much too handsome. You can't travel with him." Mère Benoît's answer was, "Well, we have to."

The vehicle was a huge station wagon. The nuns had never seen anything like this. They got in and found the priest was not alone. Another man was in the wagon, an American Catholic from Brooklyn, who effusively talked about Pope Pius XII for most of the trip. When the nuns got back to Jouarre, Mère Benoît gave the Abbess the good news about how well protected she and Mother Ethelburga had been from the handsome priest.

As Mother Benedict vividly recalled, they had gone to Paris on Sunday evening, May 19. When she got to her cousins' apartment, she called the Nunciature and asked for an appointment on the next day. To her surprise, she was treated graciously and told to be there at eleven in the morning. She and Mother Ethelburga appeared there exactly at 11:00. The waiting room was what she supposed might be a traditional Vatican drawing room, with the inevitable tapestries. After a while, they were brought to another, smaller drawing room where the Nuncio was standing. He looked up at them—"he always looked up; he wasn't very tall"— and said, "Well, what do you want?"

Mère Benoît told him she had sent him a letter petitioning him to write her a letter in turn, introducing her to the

Sacred Congregation in Rome. She told him Bishop Debray said such a request came under the Nuncio's province, not his own. Archbishop Roncalli said that wasn't true, that the Bishop should have written that letter. Mère Benoît said she agreed, but she really did need that letter.

"When?" he asked.

"Now", she answered.

"Not possible", he said. "I have a luncheon engagement. I have to consecrate a church this afternoon. I have a dinner engagement ..."

All of a sudden, as if something guided her, Mère Benoît remembered she had in her pocket the Abbess' letter spelling out the permission for her to go to Rome. She pulled it out and asked the Archbishop if he would just write a note on the statement the Abbess had written. "That I can do", he said in French, with a heavy Italian accent.

Archbishop Roncalli then took her paper and went to his desk. It was a Louis XV woman's desk, very frail, and when the heavyset man sat on the desk chair, the whole unit seemed to groan. "Come here while I write", he said to Mère Benoît. She asked him to date it, and, using an ordinary pen, the Nuncio wrote on the first page and then turned the paper to continue writing on the back. When he handed the paper back to Mère Benoît, she read in his big, round handwriting that he was happy to recommend the project, and his impression of the person requesting this was "excellent". Mère Benoît was aware that this was a very supportive clause. He also asked the Sacred Congregation to welcome her. His words were absolutely more than she could have hoped for.

Now that he had finished writing, the Nuncio addressed Mère Benoît in a very unusual way, using the familiar (*tu*) form, saying, in French, "Now that I have served you, I will ask you to do something for me." He asked that the first thing she do when she got to Rome was go to the Basilica of Saint Peter, kiss the toe of the statue and say, "Obedience and Peace". He spoke of Saint Peter as if they were buddies, and he told Mère Benoît that Saint Peter would know what that meant because it was the Nuncio's motto. He explained, "It's a motto I have lived by, and it has carried me through everything in life because there is no peace without obedience. Unless you go through obedience, you do not reach peace."

Then he asked Mère Benoît where she planned to stay in Rome, and she told him, "The Cenacle."

He said, "Oh no, that's way out. It is very far from the Vatican, and you'll have to walk. You need to find a place near the Vatican so you can comfortably expedite your business."

She was amazed at his fatherly concern and his graciousness. When she was leaving, he saw her to the door, again not a thing a man in his rank would usually do. Normally, at the door, the Nuncio would ring, and the butler would come and escort a visitor to the exit. But Archbishop Roncalli didn't do that. He opened the door himself and followed her, which she saw as signs of really carrying out, in a symbolic manner, his desire to assist and be available. His treatment of her was beyond anything she had expected, and it gave her courage and energy to proceed with what she had begun.

His response to Mère Benoît was for her like manna from Heaven. By the time she had reached the Nuncio, she was emotionally depleted and wondering if she had embarked on some kind of wild fantasy. But because this important man took her proposal so seriously and showed such sensitivity to her, and because he would extend himself to something beyond his immediate jurisdiction and concern, this charged her enthusiasm and determination to go ahead with her plan to do God's work in America.

There was no way of knowing at that time that this man, Archbishop Angelo Roncalli, would in fewer than fifteen years be Pope—and not an ordinary one, but the revered and beloved Pope John XXIII, the mover behind the Second Vatican Council of the early '60s. Looking back on her encounter with the future Pope, Mother Benedict said, "That was a great lesson for me, how this man accepted this totally unknown situation and person with a totality of response so like Christ. You can see the making of a saint in this kind of thing. This man was taken off guard yet gave a completely integrated, spontaneous response. You felt supported, that he would stand for you. And he always tried to find a connection with the spirituality of the person to whom he was talking. He was so incarnational!"

Since this was still soon after the war, and trains did not yet run frequently, Mère Benoît had made arrangements for Mother Ethelburga and herself to leave on the one train available, on May 22. This allowed for three days in Paris in which to obtain the needed paper from the Nuncio before the scheduled trip. But securing the recommendation of Archbishop Roncalli turned out to be only the first hurdle they had to cross. Abel Luthy, the husband of Mère Benoît's cousin with whom they were staying, asked if they had visas. The nuns had not thought about that. Mère Benoît was still recovering from surgery and feeling somewhat worn out, and Mother Ethelburga was too old to be trudging around buildings trying to get a visa, so Mother Mary Aline was called in. "I'll get the visas", she said, somewhat in the gutsy mode she used when she offered to go to the Gestapo to protect her friend. She also said she would get to the bank to exchange money so the nuns would have Italian currency.

Abel Luthy told her she had to get Swiss visas, which would give the nuns the right to go to Italy, and that to get these coveted visas, she would have to be at the Swiss Consulate before the doors opened at 8:30 in the morning. Mother Mary Aline stayed the night preceding their departure at Doctor Françoise Bonnenfant's apartment so that she could set out early the next morning.

At seven in the morning she left and went to the Consulate, arriving at 7:30. Already there was a line of people packed at the entrance waiting to get in. By noon, she still hadn't gotten through the doors. Now they were closing for lunch for two hours. Panic started to set in. The train was leaving that night, and if she didn't get the visas this day, her two friends would not be on it.

Taking a real chance, Mother Mary Aline left her place in the line and dashed by subway to the Swiss Embassy, gambling that she might be able to get the visas there and still make it to the Banque de France that afternoon. At the Embassy, she was told over and over that they did not issue visas, that they did not have the seal needed to stamp them. But this was a nun who wasn't going to take no for an answer. Breathlessly, she related the plight she was in, how she had to have those visas for the two nuns going to Italy that day. Finally, the Embassy contacted the Ambassador and, with his permission, did something unheard of. They put the personal seal of the Ambassador on the passports of Mère Benoît and Mother Ethelburga and did this with no charge.

Immensely grateful, Mother Mary Aline then rushed out of the building to get a subway to the bank, which was on the Rue de Croix des Petits Champs, quite far from the Embassy. There again she met a problem, because the Banque de France had no foreign currency. A supervisor explained that the bank was still on "war regime" and not allowed to have any foreign currency. She would have to go to the Office des Changes, then to the Bureau des Changes, and fill out a list with the names of the travelers and everything they needed. She also added it was useless for her to try this day, because all these offices closed at 4:00 P.M., and it was then 3:30.

Not willing to give up, Mother Mary Aline flew to the subway and arrived minutes before the offices were closing. She saw the counter where workers were giving out the blank forms that she needed, and she asked someone if she could go ahead of the others and get the papers. She was told not to try, because people were so tense and edgy that she could cause a riot by doing that. The nun decided to take her chances and with a lot of "excuse me's" got to the counter, telling her urgent story to the clerk. She was told to come back the next day, but she insisted she needed the money that day. She was told the office was closed because it was now shortly after 4:00 P.M. Something about the way Mother Mary Aline said "please" must have touched them because they gave her what she needed, a paper she could present at the next office, an adjacent bank.

Again racing, Mother Mary Aline went to that building, somehow got through the door even though the office was closed, and faced a number of French men, bureaucrats, who worked there. They were surprised that she had been able to get in and told her to come back the next day at 3:00 P.M. She said, "No, I have to have the lira now" and again told her urgent story about the two nuns who absolutely had to be on the one train going to Italy that evening. Finally they gave her a bank order that Mère Benoît would be able to exchange immediately in Italy, because, they explained, they really didn't have lira in France.

Flushed with success, Mother Mary Aline rushed to Mère Benoît's cousins' apartment, waving the visas and the bank order. This was about five o'clock, and the train was scheduled to leave much later that night. That gave the three nuns time to have dinner with the Luthys. Also with them was a dear friend of Mère Benoît's, Geneviève Dedecker, a social worker. Mère Benoît told her of the conversation she had had with the Papal Nuncio and how he had told her not to stay at the Cenacle. Mademoiselle Dedecker responded, "That's the funniest thing. This afternoon I had a hunch that ..." She paused. "Well, I went to see some nuns I know who have a house in Verona ..." The result of this conversation was that those nuns told her Mère Benoît and Mother Ethelburga could stay at their house in Monte Mario, which was just to the rear of Saint Peter's, a place called the Institut des Filles Maria Auxiliatrice, where this community of nuns, the Sisters of Mary, ran a day school and also rented rooms to guests. Mademoiselle Dedecker gave the address to Mère Benoît, who still thought at that point that they should stay at the Cenacle. Mademoiselle Dedecker got a taxi and went with the three nuns to the station, La Gare de Lyon. On May 22, 1946, Mère Benoît and Mother Ethelburga were finally on a train to Rome—and a new destiny for the American nun and doctor of Jouarre.

Chapter 8

ROME

— Abbot Langdon
— The Rome Experience
— Meeting the Pope
— The Support of Monsignor Montini

As the two nuns might have expected, the train did not leave on time, and they had no choice but to wait patiently in their compartment. Finally, a little after 10:15 P.M., the wheels started to groan, the train moved, and they were finally on their way. Part of the travel in Italy was slow because of damage from the war. They could see roads that had been destroyed. The train went along the Rhône river, traveling the alpine side of Italy. The view of the mountains, which were still topped with snow, was fuzzy because of rain and fog. The nuns occupied a nearly full compartment shared with a French pastor and two women. Mère Benoît and Mother Ethelburga had brought some food in their luggage and were very grateful to Mother Mechtilde, who had so kindly prepared the provisions for them. There was a lot of rain, but this was probably a blessing because it helped keep the compartment from becoming excessively hot.

They got to Milan after about twenty-four hours. The train tracks in Italy had been badly damaged, and there was only one track going to Rome. They were to spend the

night in this city, and since the people who would be boarding from Milan to go to Rome would get on in the morning, the nuns were able to go to another section of the
train, which was sparsely filled, and they found an empty
compartment. They were actually able to lie down and get
some much-needed relief from hours of sitting. Travel the
next day was extremely slow because although this track
had been repaired, it was still not completely safe. The nuns
found the trip tiring and were happy when the train finally
arrived in Rome at about six o'clock Friday evening, May
24, nearly two days after they had left Paris.

When they got off the train with their heavy luggage, it
was pouring rain, and they wondered what they were going
to do, being strangers here. No one they asked knew where
the Piazza di Priscilla, or the Cenacle, was, except perhaps
that it was quite a distance away. Everyone was dispersing,
except for one of the women who had shared their compartment, who was waiting for her husband to meet her.
Mère Benoît, looking at their situation realistically, as two
strangers in Italy, now decided she and Mother Ethelburga
should try to get to the religious house her friend Geneviève Dedecker had recommended, which she realized was
located much closer to where they were. She asked the
woman if she could help direct them to the Sisters of Maria
Auxiliatrice. She said her husband would help. He arrived
soon and was very pleasant, assisting the nuns with their
luggage. He had the two nuns come with him and his wife
on a trolley and then got them on a second trolley, instruct-
ing them to get off at Via Tito Livio, which would bring
them close to their destination. That second trolley left them
off on a little street. The nuns were heavily loaded with
baggage, and the street was very steep and had villas on
both sides with very large gardens. The rain had stopped,

and that was a blessing, but the walk up the hill seemed endless. The slope was so steep that they had to put their baggage down every few minutes, until they finally came to Number 24, the superb, pink-walled property of the Sisters. As they arrived, the sky suddenly cleared, and they saw the sun setting as they heard bells gentling ringing. It was a brief, comforting moment.

Somehow they dragged themselves and their luggage to the doorway of the building. The Superior, Mother Mary Ferdinand, came to the entrance and greeted the nuns graciously and warmly. She insisted, even though the kitchen was closed at that late hour, that they have something to eat, and she prepared a meal for them. With apologies, she told them that she had only a small room with two beds. The bedraggled nuns accepted this offer with gratitude.

Mère Benoît didn't waste any time the next day, Saturday, getting started with the work she had ahead of her. The first thing she had to do was get directions to the bank where she could cash her bank order. From there, she went to the French Embassy and met with a Domican priest who was Jacques Maritain's assistant, a Father Félix Darsy. Mère Benoît explained why she was in Rome and asked him about Abbot Philip Langdon, the representative in Rome for English-speaking people from Britain, to whom she had written but who had never answered her letter. Father Darsy surprised her by saying he had had dinner with Abbot Langdon just the other day. Abbot Langdon had told him that he had no use for what Mère Benoît was proposing, and that is why he hadn't answered her letter.

"Well, what does this mean?" she asked Father Darsy.

"It means you have one enemy in Rome, which is a problem."

"Well, is it insurmountable?"

"No, just get on very good terms with him. Go along with everything he says", the priest advised. He also recommended that she first see a Father de Saint David, because he was a Benedictine monk of the Abbey of Solesmes. He was in residence at a nearby abbey located at Saint Paul Outside the Walls.

Father de Saint David seemed to know why Mère Benoît had come to Rome, and he told her that as far as he could see, this was an impossible situation because Abbot Langdon was against it and therefore would probably do everything he could to make it unworkable. Mère Benoît asked, "Well then, should I give it up?"

He said, "No, you have a very good idea, and good ideas always resist time."

With that encouragement, Mère Benoît then decided she would stay firm in her mission when she saw Abbot Philip Langdon the next day. The meeting was on a Sunday, and she and Mother Ethelburga had gone to their first Mass in Rome, at Saint Paul Outside the Walls. After that, they met with Abbot Langdon. A physically big man, very forceful and intimidating, he wasted no time putting his cards on the table. He told her outright, "This doesn't make any sense." His major problem seemed to be that the way she had gone about making her proposal didn't fit into what he said conformed to the constitutions of religious. From his perspective, it would have to be the Abbey of Jouarre, and not an individual nun, that would start a Foundation. Mère Benoît was trying to establish a precedent that had never before happened in the history of the Benedictine Order. The usual procedure was that a Bishop would invite the order to come and establish a monastery, not that one member of the Order would begin with the decision to start a Foundation in a certain place and then try to find a Bishop to welcome them. Still, the Abbot, impressed with her dedication, did not send her away. He told her he would go with her the next day to the Sacred Congregation. "That's how my experience in Rome began", said Mother Benedict.

She had a promise to keep to Archbishop Roncalli, that she would kiss the toe of the statue of Saint Peter, and so that Sunday evening, she and her companion crossed the piazza of the Vatican and made their entrance into Saint Peter's. They made the Stations of the Cross, went to Vespers and then remained to go to kiss Saint Peter's foot as the Nuncio had asked. They ended the evening at Saint Peter's, where they prayed at the Chapel of the Blessed Sacrament. This first visit to Saint Peter's was a memorable experience for both nuns.

"It gave me an impression of the solidity of the Church, which was unforgettable. This monument sings in its own eloquent way the strength of the magnificence of what Christ has founded. There, all Catholicity finds itself at home. And here one finds, on both spiritual and intellectual levels, that a sense of coherence paradoxically dominates our human disparities. I will always be infinitely happy for having had this sojourn in the Eternal City in which everything finds its place and its true proportion", Mother Benedict said.

At eleven on Monday morning, she, Mother Ethelburga and Abbot Langdon went to the Sacred Congregation for Religious. The person in charge was a Spanish Bishop named Bishop Larraona, a small, meek, very precise man. Abbot Langdon started a discourse with him, explaining that this American nun was determined to start a Foundation in America, telling him also why she had to go back to the United States, because of her mother. He punctuated this explanation of her request by concluding, "You and I know this is totally impossible."

Mère Benoît was worried. She asked Bishop Larraona if he could understand French, and he said, "Only if you speak very slowly." She knew that Abbot Langdon's presentation was not very helpful, and she needed to explain her idea in her own way. After she told Bishop Larraona what she hoped to do, he asked her if she had a Bishop in America who would take her in. And did she have property, did she have money? The answer to all his questions was no. He told her she was putting the cart before the horse. "You have wonderful ideas," he said, "but the Holy See does not approve ideas."

At this point, Mère Benoît pulled out her paper from the Nuncio. Bishop Larraona read what both her Abbess and Archbishop Roncalli had written and was impressed. He described it as a "very good document" and told her, "Never lose this document. It is the only valuable thing you have." Then he said all the Sacred Congregation could do would be to give permission to the Abbess at Jouarre to send two nuns to America to see what could be done about setting up a Foundation. He also expected that Mère Benoît, and not himself, would prepare the document giving this permission. She could then send it to the Abbess for her signature and await its return.

Mère Benoît felt almost elated. To her immense relief, though Abbot Langdon apparently felt pleased that Bishop Larraona appeared to agree somewhat with his negative assessment of her plan, he, surprisingly, offered to help her draw up the document the Bishop had requested. Abbot Langdon also told her it had to be on very nice paper, which she didn't have, so he graciously provided it. With this encouragement lifting her sunken heart, Mère Benoît prepared the document and got it off immediately to Jouarre, asking the Abbess to return it as soon as possible since she and Mother Ethelburga would be able to do nothing more until this document was back in her hands. She knew this would take at least two weeks, maybe three.

During this waiting period, Mère Benoît would walk every day from Monte Mario to the Vatican. She had requested a card to the Vatican Library, and this was granted to her. "That was wonderful. I did basic study on subjects like the Rule of Saint Benedict. In the afternoon I would go with Mother Ethelburga to see the sights of Rome or a monument. She couldn't walk very fast, but she was a real trooper", Mother Benedict recalled.

Meanwhile, Abbot Langdon was beginning to show a willingness to help the nuns at least have a memorable time in Rome. Just before the Feast of the Ascension, in late May, the two nuns were waiting to take a tram to the Colosseum when a car pulled up, with Abbot Langdon at the wheel. He asked them to come with him and drove them back to Saint Paul Outside the Walls, surprising them by handing them some official-looking papers. From there, he took them to the Vatican, telling them that with these papers they could now request a special audience with the Pope. Mère Benoît was elated since she had been hoping since her first day in Rome to be able to get an audience with Pius XII.

To get to the proper room where audience requests began, they entered by the celebrated Bronze Door, a massive door guarded by two Swiss Guards in their multicolored uniforms. The colorful Guards showed the nuns the way to get to the room and the person to whom they should present their request for a special audience. The secretary there was a very pleasant Irish Brother, who took their papers and said he expected the audience would be at the end of the week. Meanwhile, he recommended that they go to the public audience that would be held at 12:15 the next day, May 30, Ascension Thursday.

Later that afternoon, the nuns were invited to the French Embassy to the Holy See and were warmly received by Ambassador Jacques Maritain, who greatly encouraged the plan for a contemplative Benedictine Foundation in the United States. He was impressed with Mère Benoît's "deeper mission", that of going to the very "root system" of the Benedictine expression. He told her that there were many Benedictines doing good work in the United States, but none of them had the contemplative dimension, and he felt strongly that America needed to see this deeper aspect of a Benedictine vocation. He also gave Mère Benoît the names of several people in the United States who might prove interested in the realization of this project, which he admitted was unquestionably difficult.

The next day, the Feast of the Ascension, the two nuns attended High Mass at Saint Peter's and then climbed innumerable stairs to get to the door of the audience chamber.

"While we were still at the door, the area already packed with soldiers, we heard a military march and applauding, which meant the Holy Father had just come in. Then the attendants in their crimson costumes permitted us to enter into the audience hall, which we did as best we could. But from then on, only tall people had any opportunity to see anything. I was climbing onto the windowsill to see, but you couldn't stay there all the time, so I'd be up and down", Mother Benedict related, as she gave an eyewitness remembrance.

"His Holiness was sitting on a throne, on top of stairs; everything was draped with red, against which his white silhouette was profiled. On either side of the Pope stood a Monsignor, and on the steps of the throne, Noble Guards, wearing white trousers and golden helmets, and Swiss Guards—the latter in full uniform with their helmets and yellow and red and blue striped uniforms. Pope Pius XII spoke copiously. His voice was strong, a well-modulated voice, very supple and pleasant. His general appearance was admirable: a very slender torso, very straight and regal carriage. The Pope's familiar gesture was to open his arms very broadly and extend his long, slender hands."

On the following Sunday, the two Jouarre nuns received the card for the papal audience, which was set for the next day. It said, however, that this would not be a private audience, but a semiprivate one, which would limit the time they could have to address the Pope but still would give them the opportunity to speak personally to him. They arrived, along with about thirty other people, and waited for the Pope to come into the room. When the word finally came that he was in the next room, attendants, dressed in black, and two Noble Guards told everyone in hushed tones that he was coming, and everyone immediately fell to their knees. When Pope Pius XII came into the room, one of the Guards told the people to stand.

The Pope then went to each person, one at a time, and spoke a few minutes to each. Mère Benoît and Mother Ethelburga were in the last third of the group. When he reached them, Mère Benoît told him that she was in Rome to prepare to start a Benedictine Foundation in the United States. He asked her, "Where are you from?" "Pittsburgh", she answered, and he repeated the name. Because people who asked for an audience with the Pope had to say what documents they had, Mère Benoît told him about the letter of support she had received from her Abbess and the Nuncio, Archbishop Roncalli in France. "Very interesting", he said, holding his hand out to receive it. Mère Benoît handed it to him, and he took the paper, reading what Archbishop Roncalli had written. Then he said to her, "I give you all my blessings." When she gestured to take the letter back, the Pope, looking at it again and noticing that the Nuncio had addressed it to "Most Holy Father", said, "Oh, this is mine", and he did not give it back to her. He said since it was addressed to him, he would keep it.

Mère Benoît was frantic. She had been told by Bishop Larraona that this was the best document she had, and now she didn't have it anymore. The Pope had it. She suppressed a temptation just to scream and yell—something like that. "My most American blood came forth", she said. But then she thought, he is my major Superior. What does a nun do in front of her major Superior? She remembered the vow of obedience and thought that if one is going to practice obedience, it has to be on the spot, in the situation, and so, at that moment, she bowed at least to reality.

But the minute she was able to leave, after the Pope gave all his Apostolic Blessing, Mère Benoît dashed to the Bronze Door and to the offices on the right, where the audiences were arranged. She went right to the Irish Brother in charge and told him that she was in serious trouble. The Pope did not return a document that was essential to her mission. The Irish Brother asked her what Monsignor Federico Torre di Canali, who was following the Pope, had done with the paper. She said he put it into a red leather folder. The Irish Brother told her to wait and that as soon as he saw the Monsignor coming back, he would find out about her paper.

About fifteen minutes later, the Monsignor came in, holding the red leather folder. The Brother practically threw himself at his feet, telling him that the Sister had to make a copy of the document the Pope took. He explained that without it she would be left in Rome without authorization for her mission. That paper was the only proof she had. The Monsignor was unmoved. He responded harshly that if the Sister did not want the Holy Father to retain her document, she should not have shown it to him. He added that if the hand of the Holy Father has touched a document, it can never be returned. He marched out of the room, slamming the door behind him. Mère Benoît then realized that her effort to get her document back was a lost cause. It would be forever lost in a papal file someplace, never to emerge again, and her heart sank.

"At that moment I was seeing the Church at her worst, when bourgeois red tape will not allow for life, when you have to obey absolutely everything because the law comes first. But the contrast at that moment between the two men was astounding. Here was the Monsignor, dressed in a magenta cape, with the flair of an actor and so self-important. And here, too, was the Brother, really interceding for me, telling me that God's presence was there, in him. I think you have to go through something like this to understand the ways that the Church works and that it takes all kinds to make a world." Mère Benoît left the Vatican, asking herself over and over, what was she to do? She realized she had to obtain a new document reconstructing the essential permission and blessing that had been given to her by her Abbess and Archbishop Roncalli. She knew she had one faithful friend who always came through in time of need, Mother Mary Aline. That very day, Mère Benoît wrote her a letter, spelling out her problem. This was the beginning of June. She knew time was getting short. She could use the postal service from the French Embassy, but even using that method, it took a week to get a letter to Paris and another week to get one back. She didn't know what kind of obstacles were ahead; she knew she would now have to depend on other people to get her what she had to have. The one positive thing that could come from this was a new version of the Abbess' statement. In the original letter, she had said she did not "oppose" the project. Since it now had to be rewritten, Mère Benoît would try to get her to say she was "seconding" her request.

She was leaving all this in Mother Mary Aline's hands, praying, too, that her friend could get to see the Nuncio and that he would still be as receptive to her plan as he had been when she had gone to see him.

Knowing that having high-level support for her proposal was getting ever more crucial, Mother Benedict now decided to see Myron Taylor, the personal representative of the President to Pope Pius XII. Jacques Maritain had recommended that she see him. A financier and the Chief Executive of the United States Steel Corporation in the 1930s, Taylor had retired from business but later held various diplomatic posts, including the position of the U.S. special envoy to the Vatican. Appointed by President Franklin Delano Roosevelt when World War II began, Taylor, a strict realist with a remarkable understanding of religious matters, was the first to hold such a post since 1867. Some American religious leaders criticized the appointment as violating separation of church and state. President Harry Truman, however, realizing the importance of having a Vatican representative, reappointed Myron Taylor to this position after President Roosevelt died in 1945.

Mère Benoît and Mother Ethelburga, without an appointment, went directly to Myron Taylor's office. The receptionist was very cordial but told them Mr. Taylor was at a meeting. In a friendly way, she said that if they didn't mind waiting, they could stay, adding, "He does want to meet you." Apparently he had heard of her plan. When Mr. Taylor returned, he, too, was very cordial and told Mère Benoît that her idea was "very interesting". He added convincingly, "I really want to help you. I can't imagine that we don't have such an institution in America."

He knew more about Mère Benoît's proposal than she could have imagined and said he wanted to send the nuns to see Monsignor Giovanni Montini, the *Sostituto*, or Under-secretary of State for the Vatican, a position that handles internal affairs. (After 1944 Pope Pius XII had no Secretary of State; he acted as his own, with the Undersecretary's assistance.) Mr. Taylor told them, "Expect a call from the Vatican." Three or four days later, that call came in. Some-one said to her, in French, "We understand that you want to speak to Monsignor Montini." She said yes. "Could you come Tuesday at eleven?" That was five days away. She answered yes.

Abbot Langdon had known that she was going to see Myron Taylor, and upon her return, he asked her what America's special representative to the Vatican had to say. She told him, "That I should see Monsignor Montini." Abbot Langdon nodded and remarked, "He's right on tar-get. Montini will be the next Pope, but one."

Mère Benoît was somewhat terrified at what she would encounter as "that famous Tuesday", as she would come to call it, arrived. She went to the Vatican and was ushered to the standard large waiting room found in the Vatican build-ings. While she was waiting, an American, Bishop Muench of Fargo, North Dakota, came in, and out of respect for his position, Mère Benoît said he could go in ahead of herself. He thanked her but said no, she was there first, and he remarked that the Vatican was "the only place in the world where a Bishop had to wait". As Mère Benoît went into the room where Monsignor Montini was, his phone rang, and he picked it up, showing exasperation for yet another of his constant interruptions. She walked back to the door to tell Bishop Muench about the delay, afraid that she would be holding him up. "I was very green, you see", she explained.

Going back into the room, the man she saw was youthful, in his late forties, with blue eyes that looked dark to her in the way they searched one. He had jet-black hair, and his hairline was beginning to recede. When he spoke to her, he was precise, warm and sympathetic. She had been told that Monsignor Montini had total authority, yet she knew instinctively it was an authority of competence.

To her surprise, Monsignor Montini knew what she wanted to talk about, and he started describing monastic life as it was lived in Europe and in the United States. He was very clear that they were two different things. In the United States, he said, the American Bishops set the agenda for religious life, and although there were a considerable number of Benedictine houses in the United States, there was not one that had the full expression of the basic Benedictine observance that the European Foundations had retained. He explained that in nineteenth-century America, religious orders had to meet the needs of people and care for them as they were, according to what would work within the American society, and that was still true for the twentieth century. In a clear way, he pointed out that this did not mean there was a loss of the fundamental monastic spirit. Benedictine life especially, he emphasized, made a case for diversity.

He asked her questions about what kind of a monastery she would set up, and Mère Benoît talked about one that would be self-supported by manual labor and farming and where spiritual strength would come from prayer and continual education in theology. The nuns would, for example, be reading the Fathers of the Church. Monsignor

Montini stopped her there, telling her she was talking too much in generalities when she had to be specific and that it wouldn't work totally to follow the Fathers of the Church, such a vast subject. He stressed that the United States was essentially a Protestant culture, but he felt, oddly enough, that this culture could provide an added opportunity to get a good reception in America—that is, *if* she and her companion understood where they were and what they were dealing with once they were situated in America. He especially noted that Americans would appreciate the practicality of manual labor, that they would look at what she was doing and draw rightful conclusions according to what the new Foundation would show itself to be.

Mère Benoît was astounded that she had met this very important man who had an intuitive understanding of what she was talking about. She was taken aback. She hadn't expected such human warmth and sympathy.

"His extraordinary genius was that he understood life could not be compressed or contained in iron-clad rules, that religious establishments had to be in harmony with the situation of the locality, that religious life had to reflect that culture", Mother Benedict said. "He had a vast grasp of the difference between Europe and America and was very astute. I learned something very fast from him. He said that Benedictine life in its traditional form was what the United States needed but that if it was too systematic, people simply wouldn't respond. Because of his position in the Vatican, he had met many American people, and he had a sense of what would fit and be needed in America for the good of the Church."

Mother Benedict would say many times in the future that the meeting with Monsignor Montini "was the crucial meeting that made everything possible". And Abbot Langdon was correct. After the death of Angelo Roncalli, who became Pope John XXIII, Giovanni Montini would one day be Pope, taking the name Pope Paul VI. More than anyone else, this man, both as Undersecretary of State and as Pope, followed closely, with great support, the Foundation that was Mother Benedict's dream.

"Pope Paul, before and during his Pontificate, constantly expressed to me that the new monastery should seek to establish a classical contemplative community formed by serious vocations, which, not infrequently, might include professional persons, whom he said should be equal or surpassing anyone in the same field. Insisting as he did on the necessity of a well-developed intellectual life in the Community, the Pope wished to emphasize that the above criterion applied to each member, whatever her background, and was not limited to those enjoying higher education. It was assumed that all those called would have an expertise of some kind. Be it ever so humble, every member would be expected to carry out her expertise with integrity as the needs of the Community would require. And finally, this Community would stress the meaning of virginity, so threatened by the chaos of present-day society."

Years after their first meeting, during a 1952 visit of Monsignor Montini to New York, Mother Benedict received a letter from him, delivered through a mutual friend, Mrs. Robert Hoguet, in which he commended her efforts in getting this monastic project to the point where it had become the Priory of Regina Laudis on September 2, 1948. Yet he was a realist; in a statement he made to Mrs. Hoguet, he predicted that there would be difficult times ahead: "There is no more difficult work in the Church than to make a monastic foundation, exposed as it is to the spiritual opposition of the evil spirits as well as to innumerable obstacles in the domain of temporalities." Mother Benedict was to reflect on these words many times in the decades ahead.

That first meeting with Monsignor Montini on this memorable Tuesday ended by taking a more practical turn. He said her next step would have to be to go to America and see if she could find a Bishop who would invite her into his diocese. He told her to work now at finding what she would need to be able to take that trip. He knew she did not have the document she needed to bring to the Sacred Congregation for Religious, the one document that would give her permission to go to a Bishop in America, since the Pope himself had taken it to keep. He told her if she did not get a new one from her Abbess and Archbishop Roncalli, she could come back to him, and he would give her a memorandum saying she had the authority to go to America to try to set up a Foundation. He also told her she should meet with the Apostolic Delegate to the United States, Archbishop Amleto Cicognani, who was coming to Rome for the canonization of Mother Cabrini. Monsignor Montini told her he definitely wanted her to stay in Rome for the canonization of this first American saint, which was set for July 7, about three weeks away.

After this refreshing and encouraging meeting with Monsignor Montini, Mère Benoît thought she should go back to see Jacques Maritain and tell him of the support the *Sostituto* had expressed. This was good news for France's Vatican Ambassador. "As long as you have that kind of advice, it's a matter of time and finding a way. So don't give up", Maritain said. And he then told her she should still see as many people as she could while she was yet in Rome, especially Benedictines. "All of them put together might be a help."

He recommended strongly that she go to see Mother Saint Luke, a Holy Child nun, who had a sister, Mrs. Robert Hoguet, in New York. "She's very high in American society and has been twenty years in Rome and is a power behind the scenes. She is well informed about how things operate. You should go and tell Mother Saint Luke your story" and gain a contact with Mrs. Hoguet, said Maritain.

Mère Benoît did as he suggested, going to see Mother Saint Luke and telling her everything about her meeting with Monsignor Montini.

Still ahead was a visit with Archbishop Cicognani to which she had agreed in order to comply with the wishes of Monsignor Montini. When the Apostolic Delegate to the United States arrived in Rome, Monsignor Montini told him about Mère Benoît's mission and arranged for her to get an appointment to see him. It was not a pleasant experience. "He was absolutely awful, a very nervous individual, who seemed to be jumping up and down as he sat", said Mother Benedict. He told her that Montini had told him what she wanted, but Archbishop Cicognani was adamant: "There's no reason for you to come to America. Benedictine Sisters are adequately represented there. It is totally useless for you to go to America."

Archbishop Cicognani was staying at a residence for visiting prelates, and as Mère Benoît was trying to explain why her Foundation would be different, in walked Bishop Muench, the man she had met in Monsignor Montini's waiting room. Archbishop Cicognani started telling him what Mère Benoît was talking about and asked if he would invite her into his diocese. Bishop Muench answered that he would like to invite her, but the conditions of his diocese—in a very Protestant area—were such that he couldn't do this. That supported Cicognani, who just kept reiterating, "You should forget about it", until Mère Benoît left. It was a dark, discouraging meeting, but she was not going to let it defeat her.

In the two weeks they would yet be in Rome, awaiting the canonization of Mother Cabrini, Mère Benoît proceeded to do all that was required of her to get to America. Good news arrived with a letter from Mother Mary Aline, who had been running to and fro to get the new document Mère Benoît needed from the Abbess and Archbishop Roncalli. While Mère Benoît felt this new endorsement from Roncalli was not as warm as the one he had given her in person, it was still affirmative. She got the document to the Sacred Congregation for Religious, and with Abbot Langdon's help, requested assistance from Monsignor Montini in getting two visas for two nuns to go to America. As it turned out, after Monsignor Montini got Mère Benoît's letter from the Abbess and Roncalli back from the Sacred Congregation, signed and approved, he sent this letter to Myron Taylor who then arranged to get the visas.

With the approval of her proposal now in hand, Mère Benoît could relax a bit, and she decided to see if she and Mother Ethelburga could visit some Benedictine establishments, as Father Darcy had recommended. She planned on returning to Jouarre immediately after the canonization. They visited the Abbey at Subiaco and met with Father Abbot Caronte, whom Monsignor Montini said they absolutely had to meet. (The Abbot was a one-time mountaineer who was personally spartan in how he lived his vocation, but he was most hospitable to others.) Then they went to the Abbey of Saint Jerome, where they met Abbot Dom Peter Solomon, author of several books on the Divine Office, and became reacquainted with Father Peter Thomas, who had given them a course on chant at Jouarre a year or so earlier.

He was a vibrant musician and an authority on Gregorian chant, and the nuns were delighted with this visit.

With only a few days to go, Mère Benoît picked up the permission document and the visas to America, extending much gratitude to Monsignor Montini.

The final joyous event for the two nuns was the canonization of the first American saint. "The canonization was baroque to the hilt, and I was totally mesmerized", said Mother Benedict. "I felt it was not by chance that this was happening now and that I was there. I saw it as a precedent for what I hoped to do. When Mother Cabrini started out on her mission, she was totally unknown also, and while her focus was different from mine, there were similarities in the obstacles we encountered. I was so grateful that such a thing as her canonization was happening. It encouraged me, and I prayed to her all the time from then on."

It seemed an appropriate—and maybe even symbolic—end to Mère Benoît's odyssey in Rome, which had, after so much effort and prayer, ended with a bon voyage—destination America. But first, she had to return to Jouarre to make final arrangements for the trip. And there was the nagging question—how was she going to pay for this new venture?

Chapter 9

GETTING STARTED IN AMERICA

— The Jouarre Response
— The Voyage to America
— Journey to Bethlehem
— Gaining Support
*— The Connecticut Bishop Reluctantly
Welcomes the Nuns*

Mère Benoît and Mother Ethelburga returned to Jouarre on July 17, 1946, to a mixed welcome. By this time, everyone in the Community knew what Mère Benoît had been doing in Rome, and many didn't feel kindly toward her for making plans to leave Jouarre and go to America. Some understood that she had to do something about her mother, knowing Elizabeth Duss could not continue to live indefinitely at Jouarre. Yet, many of them found it hard to understand why Mère Benoît had to get back to America to save her mother's citizenship. She was to learn that an even greater cause of the coldness she felt from some of her Sisters had to do with how they viewed their own future. Many of the nuns at Jouarre had expected that Mère Benoît would be the next Abbess. They had been her patients and knew how human, understanding and learned she was, qualities that were so important in an abbess. Some felt betrayed that, instead, she would be leaving them.

The Abbess did have a list of six Sisters who wanted to go with Mère Benoît, but the future foundress had received permission and visas only for herself and one other nun, and so five would have to wait. The Abbess had never wanted the responsibility of starting a Foundation, and so she had given her permission to Mère Benoît to take this mission on by herself. Yet, when the two nuns returned from Rome, the Abbess found it hard to talk to Mère Benoît about her leaving. It had never registered with her that this request by an individual nun to start a Foundation in another country could really come to fruition.

Back at Jouarre after the encouraging experiences in Rome, Mère Benoît knew there would be no turning back from her decision to leave. Her main problems were how to finance the trip to the United States, how to find a place to stay and how to find hospitality from an American Bishop. She knew she could get some financial help from her cousins, the Luthys, but this was limited. To finance travel expenses for her mother, she wrote to her brother, an attorney in Florida, but who was married and had recently become a father. He responded to her request that he pay for their mother's journey to the States, but the money he sent was just enough to cover Elizabeth Duss' fare, not for any expenses beyond that. "If only somebody would offer me five francs", Mère Benoît would say when no one was around to hear her.

There was a lot of whispering around the monastery about the nuns who would be chosen to join Mère Benoît when she got to America, and Mother Frances was determined to be one of these. Some of the nuns had been trained to do bookbinding at the Abbey, and Mère Benoît, knowing that in America she would need nuns who had a skill that would bring in money, suggested to Mother Frances that she ask the Abbess to send her to a bookbinding studio she knew about in Paris and take some lessons. This turned out to be a fortuitous suggestion. Mother Frances was not one to keep quiet, and at the studio she began talking very freely about how some of the nuns were planning to go to America. One of the women there became enormously interested in what she was saying. Her name was Marcelle Delore, and she came from a family that was very well off, having made a lot of money in the business of gas production for kitchen ranges and other equipment. She said she had a personal friend in the United States who would probably want to help.

Mademoiselle Delore wrote a letter to Mère Benoît saying she was very interested in her plan to begin a Benedictine Foundation in America and that she would help, but initially, she wanted to meet with her in Paris. This was the first good news that Mère Benoît had received that held some promise for helping her make a contact in the States, and she responded immediately. The two women met, and Mademoiselle Delore proceeded to grill the American nun on exactly what she visualized accomplishing. The French woman wanted all the facts before she would commit herself to helping to sponsor the trip. To emphasize her interest in what Mère Benoît was planning and convince her that she was one who acted on projects she believed in, Mademoiselle Delore told how she was already helping a new Foundation, one in Mexico started by two young monks from Belgium.

The wealthy French woman explained to Mère Benoît that she had a friend in the United States, an artist named Frances Delehanty, called "Fanny" by everyone, who, in turn, had a friend named Lauren Ford, also an artist. They shared a home with separate studios in a small, rural town called Bethlehem in the state of Connecticut. Both of the women artists were Oblates of the Benedictine Abbey of Solesmes and had been to France to go to that Abbey several times. Mademoiselle Delore showed Mère Benoît images of Lauren's work that had been sent to her by Fanny. She said she knew nothing about Bethlehem except through a few photos she had seen.

Impressed by Mère Benoît's story and moved by the fact that the nun had everything she needed to take the trip except sufficient money and sponsors to offer her hospitality in America, Mademoiselle Delore offered to help with the specific remaining financial needs and said she would write to Lauren Ford and Fanny Delehanty. She thought perhaps the artists would be able to provide a place for Mère Benoît and her companion to stay until they could make some contacts in the States. Lauren Ford responded almost immediately by return mail and said she and Fanny Delehanty would be happy to meet the nuns at the dock in New York and drive them to their home in Bethlehem, where they would be welcome to stay as long as was necessary.

"It all happened in the nick of time. Marcelle Delore was crucial to the project. Because she believed in the enterprise and provided our specific financial needs, we were able to proceed. All the while, from the time of the Liberation to then, I had hope, but also anguish, wondering, will it happen? Yet you couldn't be perturbed. I was doing this not for myself, but for God", said Mother Benedict.

Before Mère Benoît left Paris to return to Jouarre, she had to make a very important stop—at the building of the Nuncio. She wanted to tell Archbishop Roncalli in person about how the Holy Father was interested in her plan, so much so that he didn't return her paper with the Nuncio's blessing handwritten on it. The Nuncio welcomed her warmly and smiled, concluding that the Pope had acted "like a little boy". "Roncalli was so humble, so genuine, so good", said Mother Benedict, who was buoyed by his support for what she was doing.

Time was moving quickly now, and all that was left to do was the packing and await the decision by the Abbess as to which nun would be the companion for Mère Benoît. Mother Mary Dorothy had been the second strongest supporter of the project—after Mother Mary Aline—and originally she was to have been on the trip to Rome, but as the time grew close, her health prevented it. To Mère Benoît's relief, the Abbess gave permission to Mother Mary Aline to accompany her to the United States.

The two nuns and Elizabeth Duss left on Tuesday, August 20, 1946, for the port of Le Havre, where they had reservations to sail to America on the SS *Argentina* on the twenty-third. The port had been completely destroyed during the war, so makeshift piers served the vessels. The ship was a recently converted Army transport ship, which had not yet been refitted to have normal cabins. Women were assigned in groups of fifty, as were the men, to what were called "dormitory cabins" consisting of tiers of berths separated by narrow aisles. The nuns had the first berth by the door.

As they stood on the platform before boarding, a fine-looking prelate took notice of them. He was the seventy-two-year-old towering and revered Abbot of Solesmes, Dom Germain Cozien. He did something the nuns considered unheard of—he carried the luggage of nuns to their quarters on the ship. Mother Mary Aline was carrying a big silver bowl full of candies, with an enormous bow, which had been given to her by a Mrs. Basil Harris, owner of the steamship line. It was not something contemplative nuns are usually seen with. As for Mère Benoît, she too had an unusual package—cuttings from various trees at Jouarre that her mother had forced her to carry!

Later, when the three women sat on deck at lunchtime, they were joined by the Abbot, each opening the "picnic" food packs they had brought with them and eating in religious silence. Mother Mary Aline put a pear in front of the Abbot. He took it graciously and proceeded to tell them a very funny French story about a pear, an apple and two people. That was the end of the silence and the beginning of many fine conversations. The nuns became good friends with this man, who proved to be very humane and charming. It was upsetting to them that during the voyage someone stole his abbatial ring, a large topaz, which was never found.

The ship arrived in New York on Saturday, August 31, and the Abbot was to be met by Mrs. Justine Ward of Washington, D.C., and her companion, Agnes Lebreton.

Not familiar with how to get to the platform, Mrs. Ward was surprised and pleased to meet Lauren Ford, a longtime friend, who helped her find her way around the confusion of a ship's arrival, with people milling around noisily searching for familiar faces. These two women had been introduced to each other at the Abbey of Solesmes by Fanny Delehanty and had become good friends because of their common bond of connection with that Abbey. Lauren excitedly told Mrs. Ward about the Benedictine nuns she was to meet and their plan to start a Foundation. But Mrs. Ward, who had devised a method of Gregorian chant and had brought this to schools in France, Italy and elsewhere, had only one thing on her mind, and that was getting to the Abbot, who had come here to learn about her chant method and also to bless a Foundation Solesmes had made in Canada. The Benedictine Abbey of Solesmes was noted for being a great source of learning about the chant.[1]

In all the confusion of landing, the pier was bustling with people and activity, and Mother Benedict, as she would be called from now on, was so occupied with the responsibility of taking care of her mother that she did not have the chance to say good-bye to the Abbot. For as soon as his hostess saw him, "the Abbot became the 'personal property' of Mrs. Ward. She whisked him away to Washington, D.C.", said Mother Benedict. But she was elated when a short time later, Mrs. Ward brought him back to New York and invited the two nuns and Lauren to have dinner with them. The nuns wanted to keep a close and friendly association with this powerful and gentlemanly Benedictine Abbot. Mrs. Ward turned out to be a friend who faithfully supported the nuns in their mission.

Because Mother Mary Aline was not a citizen, it took awhile before all the paperwork was done so she could get off the ship. Meanwhile, Mother Benedict had found two women on the pier looking for two nuns and a laywoman and knew immediately that they were Lauren Ford and Fanny Delehanty. The two American artists were dressed simply, in drab-colored clothes that had a European flavor, giving them the appearance of being "quaint-looking", as Mother Benedict recalled. She couldn't help but notice in particular that both of these women artists were carrying gorgeous handbags.

With a combination of excitement and fatigue, Mother Benedict helped get their luggage into Lauren's small Ford roadster. The women then insisted they had to get something to eat and drove to the Henry Hudson Restaurant on Fifty-seventh Street. They made quite an entrance, and the waitresses lined up to get a good look at this unusual group of customers. The two women told everybody in the restaurant, "These are the nuns of *the* Foundation", as if they would know exactly what she was talking about. All of it was music to Mother Mary Aline's ears, from the way she kept smiling. Mother Benedict observed everything quietly.

The meal was fine, and Mother Mary Aline was having the time of her life, especially eating the mounds of ice cream, which she loved. But then it came time to pay for the meal. Lauren opened her impressive pocketbook and, slightly embarrassed, whispered to Fanny, "I have no money." Fanny said, "I have no money, either." Then they both confessed that they had arrived at the pier early, and so, while waiting for the ship to arrive, they had gone window shopping. However, when they saw these gorgeous pocketbooks, they couldn't resist them, and so they splurged, spending all their money to buy them.

Mother Benedict had taken fifty dollars with her on the boat. She had no choice but to pay the bill. It left her with $7.53. Lauren and Fanny accompanied them cheerfully back to the car, and now they wanted to take their visitors for a spin around Times Square. Mother Benedict would have preferred to get right to Bethlehem. She had seen Times Square before. But Mother Mary Aline was having a great time, especially when she saw an animated Mickey Mouse on a billboard—that touched her theatrical heartstrings. She also concluded that all Americans were "very holy people, since all their street signs are about saints". She was referring, of course, to the abbreviation "St."!

Finally, the five women were on their way to Bethlehem, driving along the Merritt Parkway. It was a Saturday, and there was little traffic, but all of a sudden Lauren pulled over onto the grass. Something was wrong with the car. "This never happens", Lauren said in dismay. It was dusk, and the five of them just sat there, with Mother Benedict wondering if the succession of calamities would ever end. Then a car, going in the other direction, toward New York, spun around and drove over to them. The driver turned out to be an off-duty policeman—and "an angel", said Mother Benedict. The first thing he told them was hardly consoling. He said a man had been killed there, right where they were, because this was a blind curve. Fortunately, he had an emergency road kit. He lit a flare and sent a radio message to Bridgeport, the nearest city, to send a tow truck, and then he helped push the car further up on the grass. When the truck arrived, the five women, now getting very tired, sat in the car as it was towed the several miles to a garage in Bridgeport.

The mechanics at the garage were real gentlemen and assured them they could fix the car. They were very interested in the nuns. One of the young men said he had an uncle who was a monsignor and had gone to Rome for the canonization of Mother Cabrini. That opened a conversation with the nuns. Mother Mary Aline then got out her container of candies and treated all the men at the garage. Mother Benedict realized that Lauren and Frances were mortified because they had no money, and she was worried about what this repair was going to cost since she was the only one with any money, and very little at that. When the repair was done, the bill came to $7.50. Mother Benedict paid it. She now had three cents left to begin her mission in a new country. But it was all God's work. "A safe, great freedom was better than money", she would often say later. They drove from Bridgeport, through the industrial sections of Waterbury and on to Bethlehem. The road was rustic, and the ride was so bumpy that they were "shaking like peas in a bowl". Lauren was affectionate and loving, but she talked endlessly, hopping from one subject to another,

and Mother Benedict, from her medical training, found herself wondering, was she all there?

It was midnight when they got to Crane Hollow and the
house that Lauren and Fanny called Sheepfold, which was
purchased by Lauren in 1938 and was shared by the two of
them. They went up the back stairs, with Mrs. Duss carrying on in her own way, and came to the quarters Lauren
had prepared for the nuns. She hadn't expected Mrs. Duss,
but somehow she found room for her too. The greatest
surprise for the two nuns was that this highly respected artist and Catholic convert had gone to Hartford to see Bishop
Henry J. O' Brien, specifically to seek his permission to
have an altar set up for Mass at her house. Although this
was a highly unusual request, the Bishop, who thought highly
of Lauren, granted her this permission, and so she had set
up a simple altar. At the moment when Mother Benedict
saw the altar, she knew she had come to a place that would
be "home", at least for a while.

"It was welcoming, so neat, so expressive of this lovely
woman's heart. I knew we were definitely in the right place",
she would later often say.

The next morning a priest arrived at Sheepfold to say
Mass. His name was Father Joseph Osterreicher, and he was
a Jewish convert who was well known for his theological
writings. He planned to stay a week or so in the quarters at
Sheepfold that Lauren called the "priest room". After early
Mass, he spent the morning with Mother Benedict, giving
her helpful advice and explaining to her how everything in
America was more streamlined than in Europe. He told her
she could not make comparisons between America and
Europe and that she would have to be very practical in
how she proceeded. Most important, he advised her, was
to try to get an appointment to see the Bishop, because it

would not go well for her to stay in his diocese without getting his permission. Both the priest and Mother Benedict were somewhat worried that Lauren had not told the Bishop that two nuns were coming from France to start a Benedictine Foundation and thought this omission would have dire consequences. Lauren kept apologizing, saying, "I know I should have ..." as Father Osterreicher scolded her.

At this point, Mother Benedict had no plans to stay in Connecticut. She and Mother Mary Aline had talked about settling in Virginia, a state rich in history and one with a nice climate. In fact, Mother Benedict had written to the Bishop of Richmond, asking permission to come to his diocese with the intent of locating her Foundation there. Since she had not heard from him while she was in France, she intended to get in touch with him again, so that he would know to send his response to her in Bethlehem.

Father Osterreicher advised her meanwhile to begin making contacts with people who could be of help to her. Mother Mary Aline was excited about being in America, which was her dream fulfilled, and she was ready to start working. Elizabeth Duss was not helping to make things comfortable for her daughter, since as someone who by now could stand neither Jews nor Germans, she kept her distance from Father Osterreicher.

Lauren was also making plans to help the nuns meet people who could assist them in their project, and one of these was a fine priest named Father Andrew Kelly, a cultured, influential man, with great integrity, who was in charge of the Catholic Lending Library in Hartford. He sincerely supported the nuns' mission and, putting on his best suit, called on Bishop O'Brien, asking him to accept the French nuns. The word had been coming back to Bethlehem that the

Bishop had heard of their arrival and that he kept telling whoever was listening that the nuns weren't wanted here. Father Kelly's support buoyed their spirits, particularly when it got to be late September and Mother Benedict received a letter from the Bishop in Virginia. The letter, which had been delayed in getting to her for lack of postage, told her bluntly that "regretfully" he had to decline her request to settle in his diocese.

Now it appeared that she and Mother Mary Aline should stay in Bethlehem, but this would depend on whether they could get permission from Bishop O'Brien to proceed with their work. This didn't seem likely since Father Kelly had reported that the Bishop had been "antagonistic" when he had asked him to accept the nuns. It was a difficult time for Mother Benedict, who understood the importance of having a practical plan if she was going to be able to convince the Bishop to let her start her Foundation in his diocese. But in this early September of 1946, the thirty-six-year-old nun, who became ever more convinced that she was being led by God now that she had actually gotten to America, didn't have even a hint of what the next step would be in this incredible journey on which God had set her.

❧ ❧ ❧

As September dawned, Mother Benedict would have days when she could feel truly that her journey to Bethlehem had been prepared by Divine Providence. Lauren Ford and Frances Delehanty were faithful and loving friends, willing to go out of their way to do anything necessary to get the two nuns started in their task. Lauren's one overwhelming desire in life was to paint, and it was a wrenching pain for her when she couldn't be at her work. Yet she selflessly put her own needs aside to be available to take the nuns every place she felt they should go. "Lauren had no interest in anything but painting, but she didn't touch a brush for months to be available to take us hither and yon, all over the landscape, to get us started", said Mother Benedict. "Lauren absolutely invested her name and her reputation to help us. She was a real trump card."

Lauren introduced the nuns to her Bethlehem neighbors, one being her adopted daughter, Dora Stone, who lived in the "Stone House" next door to Sheepfold. Dora had several older children, two adopted, and a five-year-old son. This boy, Anthony, named after Saint Anthony of Padua and called "Paddy" for short, was already an altar boy. Lauren's mother, Mrs. Simeon Ford, lived in Rye, New York, and at one time had created a center for artists that became a fruitful colony. She was not a Catholic, but she "was interested in esoteric things and had a great affection for me", Mother Benedict recalled. Mrs. Ford, who had a skin cancer, "was encouraged and comforted by what we [religious women] could do for her and obviously felt helped by us. Through her, I was given an introduction to aspects of society that I knew would be beneficial."

Lauren Ford had became a convert to the Catholic faith in her early thirties through the Abbey of Solesmes because of the influence of her longtime friend Frances Delehanty, who had brought her there. They had only recently begun sharing a home when the two nuns arrived. "Frances and Lauren had very different talents, but no rivalry. Both were fairly well off—Lauren's father had built hotels—and these two extraordinary women staked us to help us get started", said Mother Benedict. In their personalities, these two women were very different, very individual. "Fanny was the boss. She made the decisions about the house and meals.

Lauren took a backseat on this. She deferred to Fanny. Lauren also responded very much to Mother Mary Aline, while Fanny did to me. Most important, Lauren helped me to be clearer in the paths I had to take, though she never claimed any ownership of my mission. She had qualities that appealed to people. People loved to deal with her. She was a beneficent agent who failed no one."

At the end of their first week in Bethlehem, when Father Osterreicher left, Lauren drove the nuns and Mrs. Duss to morning Mass at Saint John's Church in nearby Watertown. Once back at Sheepfold, Mother Benedict and Mother Mary Aline would work with Lauren and Fanny on places to go and people to see so as to get support for the Foundation. Mrs. Duss gardened, planting the greenery she had insisted on bringing from France, and tried to resume her artwork, without much success. Since she was, in a sense, a self-invited guest at Sheepfold, it was very hard for her to be there, even though she would talk to everybody who was coming there to see the nuns. She also rallied to the idea of the Foundation and so seemed finally to have gotten over her earlier complaint that her daughter had wasted her medical education by becoming a nun.

Lauren lost no time in bringing the nuns to New York to meet her circle of influential friends, among them Marjorie Williams, Mr. and Mrs. Robert Hoguet, Mrs. Howell Howard and Father Vincent Donovan, a Dominican priest. Mrs. Hoguet was indeed the sister of Mother Saint Luke, the nun whom Jacques Maritain had recommended Mother Benedict meet in Rome. Mr. Hoguet had immediately told Mother Benedict and Mother Mary Aline that he would assist them with legal advice in the initial work of fundraising and setting up a corporation. Lauren and her friends gave comforting reassurance to Mother Benedict that there would be support for her undertaking. The fine American Catholic laywomen there also wanted to help the nuns become known in Catholic circles. A first invitation came from Marjorie Williams, who took the nuns for a visit to Saint Paul's Priory at Keyport, New Jersey, that September 14, where they met Father Damasus Winzen, who, surprisingly, offered to come to Bethlehem to be their chaplain if they got permission from the Bishop to start their Foundation there.

Mother Benedict did find some quiet hours in these first few weeks at Sheepfold, and, wanting to make these productive, she decided to pursue a craft she had been wanting to learn for a long time—weaving. She thought it would be nice to be able to make handwoven vestments for whoever their chaplain would one day be. She asked Lauren if she knew where she could get lessons without having to pay for them, since she and Mother Mary Aline had no money and were still financially dependent on their generous hosts. It just so happened that Lauren's neighbor, Mrs. Robert Leather, was a weaver and had big looms right on her property, adjacent to Sheepfold, in a building that was actually called the Loom House. Lauren took Mother Benedict to meet Mrs. Leather, who graciously welcomed the nun, who began lessons in weaving that very day. Mother Benedict walked from Sheepfold to the Loom House for her lessons after that, but one day about a week later, Lauren wanted to drive her—and now began another encounter that was to have a major impact on the founding of this monastery.

Mrs. Leather's husband, Robert, founder and owner of a specialized machinery company in Waterbury, Connecticut, was at the house, recovering from a heart attack. Lauren introduced Mother Benedict to him, and he began a

conversation with the two women. He was totally mysti-
fied at meeting a nun who wanted to learn weaving. "He
wanted to know why and asked me a million questions. I
explained the principles of Benedictine life, how our monasteries are dedicated [to be a manifestation of God] in the
region where they are located, and how work, especially
traditional crafts that come from local customs, is incorporated into Benedictine life. He said this was amazing. It was
a kind of spirituality he had been looking for all his life",
Mother Benedict related.

That Robert Leather was a very special person was affirmed
by a man named Richard Crane of Waterbury, Connecticut, who worked many years for him, taking over the company after Mr. Leather died on a Mediterranean cruise in
1952. In an interview, Mr. Crane[2] said that Robert Leather
was born in Birmingham, England, and moved to the United
States when he was five. His father, a master die-maker,
worked in the silver industry and settled in Waterbury. Mr.
Leather became a chemist and in 1923 founded a company
bearing his name that made abrasive products and buffing
wheels. In the later 1930s, he bought twenty-six acres in
Bethlehem, off Flanders Road, later expanding this with
land purchases across the road, bringing his property holdings up to 126 acres. The Leathers turned their first site,
with the house they lived in, into a small farm, with animals. Mr. Leather put up a building he called the "factory"
on the property across Flanders Road, specifically for the
purpose of experimenting with making better chemical products. "This was an avocation. Nothing ever came of it",
said Mr. Crane, adding that the factory was very quickly
idle and empty. Eventually, the Waterbury industrialist owned
about eight manufacturing plants around the world—in Japan,
England, Spain and Austria as well as the United States.

Mrs. Leather was a dental hygienist who had become an expert in weaving. She and her husband had no children, but they entertained customers and workers frequently at their farm home. Mr. Crane remembers her as being "a delightful woman.... And Bob was a real study. There was a great humorous side to him. He was an easy rider, relaxed, someone who loved a good laugh, but he was also a very capable individual. He wasn't predictable. He had a way of conveying happiness.

"In my opinion, he appeared to be 'aspiritual', yet in his personality, he radiated a certain spirituality that he was unaware of. He had a sense of fairness that was never so manifest as when he saw injustice. If you can say everybody likes you—and everybody liked Bob—that's spirituality. All I know is that the Good Lord works in mysterious ways His wonders to perform, and He made Bob Leather the one who would be His instrument in getting the work done that He had sent the Sisters here to do. No one was more understanding of what the nuns were going through than Bob Leather, and he didn't hesitate to help them."

As the September days passed, Mother Benedict was getting more and more anxious to see the Bishop. By now she was getting word from some of Lauren's friends, one of them Father Donovan, that the Bishop knew about their arrival and he wasn't budging on refusing to welcome them. Father Donovan put Lauren in touch with a priest named Father Thomas Stack, who was known to be a favorite of Bishop O'Brien. She invited Father Stack to come to Sheepfold to meet the two nuns and listen to their story. Father Stack took a great interest in what the nuns wanted to do and said he would talk to the Bishop. He did, but the response was hardly encouraging. Bishop O'Brien told him he had heard about these French nuns coming to Bethlehem, and he didn't want to see them. When Father Stack, who immediately had become a firm supporter of the nuns, pressed him, the Bishop put him off by saying that if the good Sisters got some land given to them, then he would let them make an appointment to come to see him in Hartford.

Lauren and the nuns felt discouraged. But Lauren, looking across Flanders Road and the property sitting there as if waiting to be occupied, decided to invite herself, Mother Benedict and Mother Mary Aline to visit the Leathers. Lauren could talk very enthusiastically about something she believed in, and, sitting with the Leathers, she began to describe the impossible situation the Bishop had put the nuns into. Where were they going to get land? If they didn't get some soon, the Bishop would throw them out of his diocese. Where would they go?

Mr. Leather, sipping a glass of wine, took it all in. And then he said the words that sounded like a miracle to the nuns. "I have a beautiful hill", he said. "It is too beautiful for one family to own, and too beautiful to be divided up for development. I want it to be a place where many people come to worship. I give it to you for your monastery."

As the three women literally gasped in surprise and joy, Mr. Leather told Mother Benedict to go and see the Bishop, and he reaffirmed, "You're going to be carrying a deed to the best fifty acres in Bethlehem."

When they left the Leathers, Lauren, with Mother Benedict and Mother Mary Aline in the car, drove off and, taking a hairpin turn, zoomed triumphantly up a hill. When they got out of the car, Lauren told the nuns this was their land, the highest point in Bethlehem. They had a circular view that encompassed miles, and "it was like being on a little island with a glorious belt of hills, an absolutely incredible scene. You felt embraced by these hills, and it was as if through them you could communicate in a heavenly way. For me, it was an expression of Gregorian chant, a harmonious connection to the Eternal. Instantaneously, we knew this was the place one day to build our church. There was a tree there. I took a medal of Saint Benedict from my pocket and buried it just beneath that tree, assuring Mother Mary Aline that we would remember that tree. She said, better yet to put some stones on this spot. We did. It was a contemplative act, but rooted to the earth", said Mother Benedict. Still in a state of glorious shock, the three women bowed their heads and thanked God for this gift, which they would forever think of as a miracle.

Now they were able to contact Father Stack with good news. The nuns had land. Would the Bishop see them now? Meanwhile, the two nuns had to become visible, and with Lauren and Fanny's help, they began to speak to groups in the area, describing the Benedictine life they wished to transplant to this country and telling how they had been given permission and a blessing by Rome to take contemplative spirituality, so linked to the transcendent grace of God, and move it into the fast-paced, postwar age into which society had now entered. They also were in touch with Lauren's New York friends, who were keeping their promise to help the nuns raise money. And daily, Mother Benedict and Mother Mary Aline went to Mass in Watertown and lived the monastic life of prayer and work. "Lauren had such empathy for what was ahead of us. She would tell people, 'I feel for that young Reverend Mother; she has everything on her shoulders.' Truth is, I still had no idea of all that would be involved in starting this Foundation", said Mother Benedict.

October flew by, and then came good news in November. Father Stack called to tell them Bishop O'Brien, who

had postponed seeing the nuns several times, was now ready
to have them come to his office in Hartford. He set the
appointment for November 19, the Feast of Saint Elizabeth
of Hungary. This saint had been a queen, loving wife and
mother of three, who was widowed, grief-stricken and exiled
at age twenty and spent the next four years devoted to her
children and God, caring for the sick and the poor, dying
too young, at age twenty-four. The feast day was a reminder
to Mother Benedict that God doesn't interfere in order to
make life easy for those who deeply love Him!

The appointment with Bishop Henry J. O'Brien was at
two o'clock, and Lauren drove the two nuns and Fanny to
Hartford. The entire circle of the artists' friends assured them
they would be praying hard for the Bishop's approval of the
nuns' proposal. During the ride, Mother Mary Aline, who
usually was bubbling with conversation and "chirping
around", as Mother Benedict put it, was intensely nervous
and absolutely speechless. Actually, none of the women was
in a mood to chat, and the drive was a silent one. When
they got to the building, they met Father Stack, and then
all were ushered into a big room and told to sit, given the
assurance that the nuns would be called when the Bishop
was ready. Some Mercy Sisters were already there, waiting,
too. "Lauren told them our sob story, saying, 'These are
the nuns of the Foundation', as if they were supposed to
know", Mother Benedict recalled with a smile. The Mercy
Sisters said they would pray all afternoon for her and Mother
Mary Aline.

By four o'clock, fatigue was setting in. The Mercy nuns
had finished their appointment and had left. Father Stack
had also left. Time dragged, but finally the Bishop's secretary came into the room and, telling Lauren and Fanny they
would have to wait there, escorted the two nuns into the

big, carpeted room where Bishop O'Brien sat at his desk. "Mother Mary Aline was stymied. She didn't have a word to say. We must have looked pale and terrified. I think the Bishop noticed that and was more tenderhearted toward us than he wanted to believe he would be. He said a few words to reassure us that he was really willing to listen to us", Mother Benedict recalled.

She was carrying a charming, small French briefcase, and he asked her, "What's in your little trunk? Is it a letter from your Abbess?" Mother Benedict said yes and showed him the permit from the Sacred Congregation for Religious.

"That's all you have?" he asked, briefly and to the point. She said yes. Bishop O'Brien then asked her what canonical conditions she had for starting a Foundation—that is, had she been invited by a Bishop of a diocese in the United States to come here? She said no. The Bishop then held out his hand to receive the document from the Sacred Congregation. It was written in Italian, with some autographed notes from the Secretary, Bishop Larraona, personally handed to her in Rome. Mother Benedict asked him if he wanted her to read it. He said no, that he knew Italian. After about a minute or so, he said, "I give up. Explain it to me."

Paragraph by paragraph, for two full pages, Mother Benedict went through the document, carefully explaining what was written there. At the end, Bishop O'Brien said, "If all that is written on that paper, I think you have a lot of imagination." Mother Benedict didn't respond. There was one moment of silence, and then he spoke four words that were forever emblazoned in her memory: "The diocese welcomes you."

"I must have looked perplexed, because he said, 'I repeat, the diocese welcomes you. And now I'll tell you everything that's against you'", Mother Benedict said.

First he told them he never blessed ideas, only facts, and he asked if they had money. No, Mother Benedict answered, "but we have land, fifty acres, and there are people in New York who have set up a committee to try to raise money for us."

He asked, "How would you build?"

"Fieldstone", she answered.

"No," he warned, "it leaks. You need to use brick. How much do you think it would cost to build?"

Mother Benedict had no idea, but knowing she should always try to answer a Bishop, she guessed, "About fifteen thousand dollars." He thought that was very naïve and told her a conservative estimate would be fifty thousand dollars. "That didn't faze me, since I didn't even have the first one thousand dollars", said Mother Benedict, recalling the incident years later. "He told me that when I had the fifty thousand dollars to come back and see him. He was sure we'd pack up and go away."

He then asked Mother Benedict if she had a chaplain. Remembering Father Winzen, she answered that she had an offer from a Benedictine priest who had come to the United States as a refugee from Germany in 1938. He was from the famous Abbey of Maria Laach, built on a lake in the Rhineland, and he had somehow come under the scrutiny of the Hitler regime but managed to get away and to America. He had been accepted at Saint Paul's Priory in the Newark, New Jersey, diocese, but he was looking for an assignment.

Bishop O'Brien nodded but then went back to the need for money, telling Mother Benedict that she had to now go out and around, telling people what she wanted to do and soliciting financial help. "I said no; he said yes", Mother Benedict said, recalling that she knew she'd have to do this, distasteful as it was to her.

Bishop O' Brien then reiterated his objections while maintaining the nuns had been accepted. However, he was adamant that they would have to start their Foundation by getting buildings. "That was not our idea of how to start", said Mother Benedict, but she believed in being obedient to her superiors, and so she accepted his orders. Bishop O'Brien later told Father Stack that he now had "some kind of new liturgical nuns" in his diocese.

On the ride back to Bethlehem, Mother Mary Aline was no longer as silent as before, but the women found it hard to talk. They were in a kind of happy shock that the Bishop, who had had no intention of accepting the nuns, had actually changed his mind once he met them. Lauren started offering suggestions about to whom Mother Benedict could write for help, in compliance with the Bishop's advice.

In the next few weeks, as Lauren made lists of names, Mother Benedict wrote letters to these people, all well-known Catholics, informing them of her project. "I composed a little essay I called 'From a French Battlefield to the Connecticut Hills' and sent it to everyone Lauren and Fanny could think of", said Mother Benedict. One of these noted and wealthy Catholics was Joseph Kennedy, father of John F. Kennedy, who would one day be President of the United States. "It was a very daring action on my part. He did write back, though, saying he couldn't help me because he was involved in other charities." Their friend Mrs. Hoguet, a well-known hostess in New York, responded by throwing a party for Mother Benedict so she could come and meet some important Catholics. One of these well-known Catholics was clearly touched by the nun's story. She was Clare Booth Luce, a convert to the faith who had taken instructions from Monsignor Fulton J. Sheen (who later became an archbishop famous for his one-man television show in the early '50s). Mrs. Luce decided she'd come to Bethlehem to meet the nuns, and when she did, she was impressed with what she saw—two courageous and intelligent women who were unwaveringly dedicated to their religious vocation. No one could have guessed at that first visit that the famous Clare Booth Luce—author, editor, war correspondent, member of Congress and wife of Henry Luce, editor of the prestigious *Life* magazine—was to be another major player in this saga of a nun's determination to bring her God-given task to fruition.

"Clare Booth Luce was top of the line, brilliant and human. She thought Fulton Sheen would be a great contact for me, and whenever he was holding forth, she dragged me there. But he said firmly, 'I will not do anything for them'", Mother Benedict revealed, adding, "I was actually glad." She had already been through too many difficult encounters with those who were cold or lukewarm.

After the visit with Bishop O'Brien and his insistence that the nuns had to go out and give talks to solicit help, it had become clear that Mother Mary Aline would be the one to put in front of a group. Speaking in public just wasn't Mother Benedict's strong point. They also knew they had to introduce young American women who might be considering the religious life to what a contemplative Benedictine life had to offer. It was decided that Mother Mary Aline would go to Catholic women's colleges to talk about the Foundation and plant the seed of interest in what was going to be built in Bethlehem. Meanwhile, one complication at Sheepfold was temporarily resolved when Mother Benedict was able to send her mother to stay with her brother John Duss and his family in Florida for an extended visit.

That first Christmas in America, in 1946—in a new Bethlehem—was a special time for the two nuns. Lauren had a special love for this holiday, and her artwork, especially paintings of the Virgin and Child, gave testimony to how strongly she was drawn to Christmas. She made this a very warm and intimate celebration of Christ's birth. "It was lovely, but I was at a point where each time I sat down to think about anything, all I could realize was that I had more and more problems", said Mother Benedict.

The need to get a building was a problem continually hanging over Mother Benedict's head since by fall she would be expecting the arrival of six nuns from Jouarre. Lauren and the lay people she knew decided to join together to help the nuns, and they went into action. With their considerable financial help, most of it from Justine Ward and Loretta Howard, Mother Benedict was able, in March 1947, to purchase her first building, a small, white farmhouse at the foot of Bird Hill, on twenty-five acres bordering Flanders Road. It had been built in 1798 and had been recently restored in exact colonial style. It would be known from then on by the name the nuns chose—Saint Gregory's.

Mother Benedict and Mother Mary Aline had been in touch with Jouarre on a regular basis. The six nuns waiting to come to America were getting anxious, and the two nuns in Bethlehem were even more anxious to establish the Community. But it was soon evident that they could not start a Foundation at Saint Gregory's. The house wasn't big enough, and the barns were beyond repair, and so they were faced again with the huge problem of where to find an adequate building.

Mr. Leather now came up with a possible solution. The factory he had built, which was hardly more than a stone's throw from Saint Gregory's and on the same side of Flanders Road, had long been empty, and he suggested that this could be remodeled in a way to fit their needs. Also adjacent to

the factory was a red barn, the interior of which was finished with a large and a smaller room on the ground floor
and one large room with nine windows in the loft. Mother
Benedict, carefully examining both these buildings, could
visualize them as being transformed into a temporary
monastery and a chaplain's house. "Mother Mary Aline was
brokenhearted. She said that we would be stuck here for
fifty years without being able to move out. I told her that
a plan to convert a factory was not our wish, but it was
what was possible, and we would have to go with what was
possible."

Mother Benedict didn't have the money for the down
payment that would be required to purchase the buildings
and land. But Mr. Leather was willing to rent them the
barn for a reasonable cost and said he would give them
permission to remodel that building as transitional living
quarters for the Community while they tried to find the
$180,000 needed to buy the building, the factory and the
land he was offering for sale. Mother Benedict also knew
she had to get permission from Bishop O'Brien before she
could proceed. With Father Stack's help, she got another
appointment with the Bishop, and he approved her request
to fix the factory building. He also gave her permission,
reluctantly, to go to Rome. This was a necessary trip because
Mother Benedict could not make a purchase for a future
monastery building without the approval of Rome. "I think
Bishop O'Brien let me go hoping that Rome would deny
me", she said.

Again, the new friends she had made, particularly Justine
Ward and Loretta Howard, came to her assistance. They
got together and raised one hundred thousand dollars for a
hefty down payment for the purchase, which would include
the factory, the barn and 175 acres. That still would leave a

mortgage of eighty thousand dollars, and Mother Benedict swallowed hard when she realized the financial responsibility she would be taking on.

It was now almost exactly one year since she had been in Rome, and this July 1947 trip was a momentous one for her. Mother Mary Aline stayed in Bethlehem to continue the work begun there, and Mother Benedict traveled to Rome, accompanied by Fanny Delehanty, anxious to bring the good news of their progress to the Sacred Congregation for Religious and request final permission to proceed with the Foundation. Once this permission was granted, she would be able to make plans for preparing a building to house the six nuns planning to arrive by September.

Everything went smoothly in Rome, with the prelates she had met a year earlier expressing some surprise at what she had achieved in so short a time yet concerned about how she was going to find the money her enterprise would require. "They kept repeating, 'You need money'", Mother Benedict said, and she knew they were rightly concerned for her. She met again with Monsignor Montini, and as before, he was positive and supportive during their meeting.

A trip to Jouarre was also on the agenda, and Mother Benedict looked forward to seeing her Abbess and fellow Sisters and introducing Fanny to the nuns of the Abbey. "The Abbess really cared for me, and she was glad to see me. I had woven a piece of cloth for her, and she was thrilled to have this gift from my hands. I also met with the nuns who were preparing to come to America to be a part of the new Foundation. I did not mask the fact that it was not going to be easy for them in Bethlehem. I told them honestly I didn't know exactly how it was all going to work", said Mother Benedict. "I actually feared that I was misleading people. I could see that what I had started to do—make a Foundation, on my own—was ridiculous. But I had to believe this task, impossible as it was, had to be done. I could see no other way."

Mother Mary Aline had been waiting nervously to get word from Mother Benedict in Rome, and before long the letter came, bringing the news that the permission to proceed with the Foundation had been granted. Mother Benedict had a signed order from the Vatican dated August 4, 1947, to go ahead with the Foundation. She had a second document listing the names of seven nuns, Mother Mary Aline and the six nuns coming from Jouarre, who, with her, would constitute the Community she would head.

Mother Mary Aline had not been wasting her time. She had met a craftsman named Walter Duda from nearby Woodbury, who had remodeled the buildings at Sheepfold for Lauren Ford. With her magnetic forcefulness, she persuaded Mr. Duda to collaborate with her in converting the red barn building into a temporary "monastery" that they would call Saint Joseph's. She asked for the work to begin on August 23, because that day marked the first anniversary of the nuns' departure from France.

The first step, she announced, would be to partition off the loft into seven monastic cells, and she made a chalk drawing on the floor so he could see her exact plan. She not only gave him detailed plans, but she also explained the meaning of Benedictine life as he began the work. With a magnetic person like Mother Mary Aline on the scene, Mr. Duda and his workers found her zeal catching, and many a night they worked late so as to get the alterations done as quickly as possible. By the first days of September, when Mother Benedict returned from Europe, she was amazed at the progress and proud of Mother Mary Aline, who gave her a grand tour of the renovations in progress and promised her that all would be ready by November. Mother Benedict recognized that Mr. Duda was a blessing, willing to work with his crew even after hours and late into the night so that the alterations could advance speedily. Any time some new purchase for materials was needed, Mother Mary Aline would give him the go-ahead, without asking Mother Benedict for approval. "Mother Mary Aline's goal was to get the work done, and my baby was the finances. I had to find the money for everything Mother Mary Aline was doing without asking. I suppose there's a virtue to that. If we waited till we had the money, that might have complicated things. Anyway, what we were doing with the buildings was the Lord's patchwork puzzle, and so it had to be right", said Mother Benedict.

On September 18, Sister Genevieve (formerly Sister Solange) and Sister Helen arrived at LaGuardia Airport from France; they were the first of the Jouarre nuns to arrive. Sister Frances and Sister Anselm landed on the twentieth, and Sister Maria Assumpta and Sister Thérèse came on the evening of September 23. The nuns traveled in groups of two on different planes for a very practical reason. Should a plane have crashed, not all of them would have been lost! The reunion at LaGuardia for each arrival was heartwarming, and after the long drive from New York to Connecticut, the nuns were settled in at Saint Gregory's.

Early on the morning of the twenty-fourth, now that all the nuns had arrived safely, the newly assembled Community of Mother Benedict Duss and seven nuns mounted the hill to the spot where their Abbey church of the future would one day stand. Here they recited the hour of Prime among the miniature pine trees, surrounded by the panoramic view of the Connecticut hills. It was a moment of joy for each of them and a time to give thanks for all that had been accomplished in the two years since Mother Benedict had made her promise to bring the gift of contemplative Benedictine life for women to America as she saw the G.I. soldiers on their white-starred tanks liberating Jouarre. But standing there, the moment of peace was short-lived for the young nun as she overwhelmingly felt the weight of the responsibility she had taken on and suddenly visualized the frightening uncertainties ahead.

Chapter 10

BUILDING A CLOISTER

— *The First Women to Hear the Call*
— *The Movie* Come to the Stable
— *The Completion of the Monastic Enclosure, 1948*

With the arrival of the six nuns from Jouarre, Lauren Ford and Fanny Delehanty had a full house at certain times of the day. Elizabeth Duss had also returned from visiting her son in Florida and had resumed her residency at Sheepfold. The nuns, who were young, all in their twenties and thirties, took their meals at Sheepfold and recited the Office in the private chapel. On September 24, Mother Benedict got them all together to practice Gregorian chant in preparation for singing at Mass, and the next day, Father Stack arrived and celebrated a sung Mass at Sheepfold. That first week, monastic life was revived for Mother Benedict and Mother Mary Aline, as they once again could recite the Divine Office as a Community. Following the advice of Father Stack, the nuns paid a few visits to local friends of their hostesses to familiarize themselves with American life. They also visited some monastic houses in New England: Dominican nuns of Springfield, Massachusetts, Trappist monks of Valley Falls and Benedictine monks of Portsmouth Priory, both in Rhode Island.

But apart from these brief excursions, the French nuns found their days brimming with the work of washing, sewing, making preserves and beginning their production of ceramics, which was to be a source of income. "Their first shock was how hard they had to work. It was a terrible blow. They had no sense of the reality they'd find here", said Mother Benedict. "We never knew where the money would come from. But God is a gentleman, and I tried to convince them that He would do His part, but we had to do our part first."

Mother Mary Aline was anxious to get the Community together at Saint Joseph's, the next step on their way to a permanent monastery, where Mr. Duda kept his workers busy. She checked on them daily to make sure the upstairs "cells" were taking form and that the kitchen, novitiate and tiny pro-chapel were well underway, still giving approval for purchases Mr. Duda deemed necessary. "I did the budgeting, and she did the spending. She was fabulous at spending", Mother Benedict remarked.

With building plans for Saint Joseph's getting close to completion, and the money for the down payment on purchasing Robert Leather's factory secured, it was time for Mother Benedict to see Bishop O'Brien again to get his authorization for the purchase. On October 9, Father Stack drove her and Mother Mary Aline to Hartford, where the Bishop graciously received them. Without hesitation, he granted them permission for the purchase and then appointed Mother Benedict as Superior of the Foundation, which they had called from the beginning Regina Laudis.[1]

When they got back to Bethlehem, Lauren, Fanny and the nuns were delighted with the news. Sheepfold had a little outdoor shrine to our Lady, a charming old Breton statue fixed to a tree near the brook, and the nuns chose this spot to celebrate Mother Benedict's installation. That very day, Father Damasus Winzen, who was to be the first chaplain, arrived and took up residence in the Stone House, owned by Lauren's adopted daughter, Dora Stone. Keyport Priory, where Father Winzen had been staying, had served its purpose as a refuge for monks driven from their monasteries by the Nazis and had been closed at the end of 1946. Its secular Oblates wanted to be associated with Regina Laudis, and with permission from the Abbot of Monte Cassino in Italy, they, along with a number of new friends of the Foundation, were able to be received at Regina Laudis with the title of Oblates of Monte Cassino.[2] Before long, however, they became known as the "New York Oblates".

The last Saturday of November 1947 was the long-awaited moving day, when all the nuns could take leave of Saint Gregory's and Sheepfold and take up their abode at Saint Joseph's, another transitional residence, but one that allowed them all to live together. A week earlier, a bell given by Lauren was hung in a rustic steeple on the roof. With the bell outside, and the small makeshift chapel inside, the fledgling Community could now celebrate the liturgy more fully, with Matins recited daily at 2:00 A.M., Lauds at 6:30, sung Mass at 8:00 A.M., Vespers at 5:00 P.M. and Compline at 7:30.[3] Mother Benedict gave them spiritual conferences, and they put time aside for singing lessons. Apart from all this, the nuns' hours were filled with work.

They had an open-door policy, however, since the enclosure had not yet been established and visitors could come in and learn about the Benedictine way of life, observing the nuns at ceramics, sewing vestments, rolling out pastry and painting. The nuns needed all the support they could get because the Foundation was plagued with poverty in these early days. Often they had to make excuses for not being able to pay the wages of Lawrence Cassidy, a farmer hired to help them, or the weekly bill given to them by Al

Rendino, their vegetable man. Some of the nuns grumbled at times over the hardships they were experiencing, such as constant work, inadequate heating, limited supplies and the lack of variety of food. "Some wanted a vocation that was pristine. But monastic life started out with the precariousness of life in the desert, and, in part, it has always reflected that austerity. The monastic idea is that we have to earn our living. And that's what we still do", said Mother Benedict.

Saint Gregory's had now become the women's guest house, where women, Catholic and non-Catholic alike, could come for a few days of rest or retreat in monastic surroundings, absorbing some of the principles of Benedictine life. To make it convenient for guests, Edythe Parsons, a friend of Fanny Delehanty, took up residence at Saint Gregory's to see to it that the guests had everything they needed, including rides from the nearest railroad station at Waterbury.

Christmas 1947, the first one to be celebrated by the Community now firmly settled in Bethlehem, was special to all the nuns. Sister Frances had made some charming ceramic crib figures and created a crèche out of a small cardboard box, in which she placed her tiny figures. The first Christmas card had been designed and sent out to friends. It showed the Infant Jesus lying on the ground under a flowering tree with a background of Connecticut hills and a red barn and a silo. A number of guests came for the Christmas liturgy, and everyone felt this was a very special time of thanks and celebration.

In January, Mother Benedict wrote to Monsignor Montini to give him news of the progress being made with the Foundation. On February 2, he responded, the first of more than a dozen letters he would send to her until he was chosen to be Pope on June 21, 1963 (taking the name Pope Paul VI).

Paternal Grandmother—
Mrs. Susannah Creese Duss

Paternal Great Grandmother—
Caroline Kroll Duss

Vera's parents, Elizabeth Vignier and John Duss

*Elizabeth Vignier Duss
with John and Vera*

Vera

Vera and John, 1925

Archbishop Curley, Vera, Elizabeth, Msgr. Louis Stickney and John in Baltimore, 1921

Vera's Passport, 1932

Vera in Paris, age 24

Vera — in medical uniform, Brevannes, April 1936

Abbess Angèle Bontemps, 1935   *Sister Mary Aline, novice*

Abbaye Notre Dame de Jouarre

Vera, May 1936

*Vera, dressed in wedding gown prior
to Investiture, January 7, 1937*

Newly clothed Soeur Benoît

Mother Benedict praying at the site where the medal of St. Benedict was buried on Bird Hill in 1946

Mother Benedict and Mother Mary Aline on Bird Hill, 1947

Mass celebrated at Sheepfold by Fr. Thomas Stack, 1947

Mother Benedict and Mother Mary Aline at Sheepfold, 1947

Lauren Ford with Mother Benedict weaving, 1947

Foundation group at Sheepfold, Fall 1947

Community chanting the Office on Bird Hill, 1947

First chapel in St. Joseph's, 1948

Nuns walking in the snow from St. Joseph's, February 5, 1948

Mother Mary Aline and Walter Duda building the choir, 1948

Mother Anselm and Walter Duda building the cells, 1948

Blessing of the Enclosure, September 2, 1948

Regina Laudis Priory, from the south, December 1948

Mother Mary Aline ringing the bell, 1948

Mother Mary Aline and Mother Benedict working in the garden

His Holiness, Pope Paul VI, and Mother Benedict, Rome, 1968

Mother Benedict outside St. Peter's Basilica, 1968

1971, Initial movements toward religious renewal and collaboration with lay professional persons and oblates in seminar on the land. James Douglas, Fr. Francis A. Prokes, S.J., Dawn Douglas, Sister Mary Ann Schmitz, F.S.P.A.

Mother Benedict on work day

Fr. Francis A. Prokes, S.J.

Closed Community and Monastic Community with
Peter Pettingell at the site of the dovecote, August 1975

Dovecote under construction

Monastic Community in procession at the dovecote, 1977

Completed dovecote – Chapter House (photo circa 2000)

Lady Abbess Benedict Duss on the occasion of her Abbatial Blessing,
February 10, 1976

*Mother Mary Aline
and Lady Abbess at
Lady Abbess' 50th Jubilee
celebration, 1988*

*R.M. Therese Critchley, Prioress of Our Lady of the Rock; Lady Abbess;
R.M. David Serna, Prioress of Regina Laudis at Lady Abbess' Jubilee
celebration, 1988*

Lady Abbess and Mother Dolores Hart, 1990

(Major) General George S. Patton, Lady Abbess, Mother Margaret Georgina Patton on the day of her final profession, August 1992

Ground breaking for the new Church of Jesu Fili Mariae, *1992*

Jesu Fili Mariae *in construction*

Jesu Fili Mariae, *view from the south, winter 1994*

Mr. Robert Leather, whose gift of thirty acres made the Foundation possible, with Mother Mary Aline inspecting the ruins following the fire at St. Martin's, 1950

Mrs. Margaret Lizauskas, early benefactor who had prayed in anticipation of the foundation of a monastery in the valley

Mrs. Ann Light, benefactor and oblate whose generous financial support made the building of the Church a reality

Nine nuns receive the blessing of Consecration to a Life of Virginity, July 11, 1998

Mother Dolores Hart, Prioress; Mother Abbess David Serna; Mother Maria Immaculata Matarese, Subprioress, in 2006 on the Hill at the site where the medal of St. Benedict was buried

*Mother Abbess David Serna and Lady Abbess Benedict Duss at the
Abbatial Blessing of Mother Abbess David, May 13, 2001*

Lady Abbess photographed by Gary Gunderson, 1989

Mother Irene Boothroyd and Mother Rosemae Pender, Foundress, F.S.E., at the coffin of Lady Abbess, October 4, 2005; photographed by Barbara Middleton

Lady Abbess' body, borne to the monastic cemetery on an oxcart, October 5, 2005

Lady Abbess Benedict Duss with Mother Irene Boothroyd near her garden on the Hill

Aerial view of the Abbey of Regina Laudis, 1980s

Lady Abbess potting plants under the plum tree, 2002

Monsignor Montini addressed Mother Benedict as "Very honored Sister" and wrote:

"Although you were telling me you did not want an answer to your words to me on 23 January, the expressions are so amiable regarding me that I cannot dispense myself from thanking you for them. This offer of a day a week of your good prayers is particularly gracious to me, and I eagerly want to tell you of all my gratitude. It is with much interest that I have acquainted myself with the news of the Community and the photographs. I send you my most cordial wish that God continue to bless your Foundation in the course of the year that has just started. Please accept, very honored Sister, the assurance of my religious devotion, in the Lord."

The next months were nonstop activity for the budding Foundation. Mother Mary Aline had taken charge of getting Mr. Leather's factory transformed into a monastery that would serve the Community until an Abbey could be built on the hill, which had long been known as Bird Hill. She was an expert on details, and though she had no formal education in architecture, she had a natural genius in this field, making her a fitting co-worker with Mr. Duda. The first step, she insisted, was to convert the storehouse attached to the factory into a chapel and choir.[4] After this, they would devote intensive efforts to the partitioning of the second floor of the factory into permanent cells for the individual nuns, a step that would allow them to move from the temporary haven of Saint Joseph's. All of this was being done on very limited funds, helped somewhat by a grant of five thousand dollars from Bishop O'Brien, who had said his contribution to Regina Laudis would be five thousand dollars a year. For the rest of what they needed—and their financial needs at this stage were enormous—they were on their own.

"Mother Mary Aline designed it all—the chapel, that wall, that gradation", said Mother Benedict, referring to the connected series of wooden panels that artistically form the wall that separates the enclosure from the monastery entrance grounds. "I had to give her something that was hers to do. I had no choice. She had to work in her own way; she had to be honest with her gift. She needed to feel the freedom of expression. And so I let her do it her way. She had a deep sense of reverence for me, and I for her. It was not easy to be in her—or my—position. We had to trust the Holy Spirit as the arbiter for our differences.

"I appointed Mother Mary Aline as cellarer. That's the one in charge of all material things. The cellarer is like a father, in the sense that she is the provider to the Community, the one who takes care of the material needs of the members. The cellarer reports back to the Abbess what inventories and supplies are needed and what maintenance has to be done. It is a very critical position, because the cellarer must be neither proud nor contentious. She's the one who gets it in the face all the time, 'Where is my . . . ?' 'Why didn't you . . . ?' and so on.

"I had no hesitation appointing Mother Mary Aline as cellarer because the people liked her so much. And she had a flair for drama in all things. At the same time, she was no cup of tea", Mother Benedict said with a smile about the nun who was frequently considered as co-foundress of Regina Laudis. "We were fighting frequently. She was so extreme in a way, prone to exaggerate in the wrong direction, and very different from the way I was. It would have caused great divisiveness if I endorsed everything she said. I had to keep my signals clear for the Community because it was sometimes hard for them to deal with Mother Mary Aline. Everything was an issue with her. I had to keep the balance.

"I knew her well from that standpoint because I had been her physician and knew how easily she could be provoked. She never had really good health, and she had a terror of illness.

"Yet she was outrageously devoted to the Foundation, to her vocation and to me, the Abbess. There was nothing she wouldn't do for the good of Regina Laudis, and she was part of the decision making from the beginning in every way", said Mother Benedict of her friend and cofoundress, Mother Mary Aline, who died on March 26, 1990, at age eighty-five.

With so many meals now having to be prepared daily to feed the eight members of the Community, Mother Benedict knew the monastery had to have the nucleus of a farm, and Sister Genevieve took this on as her major task. She found the barn adjoining the east end of the storehouse to be an adequate place for small animals, and she managed to get and care for two geese, one hundred chickens and an ever-growing progeny of rabbits. Sister Frances kept up her artistic productions, and some of her ceramics sold. But these early efforts at self-supporting work were hardly adequate for the needs of the Community.

Mother Benedict recalls this as being "a hard, cold winter, and a dreadful time of poverty. Besides having very little income, we had the $80,000 mortgage on the building that the Bishop insisted had to be paid in five years, and huge expenses in getting the factory remodeled. It was a very hard time for everybody, probably too hard for some. But we didn't get discouraged. There was no time for that. We depended entirely on prayer and God's resources", she said, knowing that her primary task as a Benedictine Superior had to be the development of a monastery.

"To make a monastic foundation, you have to have a monastery that people can come to", Mother Benedict said, explaining that Saint Benedict described a monastery as a place where everything that is needed can be found. "Thus, it is an unending task. It requires that stable relationships must be established within the community itself so that the community can be solid enough to meet the pull of the outside world and the needs of those who befriend the monastery. It is also essential to get the temper of a locality to see if it is favorable to monastic development. What we found in Bethlehem was borderline, but good. If you are too easily supported, you lose a lot of energy. To keep energy alive, you have to have a lot of crosses, difficulties of all kinds, and you have to be intelligent enough to see the truth and wisdom of this.

"I was not fully aware of that myself back then", Mother Benedict went on. "I was very tentative in what I tried to do for quite a while, truly to find out if those calling themselves friends were really so. I spent a whole year at Sheepfold without doing too much of anything that could be called monastic. I was just getting to know the local situation, the town of Bethlehem, the people around and how to relate to them." She smiled. "And we're still learning."

February 10, the Feast of Saint Scholastica, Saint Benedict's twin sister and the first Benedictine nun, was a memorable day for the new Community. Mother Mary Aline announced that the chapel was close enough to completion to allow the nuns to occupy their choir stalls for the first time, singing Vespers in honor of their revered saint. The choir and chapel were both finished in knotty pine, divided from each other by the sanctuary where the altar stood, facing the choir. Mother Benedict was extremely pleased with the "miracle" wrought by her cofoundress and Mr. Duda in designing and carrying out to completion this small, charming chapel, predominantly finished in wood,

but absolutely perfect as a beginning home for monastic worship by the budding Community.[5] A surprise gift from Lauren Ford gave the new chapel a link to the past. At an auction,
she had acquired a gilded panel, a thirteenth-century Flem-
ish wood carving of Saint Anne with the child Mary on her
left arm and the Infant Jesus on her right. She planned to give
it to Father Vincent Donovan for the chapel of Saint Paul's
Guild in New York, but they had no room for it there. Thus,
Lauren and Father Donovan graciously gave it to Mother
Benedict, who had it placed in the choir. The tabernacle, for
the repose of the Blessed Sacrament, was also a gift, being the
one that had been formerly used at the Keyport Priory, where
Father Damasus Winzen had stayed.

On the First Sunday of Lent, February 15, 1948, Mass
was sung for the first time in the new chapel. In the weeks
following, the nuns spent long hours in rehearsing the chants
they would be singing for the Holy Week and Easter liturgies. On Holy Thursday, Mother Benedict invited a dozen
very small boys of the neighborhood to take part in the
ceremony, representing the twelve apostles. They were dressed
in miniature white albs made with monks' hoods. Father
Stack was the celebrant, and he guided the boys, who carried out their parts with great seriousness. Ceremonies like
this began to make people in the area aware that a new and
rich approach to worship was in their midst with the coming of the Benedictine nuns.

On Pentecost Sunday, a most welcome sound was heard
during Vespers—the mooing of two cows. The nuns were
overjoyed when they discovered that these cows, named Cleo
and Constance, were a gift from Mr. and Mrs. Graham Carey.
This meant they would now have milk and butter, two essential foods they had badly needed to maintain good nutri-
tion. When before long, Cleo gave them a calf, they named

this new and wonderful gift Stella—which means "star", a word full of meaning for Mother Benedict.

Word had started getting around now about the new nuns who had come from France to Bethlehem, and since the story had a certain romanticism about it for American writers, some started coming around to do articles on what was happening. *Life* magazine sent a photographer, and this prestigious magazine ran a full-photo feature story on the nuns and the Foundation.

The most famous writer who came to Regina Laudis was Clare Booth Luce, well known for her plays *The Women*, *Kiss the Boys Goodbye* and *Margin for Error*, all of which were made into movies. Mrs. Luce had just completed a four-year stint in the House of Representatives as a Republican from Connecticut when she started coming to Regina Laudis. "Clare wanted to work on a movie for our benefit. She decided to write a script, to 'fix' the piece I had written, and she called hers *From a French Convent to a Bethlehem Stable*. We discussed this, back and forth. She was insistent about doing this because she felt it would be helpful to us to get known.

"Then the project was turned over to another writer, Gretta Palmer, also a convert of Fulton Sheen and a friend of Clare." Gretta had written an article entitled "The Bethlehem Story", which was to be published by *Sign* magazine in January 1949, and so she was familiar with Mother Benedict's story. "She came here, too, with Clare, but the environment of a monastery, and Sheepfold, was so foreign to them. I liked them, and they were sincere, but they were out of their element. They were more aligned with the world—unlike Lauren, who had seen and believed and was so dedicated to what a monastery means and brings to the world. They didn't understand and didn't allow the seed to germinate", said Mother Benedict.

Gretta Palmer proceeded to write a film script, never coming to consult with Mother Benedict on it. Then Twentieth Century Fox studios sent Mother Benedict a contract stipulating that they could change and modify anything they wanted in any way they wanted. Mother Benedict had to consult with Bishop O'Brien, who was adamant that she was not to sign anything. There would be no contract.

At this point, the story had become fiction, and the movie *Come to the Stable* was made. It starred Loretta Young as Mother Benedict, and Celeste Holm as Mother Mary Aline; Elsa Lanchester played Lauren Ford. The film began with the two nuns walking on a snowy night to a house in Bethlehem, and before the story was over, it had introduced gangsters and a few other plot complications. "The studio handled it exactly the way they wanted to. They wanted power, not truth, and made a farce of it. I could accept what was true in the Loretta Young role, but Celeste Holm was much too gentle for Mother Mary Aline. She didn't have her fire. Lauren congratulated Elsa but just laughed at how she was portrayed. I think Elsa was touched, but she didn't know what to make of what had come about in Bethlehem. Loretta Young never came to Regina Laudis, though Celeste Holm came here several times. We actually didn't see the movie (which came out in late 1948) until 1950, when Twentieth Century Fox sent us the film. I guess by then they had decided we would like to see it", said Mother Benedict.

"The movie was a little frosting on the cake, a tempting acclaim that had no depth. It did, however, create a stir. So many people came to look at us. Every Sunday, a contingent of people would be here wanting to meet us. We even had Sunday teas. This was the antithesis of what Lauren could appreciate, but she was only too glad that people were responding to us. Yet it meant people were invading her privacy, and that was very costly for her.

"I had to deal with this, of course. But I had a trust in God. I had taken a terrible risk, leaving France. It was crazy. And so I had to be very grateful for that attention and the respect expressed by the people who came here. We received invitations to affairs and were asked to speak. We accepted them all. I would send Mother Mary Aline to give the talks. She was totally fascinating and gorgeous, the best press agent anyone could have had. She had wanted to be an actress, and when she was standing in front of people, talking, she was totally in her element. And she did present monastic life in a convincing way to people."

Mother Benedict and the monastery of Regina Laudis didn't receive a penny from this movie at the time it was made and released, because the Bishop had not allowed her to sign a contract. Any money at this time would have been a godsend. Mother Benedict recalls this period as one where if anyone gave a gift of ten dollars, "that was a big week—we were so poor." A few years later, Twentieth Century Fox apparently had a guilty conscience, because the studio asked Clare Booth Luce to contact Mother Benedict and offer her some money for having used her story for their movie without any compensation. She received thirty thousand dollars, a sum that made a good dent in the mortgage they had to pay off before a fast-approaching deadline. *Come to the Stable* is often seen on cable TV stations during the Christmas season and is now on video.

In the spring and summer of 1948, Mother Mary Aline and Mr. Duda worked intensively at getting the second floor of the factory partitioned into individual cells for the nuns. On July 10, the eve of the Feast of Saint Benedict, the cells were ready for the nuns to move in. Getting the nuns settled became a shared project, with Mother Benedict's close lay friends carrying furnishings and personal items from Saint Joseph's to the place that would now be the monastery home of the nuns. Besides Lauren and Fanny, helpers were Mademoiselle Delore, who had come from Paris to visit Regina Laudis, and a Hungarian sculptress who had come to give art lessons to Sister Frances. The nuns still had to use the kitchen and refectory at Saint Joseph's, but the cells there were now to be used for Father Damasus Winzen, visiting priests and male guests.

Bishop O'Brien had been kept informed of the progress being made in Bethlehem, and five days after the nuns had moved to their new building, he sent word to Father Damasus that the date to mark the "enclosure" of this Foundation—that is, formally declaring it to be a Community of cloistered nuns who would from then on live behind the wall—would be September 2. He also told the chaplain that he could come himself to conduct the ceremony.

This was a time of panic for Mother Benedict. She had exactly six weeks to construct the enclosure wall, parlors, sacristy and kitchen—and no money at all. But, as in the past, the Lord didn't leave her stranded. Miraculously, a Hartford priest, Father Eugene Moriarity, knowing her plight, told some prominent Catholic laymen about the crisis facing the young Superior of this new Benedictine Foundation, and they took action. One of them provided cypress wood for the enclosure wall and a squad of workmen to erect it and raised some money by telling his friends about Regina Laudis. Volunteers came with Father Moriarity on weekends to work under his direction and that of Mother Mary Aline. Still, the preparations were enormous, and the nuns found themselves staying up well into the night to complete preparations as that very important date approached.

On the morning of September 2, a procession of clergy formed at the monastery, headed by a color guard of the Fourth-Degree Knights of Columbus from the nearby cities of Waterbury and Danbury. These men, wearing their dress swords and white and yellow satin capes, preceded some forty priests, with the last in line being Bishop O'Brien, attended by his Vicar General, Monsignor John Callahan, and some other priests. The procession came to Saint Joseph's, where the nuns were assembled, along with about two hundred guests. The Bishop greeted all, and everyone then proceeded up the incline and back to the monastery, stopping while the nuns, chanting psalms, walked past them and the Bishop. Mother Benedict was accompanied by two young key bearers: her nephew John Duss, and Lauren Ford's grandson, Paddy Stone. The procession then continued up to the Great Gate. The nuns entered the gate, with the guests and clergy remaining outside. The Bishop, following the nuns, was the last to enter the gate. There, he turned back to receive the keys of the monastery from Mother Benedict. The gates were swung shut, and Bishop O'Brien then locked them from the outside.

After that, all went into the chapel, where the Bishop officiated at the votive Mass of the Immaculate Conception, sung by the nuns in their choir. Father Damasus delivered the sermon, saying that the sacrifice of the nuns was "an answer to the materialistic spirit of the world". He continued, "In their secluded world, they will not be of the world, but their prayers and their acts of labor and love will be for the world." After the last Gospel, the Bishop himself gave a sermon, expressing his regard for this Community and his satisfaction that they had now "regained their cloister".

"His big joke was the enclosure. He said he would take the key and throw it in the lake. My brother [John Duss

from Florida] was there, and he thought he'd die when he
heard that. As for my reaction, I don't take those things too
seriously. I know what interior freedom is about. The Bishop
was demanding, yet kind. But he would never praise anyone for his work."

The next day, the Community began a retreat, preached
by Father Damasus on the theme of the Consecration of Virgins, the ceremony that had so deeply affected Mother Benedict. One of the nuns, Sister Frances, wearing the white veil,
and accompanied by Mrs. Ward and Mademoiselle Delore,
as her "godmothers", was to be consecrated. The Right Reverend Bernard Kaelin, the Abbot Primate of San Anselmo in
Rome, was invited by Mother Benedict and graciously agreed
to perform the rite of consecration. This marked the first time
that the ceremony of the Consecration of a Virgin was seen
in the United States. "I invited him to come so we could be
recognized officially. He was benevolent and encouraging."

*Mother Benedict had worked with Sister Frances at Jouarre, and they
respected each other deeply. "But the weight of religious life was too
much for her", said Mother Benedict. Sister Frances left the Community in 1970. However, she wanted to stay close to the monastery. She started a children's program for Regina Laudis and stayed
at Sheepfold. Her name was Denise Maublanc, but she asked Mother
Benedict to give her a new first name, to bless, in a way, her new chosen work. Mother Benedict asked if she would like to be known as
Hannah Eve, and she said yes, with joy. Hannah Eve Maublanc
worked with children there until her death in January 1987.*

On the following Sunday, September 12, the first temporary profession took place when Sister Anselm received the
sleeveless cowl and cream-colored veil, which from then
on were to be worn by the professed novices. Mother Benedict had decided to make the ceremony of temporary vows

more of a celebration, so she would clothe the novice with a sleeveless cowl, something not done at Jouarre. The flowing sleeves would be added at the time of the final profession.

It was very clear that the Bishop now expected the nuns of Regina Laudis to stay behind their wall. As far as he was concerned, he had locked them in and thrown away the key. But an immediate problem erupted. The farm and the garden, planted with vegetables, lay outside the wall. The Bishop's order was severe. No one but the one Lay Sister, Sister Helen, could leave the enclosure to take care of the gardens. It was impossible for her to do that much work on her own, and large portions of the crops were lost. The nuns had counted on their garden to produce the vegetables they would be able to freeze for the months ahead. Father Damasus took it upon himself to try to get the Bishop to understand this problem and its serious consequences. He went to see the Bishop and explained that in Europe, Benedictines were allowed, with certain restrictions, to work in designated fields outside their walls. The Bishop then reluctantly said he would let some of the nuns out of the enclosure to work the garden.

An urgent need now that the monastery was a reality was to create a novitiate so that American women could be received as postulants. With all the attention Regina Laudis had gotten in the press and from the movie, many American women had visited the monastery, and a number of them expressed a desire to enter. But no one could be received until additional cells were provided. Again, Providence stepped in, with two of the men who had worked on the monastery building coming forward to complete the refectory and common room free of charge. With the help of the New York Oblates, the Community was able to complete two new cells, making it possible to receive the first two American candidates. On November 12, 1948, Josephine Dinger and Alice Kortchauk entered, becoming the monastery's first American postulants. Opening their doors to American women who wanted to become Benedictine contemplative nuns would initiate a new phase in the saga of Regina Laudis, and a new level of work and responsibility for Mother Benedict.

Chapter 11

THE NUNS' LIFE IN THE FIFTIES

— Additions to the Monastery
— A New Chaplain
— Developing Talents and Attracting Visitors

The work ahead for Mother Benedict now that the Community was officially the first Benedictine cloister for women in America took on a new seriousness that would have both positive and negative effects during the next few years. For two years, the local people and visitors had been able to mix freely with the nuns; they could come into the nuns' dwelling places, watch them at work, converse with them. Now they could come to Regina Laudis and participate in the feasts and liturgies, but the wall was clearly a barrier. The contact was decidedly not the same, and some were critical, not understanding the deeper meaning of this call to serve God according to the ancient and enduring Rule of Saint Benedict, which these women were following. Lauren Ford and Fanny Delehanty felt the separation keenly, yet they understood because they had been schooled at the Benedictine Abbey of Solesmes. They came to the services daily and expressed always a great reverence for what the life represented.

The monastery was daily becoming ever more rooted in these Bethlehem hills, with its holdings that included the remodeled factory and the buildings called Saint Joseph's and Saint Gregory's. Publicity about the Bethlehem nuns' story had focused a lot of attention on the place, and visitors came frequently to see what was being built here. Young girls came to Regina Laudis to make retreats, and guests well known in Catholic circles came here to meet with the nuns and to offer lectures, among them Mother Benedict's friend from France, Jacques Maritain. Most importantly, several American women were seeking to enter the monastery, waiting until cells were completed so that the monastery could accommodate them. "We had to make a dormer for every postulant, and each one cost two thousand dollars", said Mother Benedict, who at this stage still had no bank account and no idea of where the next penny would come from.

The work of the first few years had taken a toll on Mother Benedict, and as the Community prepared to celebrate its first Christmas in the enclosure, she became very ill with a sinus infection. Somehow she recovered enough to be with the other nuns as they prayed and enjoyed recreation around the Christmas tree. She even distributed gifts that had been sent by devoted friends to all the Sisters. On the Feast of the Epiphany on January 6, Mother Benedict was able to greet Ann Eichelman (later Mother Cecilia), a musician from Maryland, who was then a candidate for the religious life. But a few days later, the foundress collapsed from a case of severe anemia and was taken to a hospital in Hartford for treatment and rest. She had to stay there three weeks, and upon her return, she had a recurrence of the sinus infection. This was a dark time for the young Superior, who had so much to do and so much on her shoulders, especially the need to find money to pay bills, support the Community and stay out of debt.

"I was truly absorbed by the formation of this Foundation, which was fantastically difficult and often seemed a
thankless task. I was dealing with the shock of being in this
moment, not knowing exactly what it all meant. The needs
were like those of a young family, having to get started
with everything, from pots and pans for the kitchen and so
on. We were starting from scratch, hoping to get little by
little to the fullness of life. But certainly, we didn't have it
to start with", said Mother Benedict, emphasizing that everything had to be done "in an honest and impeccable way, so
that we remained true to the starkness of the vocation".

She appreciated anything that was a momentary ray of
light—like the news from her New York friends that they
had arranged for a lecture to be held at the Waldorf in
New York for the benefit of Regina Laudis. It would be
held on Ash Wednesday, which in 1949 fell on March 2,
and the speaker was the renowned British author Evelyn
Waugh. Other friends also came through with help, one
holding a bridge game in Hartford to raise money, and
another offering her services as an accountant to assist Mother
Benedict in keeping the monastery account books. Then,
on March 21, another American woman, Ruth Wilson,
entered as a postulant.

In late April, Clare Booth Luce came back to Regina
Laudis to make a retreat. She had received the Bishop's
permission to spend three days inside the enclosure with
the Community. Mother Benedict would recall later that
Mrs. Luce proved to be a charming and tactful guest, carrying out all the monastic customs with great humility.
Even more, Mother Benedict would remember the practical "thank yous" that came from Mrs. Luce—especially
a station wagon that was so crucially needed. At her request,
a friend of Mrs. Luce provided the money needed by

Mother Benedict to equip their small kitchen with cupboards and a dishwasher.

In mid-May, Regina Laudis conducted an ancient ceremony on the monastery grounds, one called the "Baptism of the Bells". The nuns had acquired four bells to be placed in the steeple of their monastery, and each had a history and would be given a name. The first, named Francis-Julia, was a shiny locomotive bell from the New York, New Haven and Hartford railroad. The second, Lauren-Francesca, had formerly belonged to a Canadian farm. The third, Simeon-John-Ascension, had once been used by a Protestant church in Pennsylvania. The most unusual of the four, Mary-Eugene-Benedict, was a bronze bell cast in 1746 from the French village of Mouans-Sarthoux in the Maritime Alps. It had been used there in the ancient chapel of Saint Bernardin until the death in 1929 of the last member of the brotherhood, the "Confrérie" to which the chapel belonged. It had come to Connecticut on the French "Merci Train" [1] and had been destined for the state library. But when it became known that the nuns in Bethlehem were interested in this bell, which came from the country they had left so short a time before, some friends arranged that this bell, one of the oldest now in America, be given to Regina Laudis.

On June 6, 1949, the Feast of Pentecost, a new postulant arrived, Patricia Fullerton of Saint Paul, Minnesota, an accomplished singer. Mother Benedict was expecting two more nuns from Jouarre, Mother Ida and Mother Paule, to be arriving at around the same time to be "seniors" of the developing Community. Mother Ida would be in charge of the sacristy, responsible for all the items needed for the liturgy, as well as the sewing—making wimples, bandeaux and habits. Mother Paule would become librarian and guest mistress while helping with other chores—even peeling

vegetables—if needed. Activity to get the carpentry work
finished in the factory building went on at a feverish pace,
with Mother Mary Aline pushing Mr. Duda to put the
finishing touches on the library, getting carpenters to partition off new cells in the attic and assigning volunteer
workmen to arrange the laundry and sewing room in the
basement as well as finishing storerooms for the sacristan
and the cellarer. When the Jouarre nuns arrived on June
13, all was ready, and they were greeted by the joyous
pealing of the newly "baptized" bells.

That summer was one of the hottest anyone could remember. Because of the record-breaking heat, Mother Benedict, relying on her medical knowledge and common sense
with a priority on well-balanced freedom and wisdom,
changed the order of the day so that the garden work—
which required everyone's help—could be done during the
least oppressive hours. And instead of eating in a sweltering
refectory, the nuns were allowed to combine meals with
recreation by having picnics in their woods. By August,
when the weather had become more tolerable, Justine Ward
came to visit, offering to coach the nuns in the chant that
was her expertise. She came for eight successive Thursdays
to give the nuns singing lessons, a gift that made Mother
Benedict very happy.

In early October, the Regina Laudis Community had a
surprise visit that also brought them great joy. Mrs. Ward
brought the Abbot of Solesmes, Dom Germain Cozien, for
his first visit to the new Foundation. His coming coincided
with the investiture of Miss Ruth Wilson, who would receive
the name Sister Mildred, and he consented to be the celebrant for the ceremony. Shortly before the Abbot was ready
to put on the vestments, Lauren Ford took a color photograph of the altar. The photo proved to be so striking that

it was printed in a postcard form and sold in the art shop for years.

Back in August, two more American women had arrived at Regina Laudis seeking to be postulants: Mary Marko of Fairfield, Connecticut, and Patricia Dempsey of Brooklyn, New York. Of the six American women who had entered the monastery before "the Dempsey girl from Brooklyn"— who was given the name Mother Placid—none remained there permanently, leaving for reasons ranging from poor health to an inability to adapt to the demands of religious life. "The gap between what they expected and the reality of the life was too much for some. What they found here was not the beautiful mirage they had envisioned", said Mother Benedict.

"Mother Placid was the first serious candidate", she continued. "She started bravely, as did the others, who were, however, less able to bridge gaps between what they left and what they were coming into. She could understand the vision", said Mother Benedict. As recounted earlier, after celebrating her Golden Jubilee, Mother Placid was fond of saying, "Entering is like the first day of creation for you. You come to find out what God has put you here for. You walk in, and this place will set off all the light and dark places in you." She likened a monastery to a pressure cooker: "all the trials you need to clean up your act and learn to love".

Miss Patricia Dempsey had first heard of Regina Laudis in 1947 when Mother Mary Aline came to the college she was attending, Marymount in Tarrytown, New York, to tell the young women students about this new Foundation. "I had been in Catholic school for sixteen years, but there was something different in what this nun was saying", said Mother Placid. Curious, she and three friends decided to go to Bethlehem during the Christmas vacation. They arrived during a blizzard and were put up at Saint Joseph's, where the Community then still lived. She remembers the next morning, seeing the lovely, snow-covered fields, having breakfast, drinking coffee out of little bowls—and meeting Mother Benedict.

"She came over to us, knelt down, put her hand on my shoulder and talked to us. I had never met a nun like that in my whole life. She was so real, totally dignified, not coming on like a big personality, but such a presence", Mother Placid recalled. "She had a soft voice, like air, and something emanated from her. She was different. I couldn't put my finger on it, but I knew she wasn't one to try to impress you with her personality. I felt she was tied into another dimension."

It had not been Patricia's intention to enter the monastery at that time, but after her graduation from college, the aspiring artist, who had returned twice to Bethlehem, came again in August of 1949, this time for good. She knew she was looking for "something deeper. When I came, there was still a dirt road. I saw the nuns in sandals, doing their farm work. It was so cultured, so simple—like a Lauren Ford painting. It was like morning had never been before. There was a freshness here, a mystery—like going into some huge stillness, going into God", she said.

Miss Patricia's first assignment was to work on the farm with Sister Genevieve, and that was a truly new experience for someone who had been raised in Brooklyn. Because she was a talented artist, she was also placed as an assistant to Mother Frances. Meals were very different from what she had been used to before, often including wild plants, like dandelions and mustard greens. A small tragedy hit on October 18, 1949, when one of their three cows, Constance, died. Somehow Constance had gotten out of sight long enough to eat a huge number of green apples, and she became so sick that nothing could be done to save her life. "I remember we were all called into the common room, and Lady Abbess gave us the terrible news. She said things would be different now that our milk would be so limited, no more than one glass a day. We were young girls, and we liked milk. We sensed this would change our whole economy", said Mother Placid.

The days brought consolations, however. There were impressive visitors like the respected Fordham philosophy professor and writer Doctor Dietrich von Hildebrand. Also, some financial gifts allowed work to begin on the monastery grounds. Bulldozers, a backhoe and trucks arrived, and the operation began, including draining; grading and surfacing the large parking space northeast of the monastery; making solid driveways to connect Saint Joseph's, the monastery and the parking place with Flanders Road; and excavating a large ditch to carry off spring water, which, especially in rainy weather, seeped through the walls of Saint Joseph's. This was progress, and prayers of thanksgiving were in the hearts of all, especially when another gift came in November, allowing the Community to purchase two more cows to take the place of Constance! For these new and most welcomed additions, Sister Genevieve picked names with a monastic touch—and milking time reminder—Matutina and Vespertina.

On November 10, another woman arrived to enter Regina Laudis, this time a nun from another order who had obtained the required authorization to be admitted as a transfer. She was immediately invested with the monastic habit and was given the name Sister Columba. In later years, Mother Columba and Mother Placid would collaborate as writer and artist for some books in the Paulist Press series Classics of Western Spirituality.

With Christmas approaching, the monastery received another surprise gift, a magnificent Neapolitan crèche that dated from the eighteenth century. The crèche had been offered for sale in New York for several months, but with more than sixty figures, it required a large room in order to display it adequately, and it was very expensive, a double impediment, even for collectors. Loretta Howard, one of Regina Laudis' great friends, had seen the crèche and become enamored of it. She bought it and decided to give it to the monastery as a memorial to her deceased husband.

Now the problem that loomed for Mother Benedict, who still had no discretionary funds, was where and how to display this gorgeous gift. A very well-known woman in Bethlehem, Caroline Ferriday,[2] a former actress, came to the rescue. Miss Ferriday's family had bought the house that once belonged to noted Protestant clergyman Joseph Bellamy, who ran the first Protestant seminary in the United States and was locally known as "the Pope of Litchfield County". Miss Ferriday offered Mother Benedict a colonial barn from the Bellamy property, now her family estate, which could be moved to property owned by Regina Laudis. Not wasting any time, Mother Benedict hired workmen to break ground just to the northeast of Saint Gregory's, at the foot of Bird Hill, to prepare the foundation for the barn. Mrs. Howard was ecstatic. The formal opening of the Crèche—as the Neapolitan creation set behind glass in this relocated barn would from then on be called—was expected to be in 1950. To Mrs. Howard's joy, the work was completed by Christmas, and a celebration was planned.

"I was told to make a map to show how to get to the Crèche. I did a kind of stand-up card, which everybody thought was creative", said Mother Placid. "Mrs. Howard had arranged for the Paulist Boys' Choir from New York to come and sing, and many local people came. I was standing next to Mrs. Howard when everybody started to sing. She was transfixed." The official opening and blessing of the Crèche took place on February 19, 1950. Father John J. Dougherty, distinguished professor of Scripture at Immaculate Conception Seminary in Darlington, New Jersey, delivered the sermon.

The Crèche has ever since been an oasis for visitors, who come from far and wide to see this magnificent rendition of townspeople in Italy going to the stable to see Mary, Joseph and the Babe.[3]

As the new decade of the '50s began, Mother Benedict continued working to meet what she anticipated would be immediate and future needs of the Community. An important undertaking was the acquisition of a small hand proof press, which inaugurated the founding of their monastic press. The little machine was installed on a table in the library, and a friend, Raymond Healy, came and taught Mother Benedict and Mother Assumpta the printer's art. Following this, the resourceful Superior added a new enterprise, a "scriptorium", to focus on the art of producing beautiful books. She had an artist's table installed by the window of the library and invited another friend, Nancy Wayne, to teach Sister Anselm the art of lettering and illumination.

On Saint Patrick's Day, the Community welcomed another new candidate, Anne MacDonald, a professional woman who was a Benedictine Oblate and a longtime resident of Hartford, Connecticut. Miss Anne, who later received the name Sister Maria Joseph, brought business skills and a good knowledge of Connecticut to Regina Laudis. She became the official chauffeur for the Community, but even more importantly, she took charge of business correspondence and the account books, relieving Mother Benedict of these trying chores.

Work to make the monastery a fitting living place went on, with Mother Benedict ordering installation of an automatic fire alarm system in all parts of the monastery, chapel and barn. To reduce the coldness of the building, she also had the building insulated. Mother Mary Aline continued to see to it that the development of the monastery building progressed at a brisk pace. Under her keen supervision, the exterior walls also received attention and were covered with rough-finished shingles that were about the same color as the original gray cinder blocks. Some of the workmen would come on weekends to continue putting in dormer windows and partitioning cells on the third floor, planned to be the novitiate dormitory, to ready the monastery to receive more postulants as they petitioned to enter Regina Laudis.

As spring of 1950 got under way, Regina Laudis was becoming a thriving Community, with twenty-two women living together as postulants, novices and full-fledged nuns. Expansion was necessary, and the best solution seemed to be converting the monastery barn into workrooms and a dormitory. This could be done only if another shelter could be found for the livestock, the hay and the farm implements. Mother Benedict was aware that a farm adjoining their Bird Hill property on the east was being offered for sale. It consisted of 140 acres of land, a large modern dairy barn with a silo, a ten-room farmhouse and numerous outbuildings. She had shared her dream of being able to buy this property with her friend Lauren Ford, and to her great surprise and gratitude, Lauren, insisting on anonymity, generously came forward to provide the needed money.

After the purchase, the Community named that property Saint Martin's. Understandably, the farm now became an absorbing problem for the Community. The herd had been moved to the new barn and pastureland, but the labor was more than the nuns could handle on their own. Mother Benedict had met a man named Norman Langlois, a Benedictine Oblate and a farmer, on her visit to Saint Paul's Priory in Keyport shortly after her arrival in Bethlehem. They had stayed in touch, and now she contacted him and asked if he would come with his family to Regina Laudis to be auxiliaries of the monastery and work the farm. He and his wife, also a Benedictine Oblate, and their six children moved into the farmhouse in July and immediately began the work of rehabilitating this long-neglected farm.

In the months that followed, the herd was enlarged from five head of cattle to seventeen, and modern dairy equipment was installed. Mother Assumpta and some of the novices went every day to work in the dairy and care for the livestock. Mother Frances went to the farm twice a week to make butter. When it came time to cut, bale and get in the hay crop, neighboring farmers pitched in to help.

This should have been a time for Mother Benedict to be able to catch her breath and relax a bit, but bad news came suddenly in early September. Mrs. Langlois telephoned in a panic, telling the Superior that their great barn was on fire and her husband was in Hartford. The nuns could hardly believe the news until they looked out and saw a huge column of black smoke rising from behind Bird Hill. In spite of efforts of firefighters to control the blaze, within about one hour the fire destroyed the barn, dairy and silo, as well as the entire hay crop, the tractor, the electric milker and most of the other dairy equipment.

Neighbors who had hurried to the scene of the disaster were full of sympathy. One of them was Mr. Leather, who said he wanted to be the first to present Mother Benedict with a donation for rebuilding the barn. The nuns, need-ing to renew their trust in the Lord, felt it was more impor-tant than ever to be in the choir that day to sing Vespers. After Vespers, Mother Benedict went back to the scene of the fire. It had started to rain, and so she put on a hooded rubber jacket while she was outdoors assessing the damage. She went to the house carrying a present of homemade bread and wine to reassure the Langlois family that all would be well. Norman had returned from Hartford, not know-ing that he was going to find the barn in ruins. He simply broke down in tears, devastated by the disaster that had hap-pened with no warning. (Later, they discovered that the fire had been started when a neighbor's child, playing in the barn, had struck a match.)

Now that there was no place to keep the herd and no fodder to feed them, it became necessary to sell all but two of the cows. Neighbors and friends did all they could to help, bringing bales of hay and contributing money and building materials toward the erection of a new barn. But even with this help, and the insurance money, there was not enough for the undertaking. Fortunately, the stone foun-dation of the barn, which was all that remained, was solid. They covered it with boards to protect it from frost, hop-ing that they could rebuild come spring.

About a month after the fire, their chaplain, Father Dam-asus, went to Rome with a few of the New York Oblates. Mother Benedict thought he was there for a holiday, but as it turned out, Father Damasus had another plan in mind. He requested and obtained permission to start a Founda-tion in Elmira, New York, which would be called Mount Saviour Monastery. He, along with Father Gregory Borg-stedt, Father Bernard Burns and Father Placid Cormey, would be the first members. While Father Damasus was away, Father Bernard Burns stayed at Regina Laudis as temporary chaplain.

Mother Benedict, who remembered Father Damasus as being very scholarly, having his own private library and being a fine preacher, later spoke of his plan to start his own Foundation—without ever having notified Regina Laudis—as painful for her. "We seemed to be a stepping stone for him. Many of the New York Oblates had come here because they had known him at Saint Paul's Priory in Keyport, and they more or less installed themselves at Regina Laudis. We received them because they were following him. They meant well, and some stayed with both Foundations", Mother Benedict recalled. "But he also asked people supporting us to support him, and they left. I don't know if he could have gone through what we did. Perhaps he had to find something already in motion, and ultimately God called him to do that in Elmira."

Father Damasus returned at the end of October, but since his plans for the future meant he could no longer be chaplain at Regina Laudis, Mother Benedict had two pressing new problems—the need to find a new chaplain, and the necessity of obtaining replacements for much of the chapel equipment. The side altar, the main altar, the tabernacle, the sanctuary lamp, candlesticks, a chalice, some vestments and the choir stalls had all been brought to Regina Laudis by Father Damasus from Keyport. He now needed to take these with him to establish his new Foundation. He gave the monastery the choir stalls and the main altar and said they would have several months to replace what he would be taking away.

The more pressing problem was the need to find a chaplain immediately. Mother Benedict had invited Abbot Ignatius Esser from the Abbey at Saint Meinrad, Indiana, to

come to Regina Laudis to officiate at the ceremony of investiture of the three eldest postulants, who received the monastic habit with their new names, Sister Michael, Sister Martin
and Sister John the Baptist. Mother Benedict now called
on him for help in finding a chaplain. Abbot Esser promised a monk from Saint Meinrad's, who arrived a few weeks
later. He was a venerable monk with forty-eight years of
service, Father Eberhard Olinger, well known as an authority on Scripture and translator of the Book of Psalms that
was part of a new English translation of the Bible spon-
sored by the Confraternity of Christian Doctrine. He began
a course on the Psalms for the nuns, who regularly were
being given courses and lectures by visiting scholars and
writers, both priests and laymen. One of these noted guest-
teachers was Frank Sheed, well-known publisher and author,
who spoke on the subject of "The Catholic Intellectual
Revival" when he came to Regina Laudis in 1951.

Before the end of 1950, the nuns had accomplished an
impressive work, the firstfruit of their monastery press. This
was a small, paper-covered book of poems by Justine Ward
entitled *Flowers of the Days and Hours*. This title was very
much in keeping with the tremendous devotion Mother
Benedict had had for gardens all her life. In fact, at Regina
Laudis, with the help of some lay garden enthusiasts, she
had been able to create a formal garden, which was greatly
admired by all who saw it. Mrs. Ward's booklet was the
first printed at Regina Laudis, and copies were placed on
sale in the art shop.

On the eve of New Year's Day 1951, Mother Benedict
contemplated the major work to be done in the months
ahead. It would have to start with the rebuilding of the
barn at Saint Martin's and the making of an additional
dormitory in the hay loft on the second floor of the space

adjacent to the monastery, where the scriptorium, ceramics, arts and printing departments had been moved. Refurnishing the chapel was also planned. What she didn't know was that the problem of finding a chaplain would surface again almost immediately, when Father Eberhard suddenly fell too ill to carry out his duties. He remained several months as an invalid at Regina Laudis while the nuns cared for him.

Providence came to the rescue on January 11, when Father Vincent Donovan, a Dominican priest who was one of the first friends of the monastery, showed up to visit Mother Benedict. She told him of her most pressing need—to find a chaplain. To her surprise, he said he'd love to fill that vacancy. Wasting no time, he got permission from his Superior to take on this position. On the first day of February, Norman Langlois drove to New York, picked up Father Donovan, loaded his trucks with the priest's belongings, which included a library-sized collection of books, and brought Regina Laudis their new chaplain. Father Donovan, well known for his enthusiasm for Gregorian chant, had a large following, and he brought that following with him to Regina Laudis, often giving weekend retreats to small groups at the monastery.

At the end of May, a truck pulled up to the monastery to remove all of Father Damasus' equipment from the chapel and bring it to Mount Saviour. Plans began immediately by friends of Regina Laudis to replace these pieces. Mr. Duda, with Mother Mary Aline urging him on, made the side altar, careful to make sure it matched the other pieces. They obtained a new altar stone containing relics of Saints Fulgentius and Constantius. Mr. Duda also started building a new oak tabernacle, which was completed and ready for use by July 8. The door of the tabernacle was made from a fifteenth-century ivory piece donated by Justine Ward. Mother Benedict and Mother Frances worked at sewing to replace some of the vestments.

While all this was going on, Norman Langlois was busy with the work of getting the barn rebuilt. And that April, Mother Benedict had had a visit from Edward Combs of Yonkers, New York. He said he had heard she needed construction help, and he offered to recruit friends and come weekends to do the job. She told him, "Welcome!"

The hammering began on May 11, and since nine cells were to be constructed, the work took many weekends. The addition needed a bathroom, septic tank and heating unit, so this lengthened the completion time. A year later, Mr. Combs and his friends, who did all the work, could look with satisfaction on what they had accomplished.

As the year 1951 wound down, the Community could look back and see the enormous progress that had been made. Their labors in the garden and on the farm had produced solid quantities of food that were preserved— green beans, squash, peas, tomatoes, corn on the cob, and peaches. They had put up a good supply of jams and jellies and had regular supplies of milk, eggs, butter and cottage cheese, along with chickens and rabbits. Friends continued to help the nuns get food they couldn't produce.

"Mrs. Ward got the idea that it would be nice on a feast day if we didn't have to cook, and she arranged with Curtis House [a nearby restaurant in Woodbury] to bring us the meal. After that, Curtis House gave us leftovers at night on a regular basis", said Mother Placid, commenting on how this gift of food was a blessing in the monastery's early and lean years. Curtis House is touted as being the oldest inn and restaurant in Connecticut.

Mother Placid also told of a couple, Robert and Ann Clark, who owned Merryvale, a bed-and-breakfast in Woodbury, who also saw to it that food was sent to Regina Laudis. They provided the monastery with supplies from a local grocery store over a period of many years. Clearly, neighbors who had seen the devoted and hard work being done by the nuns respected them and wanted to help out when they could.

But while hard work was required and hospitality for the varied guests who came was always generously and graciously given, there was a third side to the Benedictine life that was never ignored—the necessity of study and reading. Mother Benedict gave conferences regularly for both the novitiate and the whole Community on subjects that included the history of the liturgy, the meaning of contemplation, the mechanical structure and literal sense of the Bible and the Holy Rule of Saint Benedict. This Rule was the rock upon which the Foundation was being built, and it was crucial for the growing Community to understand it.

"The Rule of Saint Benedict is based on maintaining and improving our relationship to God. That is stressed by the Rule. God created us to be His workers, His 'hired labor'. It is that stringent. That's our identity. It follows us through every event or status in life or series of strange events and apparent coincidences. You can't change that relationship. You can only improve and own it. And it's not as simple as it seems. It means if you choose that identity, then the manifestation of your fidelity to that commitment needs to be expressed throughout every happening", Mother Benedict explained.

"When you introduce stability, that is, never leaving, then this works very well. For this, you need structure, which, Saint Benedict said, has a stability of its own. He was the first to introduce this characteristic of monastic life—that you stay where you entered. The monastic profession is based on the fact that we make particular vows of obedience, poverty and chastity. Saint Benedict added stability. You'll stay put. You'll stay here. That's an additional strain on our native desire to be free. It takes a conversion of heart to acknowledge that this is right. Obedience is the vow that defines the monastic state. Then the vow of stability maintains your battlefield in this one place. You can't default, get in the car and take off.

"Now, obedience must never mean slavery to a system. The old idea of monastic obedience was often an abuse of power. Obedience has to do with helping you convert your manner of being. It can't be only to submit to strict authority, because this would simply cause revulsion. The orders a Superior gives have to be just. Obedience means you're going to have to work on your attitude, that aspects of your being will have to be changed and modified to be consistent with God's will. This is a work never finished. A Benedictine is being educated to seek the higher good, and that is where obedience is a formation tool. And what must be remembered is that Saint Benedict says you can't obey except out of love.

"And yet love of God is the last thing they're thinking about when they come to enter a monastery. They may think they are. But it is so difficult to love God. It takes so long to get there. Saint Benedict says all you have to bring to Christ is the offering to share in His Passion, and you go through a rigorous process to discern how to get there. If you choose this path, it propels you into the Passion of Christ. Saint Benedict defines this whole process as being patient—it comes from the word *patior*, meaning 'to suffer'. You have to suffer to continue the work of redemption, even while you never know who you are redeeming. This is all a mystery; we can never understand this rationally, and only by grace can we choose the redemptive path that Christ opened to us. In a small way, or a big way, we have to die within ourselves to further the movement of the Church", said Mother Benedict.

✤ ✤ ✤

The decade of the '50s would be one of progress on all levels for the fledgling monastery, but not without setbacks and problems as the Community dealt with the growing pains endemic to those who make a radical change in their life and relationships. The American women entering Regina Laudis in the first six years were "all city girls", said Mother Benedict, and several of them left. "The monastery's first practical responsibility was to sustain itself. We had to make a living, and that required care of the land, but within a monastic tradition. They had no idea of that aspect", said Mother Benedict, explaining that to follow the Rule of Saint Benedict, who said all things must be treated as "sacred vessels of the altar". His followers had to be willing to "work with their hands, study with their minds and pray with their beings."

The foundress stated often that Bishop Henry O'Brien was never convinced that she would be able to develop a successful farm. "He told me, 'You're never going to find American women to do that kind of work.' I trusted that we would in time."

But Mother Benedict didn't focus just on farm work. She early on had put a priority on "elevating the consciousness of the monastery to creative dimensions of work" that would make Regina Laudis known and bring in money. She found that several of the women entering the monastery became quickly skilled as craftsmen, including a potter, candlemaker and bookbinder. By late winter of 1952, one of the trusted workmen began to construct a bakery at the east end of the monastery building so that the nuns could add another craft to their list, that of producing fine baked products. By summer, when the work was done, and a new gas oven installed, Mother Benedict herself put the first loaf of bread into the oven.

But never was the Superior naïve about what was required of a woman becoming a Benedictine nun. She was always conscious of the tension between personal satisfaction gained from working at a particular specialization or project and the basic demands of supporting the growth of the Community. "The fulfillment of a woman in the Benedictine life depends on achieving a balance between the project dimension and the survival dimension. If the survival dimension is at peace, then you can do the individual development work that is also essential. But if you are stripped to the survival dimension alone, or the project dimension alone, then there is disruption", said Mother Benedict. She added reflectively, "There's a difference between grace and altruism." A woman could be determined to stay in a monastery, thinking altruism could get her through the demands of the life. But grace is what makes the difference, "otherwise you're just ravaged", she said.

Building a Community is "very precarious", she went on. "You can lose it in three minutes. I thank God when I see everybody at Compline who was there in the morning. To me it's a miracle—astounding that they have made that free-will decision to stay. All of us here have to confront that option every day of our lives."

Mother Benedict was aware that times ahead would be rocky for some of the young women who had entered as reality set in, and they would find it more and more difficult to make a free-will decision to remain. But the days now were full of hope. People from the area and beyond brought new energy to the monastery with their encouraging affirmations of respect for Regina Laudis, and many guests—including notable priests and scholars—found their way to Bethlehem.

One of these visitors was the prominent English writer Father Gerald Vann, known for his very human spiritual treatise *The Heart of Man*. He visited the monastery at the end of January 1952 and gave the Community a conference on Mary's canticle, the Magnificat. But he also brought a story that gave the nuns a smile about how the movie inspired by the founding of Regina Laudis—*Come to the Stable*—had come to have its title. He told them that one day he happened to be with Clare Booth Luce and some of their mutual friends, listening to a radio broadcast of Christmas music. Hearing a familiar air, he remarked to Mrs. Luce, "That's an English carol." She then asked him for its name. Father Vann replied, "It's 'Come to the Stable'." At that, Mrs. Luce exclaimed, "Why, that's just what I need for the title of my motion picture!"

Father Vann smiled and went on, telling the nuns that the odd part of the story was that a day or so later, it hit him that the name of the carol was not "Come to the Stable" at all. It was "Come to the Manger".

Having been led to Bethlehem, Mother Benedict was not surprised that the monastery would get special attention at the Christmas season. The demand in 1951 for Christmas cards made and painted by the nuns had taken all of them by surprise, and so the decision was made that they would begin making the cards for Christmas 1952 early in the year, with new designs added to their assortment. Meanwhile, the print shop took on a most ambitious project, producing one thousand books of poems by Raïssa Maritain, wife of Mother Benedict's friend Jacques Maritain. In this book each poem was printed both in French and in its English translation. Today, these books, featuring the work of this renowned woman scholar, a Russian Jewish convert to Catholicism, are collector's items.

A special surprise awaited the Community on Easter Monday when Mother Benedict announced that, thanks to a gift from a benefactor, the mortgage on the monastery would be completely paid off in a few months. Bishop O'Brien had been adamant that this debt be paid within five years, and now Mother Benedict could say, for the record, that she had been able to meet this obligation before the Bishop's deadline.

A few weeks later, the Community welcomed as a visitor Dorothy Day, the highly respected foundress of the Catholic Worker Movement. Miss Day and Miss Harriet Schuyler, foundress of the Mother Cabrini Circle and a leader in interracial activities in Rochester, New York, were at the monastery to be attendants for Miss Mary Agnes' solemn investiture, when she was given the name Sister Prisca. Miss Mary Agnes had been affiliated with the Catholic Worker Movement in Rochester. She made a striking figure on this day because, at the beginning of the service, instead of wearing the traditional white wedding gown, which is then exchanged for the black habit and white veil, this postulant chose to wear a black gown with gold accessories.

A very painful situation developed for Mother Benedict as summer approached. Mother Assumpta, who had come from France, had a psychiatric breakdown and had to be temporarily hospitalized. She was a very attractive woman, with charisma and a way of captivating people, and she had been a key person in the first few years of the Foundation. But she clearly had severe psychological problems, which probably stemmed from her childhood. Her parents had been killed when she and her two brothers were quite young. They lived in poverty, often not having enough to eat, a trauma that had given her recurring problems with food. Mother Benedict wisely arranged private therapy sessions for her, but these did not prevent a breakdown. Unfortunately, Mother Assumpta developed an animosity against Mother Benedict and sowed a great deal of discord. She was charming enough to get the ear of people coming to the monastery and easily would make them her audience as she complained that she was being badly treated by Mother Benedict. This was a painful time for the foundress, who dealt with this first serious conflict between herself and one of the nuns by getting Mother Assumpta the professional help she needed, guarding her privacy and responding with silence and love despite the discord she had churned up.

One consolation for the Superior during Mother Assumpta's time away was that the garden was thriving, with an assortment of vegetables and fruits. A joyous occasion was when Sister Genevieve and the postulants helping her counted the strawberries they had picked and could announce the amount as nearly six hundred quarts. A number of guests helped that summer with gathering vegetables. Some of them were high school girls from the small town called Herkimer in upstate New York who had come for a retreat but worked in the garden between meditations.

Mother Benedict saw the garden as "one way of giving service to creation. We draw out of creation our sustenance, and we teach people to reverence that, so as to restore the order that God wanted." She explained, "God created a garden that was meant to be the medium for His first man and woman to do good. Whenever we make a garden, it is Paradise restored in some sense—and people will latch

on to that. To see a garden is to increase the sense of wonder of life and what is possible. This has a transforming
effect on people."

In October, another well-known group came to visit
Regina Laudis, the famous von Trapp Family. Their chaplain, Monsignor Franz Wasner, had preached a retreat at
the monastery a month earlier, but now he had come back
with the family of singers, who sang and played their current concert program for the nuns. The von Trapps and the
Community felt an immediate rapport, and when it came
time to leave, the visitors were so reluctant to go that they
lingered in the October sunshine, taking out their instru-
ments and performing a few more songs. Mother Benedict
and Mrs. von Trapp formed an instant and strong friendship. When she was back at her home in Vermont, Mrs.
von Trapp sent Mother Benedict an autographed copy of
her most recent book, which then was *Yesterday, Today and
Forever*, and she continued writing periodically to the
foundress for many years after.

At Christmastime, yet another first-time event took place
at Regina Laudis. Mother Frances had started a catechism
class for children and had arranged a surprise for their parents and friends of the monastery. She and the children had
prepared an Advent play based on the prophecies of Isaiah.
On December 20, the children put on the play at the Crèche.
Some two hundred people of all denominations crowded
into the old barn that houses the Crèche to see what the
children had accomplished. Afterward, all the visitors were
invited to tea at Saint Joseph's. Never did this monastery
waver when it came to hospitality in the spirit of Saint
Benedict.

Christmas week brought a touching letter, sent to Mother
Benedict by Mrs. Robert Hoguet, who had just been to

Rome and had met with Monsignor Montini. She wrote as follows:

"Just before we left, Monsignor Montini paid us the glad honor of coming to see my husband and me at the Grand Hotel, and I was deeply touched by the way he spoke of you and of his great admiration for what you have done and for the way in which you have done it. I asked if I might tell you all he said, and he seemed pleased to have it all repeated to you. I have rarely heard greater admiration voiced or greater enthusiasm shown for any project or the realization of any project. He is so wonderful himself, and all he said made a great impression on me.

"You are always in our thoughts and in our hearts, and may I say my admiration and affection equals that of Monsignor Montini."

As 1953 dawned, Mother Benedict responded to a request by some of the New York Oblates who wanted to form a study group focused on Scripture. The foundress agreed to give them conferences on Scripture once a month. She also gave weekly conferences to the nuns on monasticism, the meaning of asceticism, on the imitation of Christ and on many other subjects, with her teaching firmly grounded in Scripture and the works of the Fathers of the Church.

The monastery was getting a reputation for being a place where both children and adults could come to learn more about the faith. Sister Frances asked Father Donovan if he would take on a new responsibility—that of teaching a weekly course on the fundamentals of the Catholic faith for boys in Bethlehem between the ages of eleven and fourteen. She was teaching the younger children. The priest agreed, and to the happy surprise of the boys, after class he would often give them lessons in boxing, a sport in which he proved to be an able instructor. Meanwhile, Mother Mary

Aline was organizing retreats for married couples, which were also very well received.

In mid-January came another letter that warmed the heart of the foundress, from Monsignor Montini, *Sostituto* (Undersecretary of State) for the Vatican. Monsignor Montini wrote, "On my part I do not forget you, and with all my heart, I wish that the year that is beginning would mark a new stage in this 'totally interior growing', as you so rightly describe it, in the souls that have been confided to you. With these wishes and the assurance of my faithful remembrance before God, please accept the assurances, my Reverend Mother, of my very devoted sentiments in our Lord."

There was also a fun side to the goings-on at the monastery from the very beginning because Mother Benedict had a great sense of humor and was very conscious of the importance of seeing the light side of life's events. The novices had a grand opportunity to share some fun when Monsignor Franz Wasner, the von Trapp Family chaplain, came back for a short stay at Regina Laudis, offering to give the Community singing lessons focused on harmony. In preparation for the March celebration of the Feast of Saint Benedict, Monsignor Wasner and the novices composed a four-part round in honor of Mother Benedict, followed by a puppet show, a spoof that gave everyone a chance to laugh at herself.

The monastery now discovered that it was developing a reputation for producing fine Christian art. Mother Frances and Sister Placid had undertaken a serious study of Christian art with special emphasis on the Byzantine period and found in it a means of deepening the spiritual qualities of their own individual talents. At the same time, the small art shop set up on the monastery grounds was constantly getting depleted, needing new materials for sale. This meant everyone had to try her hand at art. Mother Benedict, reflecting on this time, says, "The artistic endeavor of Regina Laudis had become a family affair."

Sister Prisca had embarked on her own art form, taking orders for stained-glass medallions. With the help of Sister Placid, she added to her original patterns of stars and crosses some lovely figures of our Lady and the saints. She was also helped by a well-known artist named Carl Paulsen and received generous donations of stained glass from various companies throughout the country. One of her big orders was to produce six medallions for a church in the Midwest. Seeing such spectacular artwork, the monastery's old friend, Father Stack, took some samples to an exhibit of Christian art in New Rochelle, New York. That generated many new orders and enhanced the reputation of Regina Laudis as a center for sophisticated and creative Christian art.

Books produced in the print shop were also getting noticed. Sister James and Sister Lawrence had produced one thousand booklets on Regina Laudis, and these were sold out. They immediately did a second printing of 1,500 copies while also supplying the art shop with cards and filling orders. Business was getting brisk, and Regina Laudis was getting ever better known.

In August, two of the postulants left the monastery. Mother Benedict gave them her blessing but then decided to make a change in accepting candidates. The guest house was frequently inhabited by young women questioning if they had a vocation and wanting to try this out by entering Regina Laudis. Now, after the experience of several candidates having left, Mother Benedict decided a more thorough investigation should be made to try to assess the possibility that the call was true when someone came knocking at the door. Applicants from then on were asked to make a two-week retreat at Saint Gregory's so that more insight would be available before a decision on acceptance was reached.

"I have always given the benefit of the doubt to a woman who wants to enter, maybe to the far limit of prudence. I don't regret that. I always give them an opportunity, even if it's misused. When someone comes here, I try to clarify what her motives might be. There's a drive in people to look for security, and from the outside, it might look like this is the ideal place for security. But it's not. The monastery is a dynamic challenge. It requires that you do something to change, to become more pliable so that you can take on Christ in a new way. This is a lifetime process. Either it works, or it doesn't. I tend to extend these periods of learning. Maybe I'm tolerant in an exaggerated way, but God is patient that way, too. Yet, if a person has no vocation, I have to tell her. There's no use in her staying. People who come in really have no idea of what they're coming into. It's a shock. It's in the more subtle forms that demands are made on your life and where difficulties reside— like having to contend with individual Community members.

"My principle is to try to have a clear grasp on how this person is presenting herself. Is she really seriously seeking the life of conversion that religious life represents? This is what she will have to deal with all the time.

"Some have no capacity for this. They're not able to live this way. They then must exercise their freedom to leave", said Mother Benedict. And she emphasized, "I'm a staunch advocate of freedom before God."

The vegetable garden was flourishing again that summer, now under the care of Sister Cecelia, Sister Lawrence and Miss Santina (later Mother Luke). Knowing how important it was to the Community to have good crops, the nuns had sent samples of their soil to the Agriculture College at the

University of Connecticut for analysis and recommendations. The report was not encouraging, saying the soil was not good enough for a thriving farm, but the college did recommend different fertilizers to be used for each of the crops. Between devoted care and prayer, and these specific fertilizers, the crops turned out to be superb, excellent enough for the nuns to enter some in the vegetable contest at the Bethlehem Annual Fair. The entries from the monastery received six first-place and two second-place awards. Only one entry, the green peppers, failed to impress the judges.

Help still came to the nuns, who saw this always as a reflection of the loving kindness of their Father in Heaven. In one short period of time, a workman came and installed a burglar alarm, a long and complicated task. He didn't charge for his labor. A Jewish garage man was called to repair a car on their parking lot, and he requested that the fee for his services be given to the monastery instead of to him. A pint of small coins appeared in the chapel, the gift of unknown children. And a window washer refused to accept payment for his work because he was a Knight of Columbus. To have this kind of support from strangers was a great affirmation for what Mother Benedict and the Sisters were achieving.

On September 7, 1953, Regina Laudis opened its gates to receive Miss Mary Prokes as a postulant. Born and raised on a Minnesota farm, Miss Mary had heard of the fledgling monastery of Regina Laudis while she was teaching English and physical education at a Benedictine school in Yankton, South Dakota. She was attracted by what she heard of the liturgy and the rhythm of the life at Regina Laudis. But when she came to Bethlehem to see and experience the monastery, something else happened. She later said: "They were exceedingly poor, just starting out. I felt the genuineness of the poverty—and that spoke to my soul." To have an experienced farmer now at the monastery was exactly what was needed to transform the land into a working farm.

A month later, the Community was on retreat when the news came that the Hartford diocese was undergoing a major change. The diocese was being divided into three parts, with Hartford becoming an Archdiocese, and the other divisions being the dioceses of Bridgeport and Norwich. The Most Reverend Henry J. O'Brien would now be the Archbishop of the newly created Archdiocese of Hartford. Regina Laudis would remain under the paternal jurisdiction of the new Archbishop. On November 5, Archbishop O'Brien paid a short visit to Regina Laudis to confer with Mother Benedict and later assured the Community of his deep interest in their welfare. He gave them his paternal blessing before he left.

Mother Benedict had received another letter that fall from Monsignor Montini, who wrote, "I send heartfelt wishes that God may continue his protection over your Community. . . . The fidelity of your remembrance touches me deeply. I beg you to continue to keep me continually in your prayers, of which I have a great need in the difficulties of my office. Please accept, my Reverend Mother, my very devoted sentiments in our Lord."

Chapter 12

CHANGES IN THE SIXTIES

— The Upheaval of the '60s
— The Arrival of Father Prokes
— Pope Paul VI Supports Mother Benedict

As the months went by in the year of 1956, Mother Benedict began to think ahead, knowing that before her was the task of writing a specific constitution for Regina Laudis. Unexpectedly, Father Bernard Sause, a Benedictine from Atchison, Kansas, paid a flying visit to Regina Laudis and gave two conferences to the Community in which he stressed exactly what was on her mind—the matter of a constitution specifically adapted to the needs of this monastery. He showed that he really understood the uniqueness of this Foundation when he emphatically told all of the nuns that they were pioneers, not only because of the newness of their Community, but also because they were designing a new concept of cloistered life that was the right fit for the United States.

Father Sause didn't mince words when it came to underscoring that they would need enormous patience and generosity to deal with the hardships that are inevitably part of building a new Foundation. He also emphasized that there should be unity within the monastic family and that, while each member should seek individual development, the motivation should be precisely to enhance the common design and to contribute to the unity of the common life. He also told them that it was necessary for them to see what their place should be in the neighboring community of Bethlehem and to have a clear perception of the contribution they would be able to make to their neighbors.

"We all appreciated the confidence he placed in us and the encouragement he left with us", Mother Benedict would say. "My desire to have Regina Laudis compose its own Constitution was based on the fact that each monastery must assert its autonomy. There is no central body that is in control of Benedictines. Each monastery derives its authority directly from Saint Benedict himself, and it is exclusive to each one. Historically, since the fourteenth and fifteenth centuries, attempts have been made to try to centralize the Benedictine order, but these have failed. Each monastery has its own structure. We kept the Constitution of Jouarre at first, but it was my intention always to work to have our own. Then, by the late '60s, Rome asked us to prepare our own Constitution, which we did."

In June of 1957, Mother Benedict welcomed a newly ordained Jesuit priest who was to become a major player in the continuing development of this monastery. He was Father Francis Prokes, S.J., the brother of Mary Prokes, now Sister Stephen. Mother Benedict had invited him to say his first solemn High Mass in their chapel on Trinity Sunday. With great joy, the Community prepared for this event, with everybody finding a way to make a contribution, from making vestments to printing programs. On that Sunday, all the Prokes family members—father, mother and five sisters, three of them nuns—were present. After a few days, Father Prokes went back to his Wisconsin province, saying as he left how deeply he had been impressed by the spirit of the monastery.

The rest of the year was filled with memorable progress on the buildings. The little art shop that had been located in the small parlor at the monastery entrance had to be moved, and while the Community debated where to move it, the Knights of Columbus from Hartford arrived with a solution. Edward Crofton, a close friend of the Abbey, offered to erect a separate building for this shop that would permanently be named the "Little Art Shop". Help came from individuals and companies for everything needed, from the excavation of the building site to digging a drainage canal to laying the floor, then putting in display cases, installing doors and windows and adding the finishing touch, venetian blinds. The Community offered its boundless gratitude to these friends, who worked two years to complete this building. The Little Art Shop, which sells unique products made by the Regina Laudis nuns, has ever since been a favorite place, frequented by visitors, tourists, friends and neighbors.

Another building under construction that summer was a garage. Sister Stephen was gaining friends among the neighboring farmers, who respected the nuns and encouraged them to continue to try to turn their land into a thriving farm, in spite of the poor equipment they had. Surprising her, Paul Hanrahan, a man who had come occasionally to the monastery, donated a new tractor to the monastery. He said he had been impressed by the nuns, who had to work under difficult conditions, and he admired Sister Stephen for her competence as a gardener. The monastery garage, however, couldn't accommodate the monastery's prized new tractor. That didn't faze Sister Stephen, who, with the help mostly of college student volunteers, built a new garage.

Again, a letter came from Rome in August that warmed Mother Benedict's heart. It was from her friend Monsignor Montini, now an Archbishop, who addressed her as "Very

Reverend Benedicta Duss"(!) and wrote, "I have not thanked you for your many dear and good letters! I still keep them here, spread out on my table. Now, here is your letter of 5 January, with the beautiful image of the Magi and an enclosed offering of fifty dollars", and he went on to respond to her other letters and gifts. Continuing, he wrote, "You can always count on my good reception of your writing, even if time is not always given to me to answer immediately. You can be sure of the communion of prayer and charity that holds me close to that hearth where family reunites with religious life. I am happy to see that your flame is fed by the Spirit of God and from the wind, for this world that is truly miserable needs so much to be illuminated by the contemplative life. I am in contact with the Viboldone Community, to which I send your offerings. They are in need of a new monastery. Their house is still in difficulty, but we hope to be able to defend and help them.... I send to you and your Community my blessing."

Mother Benedict always spoke of how she cherished the letters received from this friend, who later became Pope and who so warmly affirmed her mission. She always shared these words of support and encouragement with the Community.

"Sometimes the tremendous responsibilities I was carrying almost overwhelmed me, but one thing always came to my rescue, and it was that I had always been able to keep a sense of humor. I always made sure that the Community kept a sense of fun, and some occasions, like the October Feast of Saint Placid, seemed to be a good time to remember the light side. The nuns here had always managed to come up with some enjoyable entertainment for themselves, and I remember that the event they planned for

October of 1957 was exceptionally funny. In spite of the fact that they were enormously busy, they decided to put on a variety show that would portray the trials and tribulations of the typical novice, whom they called Sister Placid. They would work in pairs, and I was teamed with Mother Mary Aline. Each couple had to come up with their own skit, which was to be kept a secret until the very opening of the play", Mother Benedict recalled.

"When the day came and the curtain rose, the show began with two senior novices grumbling over the prospect of putting on another Saint Placid's Day entertainment when obviously the theme had been worn out centuries ago. Then there was the disillusioned Sister Placid, who had expected to find a leisurely life as a contemplative and instead had to work on a farm.

"The finale was the skit that Mother Mary Aline and I had prepared. We were both dressed, rather outrageously, as postulants. We stood before the monastery gate—the prop was a door from one of the cells still under construction— and sang, in original verse, the scruples we were wrestling with as we were taking that step over the threshold. Finally, with heroic resolution and hands outstretched to receive the palm of martyrdom, we made our entrance. Apparently, from the applause and response, our presentation was the high point of the entertainment. We all did a lot of laughing and had a great time."

There were also opportunities for the Community to get firsthand information about current events and developments in other countries. This interest was in keeping with Mother Benedict's insistence that the Community stay informed about what is happening in the world. "At Jouarre, a nun had to hide the Bible under her pillow. Traditionally, there was not an emphasis on intellectual life. I think when we left they began to wake up and see there was more to monastic life. I was determined to have a high intellectual and spiritual life here at Regina Laudis. We weren't just going to do peasant work", she emphasized.

Complementing this devotion to learning was another project Mother Benedict felt would be appropriate for Regina Laudis, the opening of a lending library of books on theology, spirituality, the saints, inspiration and religion for the use of their lay neighbors. In charge she put Mother Lawrence, who worked with some Catholic women of Bethlehem to plan and publicize the venture. They came up with the idea of placing shelves for the books in the entrance parlor so that Mother Lawrence could greet borrowers from behind the portress' grille. Seeing this important educational development, an anonymous donor gave the monastery a donation allowing them to buy children's books to add this component to the library. In the spring, a weekly story hour was added, and each Saturday, the large parlor was filled with lively, enthusiastic children hearing tales and bringing books home to read during the week. The library project was yet another phase of their continuing ministry to include serving the spiritual needs of neighbors as a complement to their mission.

On the tenth anniversary of the Community's first Christmas in Bethlehem, celebrations were creative and joyful. Mother Mary Aline supervised the novices as they gathered pine boughs from the woods to shape into a large Advent wreath hung from the ceiling of the refectory, a tradition they kept ever after.

On one Sunday just before Christmas, the Community sang several Christmas selections for a tape-recorded broadcast on a Hartford radio station. Musician Stanley Roth, a longtime friend, brought his adult choir from Waterbury to sing traditional Christmas carols outside the monastery. Lights from the windows highlighted the white snow that had just fallen, making a perfect setting for the beautiful songs. The carollers were then thawed out by coffee at Saint Joseph's. The visitors wanted to know why some nuns didn't have to stay in the enclosure. They explained that some of those who enter are called "Oblate Sisters", and they are a connecting link between the "choir nuns", who mainly stay within the enclosure, and the outside world.[1]

The new year of 1958 began as a season of promise for the monastery, but with one recurring problem for Mother Benedict—the continuing care of her mother. "She had been a resident at the monastery since our arrival from France, leaving occasionally to visit my brother in Florida or friends in New York State. At Regina Laudis, she helped with the gardens and the animals, had taken an interest in beekeeping and had even been a teacher for several months, giving French lessons to a young Trappist monk named Frater Liguori. But recurringly, my mother would have severe health problems, which I would have to deal with. And then there was always an uncertainty about my mother's behavior. You never knew if she'd be difficult or nice to guests. She could be lovely, and she could lash out. You never knew what she would do. Mother Mary Aline was the one who dealt with her. They could get along. But worries about my mother were always hanging over my head", Mother Benedict said.

In March the nuns rejoiced at the clothing of another Oblate Sister, Melanie von Nagel Mussayassul, who had been brought up in Italy and Bavaria and whose father had been a highborn general in the Bavarian Army. She had been married to an acclaimed portrait painter in Munich, who died in 1949. Melanie was a convert and a historian. She knew that European abbeys had always accepted widows, and she found herself beginning to think of religious life "from some sudden impulse", as she put it. She had hoped to find a Carmelite monastery in America that would take her but then came to the Benedictines by mistake. She was in Connecticut, and a friend brought her to Regina Laudis. She asked if she could be accepted here, admitting this was "totally irrational", but she said this place spoke to her of "something real". Regina Laudis was actually the only monastery in America in the late '50s that would accept her, a widow, who was forty-eight years old.

She was striking as she walked in on the day of her clothing, wearing a plum-colored coat dress, embroidered and belted in gold, over a white silk dress. Her white veil was held by a gold brocade skullcap. The costume was North Caucasian and had come to her through her husband's close connections with the nobility of that region. Mother Benedict gave her the name Sister Jerome.

"It was unusual that the Archdiocese accepted me, a widow, and it was wonderful that Regina Laudis accepted me. I was shown the broad heart of Mother Benedict", recalled Mother Jerome. Thinking of the sadness of her husband's early death from a heart attack and her subsequent call to the religious life, Mother Jerome stated, "The Lord closes doors in your face while pushing you out another door."

Mother Placid and Mother Cecelia, who had been on a visit to Jouarre, had now returned, and their arrival back home brought a novel excitement to the Community. Those who had never seen Jouarre found it difficult to picture life there and kept wanting to hear more and more accounts of life at the ancient, 1,300-year-old monastery. Mother Placid and Mother Cecelia had brought back gifts from the nuns of Jouarre and arranged them in the common room so that the entire Community could examine these souvenirs. Over and over, the two nuns kept talking about the wonderful kindness that had been shown in every way to the two visitors and the warmth of affectionate interest in Regina Laudis that had been expressed by all at Jouarre. Mother Placid also told them that everyone told her "your Reverend Mother would have been Abbess if she stayed." Mother Placid also found a mentor there, Mother Jean Marie Vianney, an artist like herself, who became her friend for life. This was the same Mother Jean Marie whose brothers had helped Mère Benoît obtain her false identity card during the occupation.

Mother Placid wanted Mother Benedict to know she had learned something ever so important. "I saw that we were carrying monastic life forward without the encumbrances of the nineteenth century. We found we were better formed than they were at Jouarre for contemporary challenges. We were in the tradition of Saint Benedict, and so I had a sense of that from which it all came. But I could see what we were doing under Mother Benedict's guidance—bringing something new from something old. In a true sense we were doing what monasticism was doing in the early days of Europe, forming beautiful stories. We were forming beautiful stories at Regina Laudis. We were going back to that fresh thing. We had the essence and were taking it forward, in a new country. I saw this as an exciting thing", said Mother Placid.

As the year progressed, Regina Laudis was making a fine beginning launching its second decade as a Foundation. By this time, between land purchases and donations, they now had three hundred acres at their Bethlehem location. Out of her deep respect for nature and all its creatures, with the rousing support of Connecticut's conservation program, Mother Benedict declared these acres to be a bird sanctuary. This meant that no feathered friends would ever be shot on these acres. As a sign of gratitude, the Conservation Department supplied the monastery with bushes particularly attractive to birds, which were immediately planted in the wild garden refuge they had named Saint Mary's.

That summer, the nuns opened the Monastery Garden Shop, which would be run by the Oblate Sisters under the direction of Sister Prisca. Friends from the Bantam Lumber Company in Litchfield built a cedar building, fifteen feet long and eight feet wide, next to the Little Art Shop. Now the nuns could sell their garden produce, jellies, herbs, plants and crafts, like handmade candles and marvelously scented soaps. The new garden shop was a hit that summer at the monastery fair, put on for many summers by the nuns, as was another innovation—the outdoor presentation of *The Boy with the Cart*, Christopher Fry's verse-play based on the life of Saint Cuthman. In the years to come, Regina Laudis would become known for the outstanding theatrical productions that were both brought there and nurtured there for the benefit of friends and the public at large.

The word came in early fall of '58 that Pope Pius XII had died, on October 9. Mother Benedict, who had met him in 1946, when she was in Rome, shared her reminiscences with the Community.

But the news that came on October 28, the Feast of Saints Simon and Jude, gave a jolt of surprise and great joy. "We were having dinner when the news came through the radio that the priest who had been elected the new Pope was none other than my old friend Angelo Roncalli, who had taken the name John XXIII. I immediately called the Community together to tell them the news. Then I told them in detail of my three interviews with this fine man at the time he was Apostolic Nuncio to France, and I was beginning to plan an American Foundation. Instantly, the nuns all took this man into their hearts.

"We celebrated the coronation of Pope John XXIII with a festive dinner. I had my table covered with a white and gold cloth that had a large papal coat of arms on the front. It draped to the floor, majestically, fitting for the occasion. The desserts that day were covered with white meringue topped with tiny papal flags. The next day, using a borrowed television set, we watched the ceremony of the making of a Pope, kneeling, like all those in Rome, when he pronounced his apostolic blessing on all in the world."

Mother Benedict continued, "At that moment, no one knew that this roly-poly, simple man from peasant stock, approaching his seventy-seventh birthday, would astonish the world by calling an ecumenical council precisely to initiate a period of major renewal and reform of the Catholic Church. He would tell the world that 'we are not born to be museum keepers, but to cultivate a flourishing garden of life.' He was seeking nothing less than a burgeoning new life in the Church, and to make sure this was understood, he called this Second Vatican Council 'a new Pentecost'.[2] Pope John had used the symbolism of opening a window to let the fresh air in, and for me this was both a comfort and an affirmation for what I had seen to be my call. For a long time now, I had been letting the fresh air in."

As the year came to a close, Mother Benedict received another woman seeking entrance to the monastery. This was the fifth American woman that year to come to the Abbey asking to become a Benedictine, and while Mother Benedict could add up the numbers and be grateful that twenty-two women had received the habit at Regina Laudis, she would say she always had a certain uneasiness knowing some would not stay. She received six more candidates in 1959, but of these only two would stay, one being Anne Serna, who was given the name Sister David and replaced Mother Benedict as Abbess of Regina Laudis in 2001. A social worker, Anne had gone to Puerto Rico in 1956 to work with the people there after she graduated from the College of New Rochelle in New York State. During her year in Puerto Rico, she had met Melanie von Nagel Mussayassul, a visitor from the States who was acquainted with a monastery called Regina Laudis in Bethlehem, Connecticut. They had lunch together the next day and ended up sitting in the blazing sun in the plaza of San Juan Cathedral, talking about the contemplative life. Anne Serna entered Regina Laudis in 1959, two years after her luncheon companion, who was to be the future Mother Jerome, had entered.

Looking back on those years, Anne, now Mother David, spoke personally of the confusion she felt even as she was drawn to the religious life. As she more and more felt God's call, she also resisted. "There's so much of you that wants to hear, and so much of you that doesn't." But she couldn't deny that something essential in her life was missing, and she felt "God was trying to tell me something." She entered the Benedictines, but it wasn't easy. She spoke of how difficult the passage was to become refashioned, "putting on Christ". "I almost died abornin'", Mother David told me with a smile. "To enter the contemplative life you have to go through a deep, narrow, lonely place in your being where you face all your fears and selfish patterns, even when you don't know what these are. I thought I was very grown up, very mature. You don't realize what a child you are until God tests the heart and you go through that deep place all of us have to go through."

She acknowledged it is not at all hard to understand why someone could enter with the finest intentions of taking on this life and yet not make it.

Regina Laudis was increasingly becoming known as a spiritual place of welcome for both priests and lay guests. Regularly throughout this last year of the decade of the '50s, people came seeking a respite at this Bethlehem monastery, many of them leaving a gift of themselves. One week came with a double surprise, a visit by a friend and singing teacher, Miss Iva Hiatt, who spent four days giving the nuns singing lessons. Before the week was over, they received Dom Joseph Gajard, the choirmaster from the Abbey of Solesmes, who had come for a brief visit. He also gave singing lessons to the Community during his stay. Mother Benedict would say she never missed an opportunity to heighten the quality of the Gregorian chant sung by the Community. She was always wanting the nuns to develop their perception of the spirit as well as the intricacies of this musical form, which is sung prayer that seeks to speak of our love for God.

One day in 1959, a visitor came to Regina Laudis who could not avoid being noticed. She was young, blonde, beautiful and well known from Hollywood to New York. Her name—Dolores Hart—was associated with actors like Elvis Presley and George Hamilton. She didn't really know why she had come—but somehow she had been drawn to visit this unusual monastery. For now, it was just a visit.

As Mother Dolores relates, "In 1959, after having done a number of films and a Broadway show, I was at a turning point and terribly uneasy. At the time, I was on Broadway, playing in *The Pleasure of His Company*. I was the only cast member with no country home. The other players, like Cyril Ritchard, Cornelia Otis Skinner and Walter Abel, were 'old theater', and on weekends they had a place to go to rest", said Mother Dolores. "I was twenty-one, far from home and staying with a roommate, Winnie Allen. Her friend, Faith McFadden, had recommended the monastery of Regina Laudis as a good place to get away for a weekend. I was not enchanted with this. I was having a struggle at that point maintaining a relationship with the Church and my industry. I felt confused by a bourgeois mentality in the institutional Church. I couldn't integrate my professional life with what I was feeling about the Church. I was up against a lot of questions, though not theological ones. Mine were more like, what do you do as an actress when in confession a priest tells you your profession is an occasion of sin?

"That rigid, Jansenist thinking was difficult for me, and the thought of coming to a monastery of nuns didn't seem to be anything that I was ready for.

"My first introduction was Mother Placid, and she made me feel welcome. But then, the moment I met Mother Benedict, I felt immediately that I was in touch with a spiritual master. She had a depth of understanding that astounded me. She was a woman with professional experience, a doctor. She could put the tension I was feeling into perspective for me. Mother Benedict didn't make 'absolutes'. She had an incredible capacity for putting my questions together ... with a womanly integration and perspective that I could understand.

"After that, I came back every six months. I began to realize that my center was here, not in Hollywood."

As 1959 came to an end, Mother Benedict would say she could feel the winds of change. "I knew now I had received into the monastery some exceptional women who would dedicate their entire lives to serving God as Benedictines. Now it was time to think ahead and plan for what Regina Laudis would look like in the coming years—what kind of buildings would it have, what connections to the outside world, what would be the ever-evolving spiritual formation of a growing Community, what would be included in a constitution specific for this monastery, and, most important, who would be the candidates knocking on our door in the next decade?

"I looked ahead to the new year, the one in which I would celebrate a pivotal birthday, reaching the age of fifty. I sensed strongly Regina Laudis and I both stood on the brink of change. Early in the new year, on January 11, I received a handwritten note from my faithful friend and correspondent Archbishop Montini. We had something in common, for he, too, faced the prospect of needing to build. His task was to construct a new church in Milan. His letter said, 'Thank you also for the wishes you have expressed for the architects of the new churches of Milan. They will not easily be disposed to let themselves be guided by the mysterious breath [of the Spirit] that you would anticipate and wish for them; but one must not despair! The solution for Viboldone is still uncertain; we need a victory that only prayer can obtain: I recommend this to your prayers. Many, many wishes for every good thing for you and for all in your Community. Devotedly in Christ.'

"I pondered that letter, looking ahead to what might be my own troubles one day working with an architect in designing the monastery building and church Regina Laudis would need. What I didn't know as the '60s began was that an architect I had met and respected would be the answer to my prayers as I faced these new responsibilities and challenges—the priest who had said his first Mass in the rustic chapel, Father Francis Prokes, S.J."

⚜ ⚜ ⚜

Mother Benedict was now at a point in life where she found herself, at age fifty, with so much work ahead of her that it made her increasingly conscious of being on the verge of change. She felt, too, an uncertainty stemming from the signs of the times—the ever-building crises as the nuclear threat grew between the Western and Communist nations; the change in society as modern women began to seek equal rights; the explosive sexual revolution; the escalating dominance of the media; and the lessening influence of religion. She was feeling sure that the monastery would stagnate if it were to be kept in the environment of the '40s and the '50s. But she worried that some of the Community members would want that first pastoral era of Regina Laudis to remain unchanged, even as she knew it couldn't do that. Her responsibility would be to learn what would go and what would stay as they faced the future.

A few of the nuns, for example, Sister David, were already starting to communicate some of the problems they were facing. Mother Benedict would not forget how Sister David complained about a chart in the laundry room that gave instructions on how everything had to be folded. She thought this was a waste of hours and energy and that it was time to be more efficient in how things were done. Many years later, Mother Abbess David spoke honestly of the "radical difficulty" she felt when she arrived.

"I was a social worker. Maybe because of that, and my family background, I had a great desire to participate with my Sisters on a deeper level. But my impression when I came was that in the life being led here the orientation was still very hermetical in its base. Even though there was a fraternity, it seemed to be a side-by-side-to-God approach, with no crossing over.... Each woman was alone in her relationship with God", said Mother David. "But that wasn't who I was." That ideal of contemplative life, which was still based on the old European-style monastic life, didn't meet the human dimension she believed was needed. The concept was still that you were told what to do, and you were trained to work accordingly.

"I was with a group of six postulants when I entered," she went on, "and we were all pressing for change. Novices were not very involved with the life of the monastery. As a novice, I was caught between two worlds. I even wrote a paper on the renovation of a monastery", Mother David recalled. "There was a lot of confusion and unrest in the Community. Mother Benedict had to try to meet the new generations coming."

"I was very conscious of the unrest", Mother Benedict would admit, yet she held to her belief that their work and mission would have to be broader and more to the point of what would be needed in these changing times. "I absolutely understood the importance of education—as Archbishop Montini had always emphasized to me. Without continuing education, we would not be prepared to grasp what the contemporary world was all about or meet the demands that the world would place on each of us.

"I knew, however, that once I initiated changes in that direction, I would have to deal with the consequences of my actions, and this would not be an easy time for me. For a long time, I pondered in my heart the need for the new versus the comfort and security of the old. You have to pioneer your paths before you can share them. But if you do what you have to do, you can't worry about the consequences. All that opponents can do is constrict you. They cannot destroy what's right to do."

Guiding her always was the Rule of Saint Benedict, and she believed in being faithful to the inheritance of his Benedictine principles—to be a Christ-lover, continuously engaged

in living the Gospel and sharing it with all. Yet Mother
Benedict believed a Superior always had to help a new generation grasp and bring forward what was traditional into
their new times.

"I realized that many of the young women coming here
had pious reasons for becoming nuns. Their coming wasn't
the result of deep, interior reflection. You take on a habit
and a cowl. But what do those symbols mean? To what are
they awakening you? I felt I was being pressed into leading
the members of the Community to a place where they would
want to probe and explore the interior meaning of their
life, not only as individuals, but also as members of the
corporate body of Christ, living in a complementary relationship with each other and with the world. But where
and how was I going to begin this new chapter in the life
of Regina Laudis?" she would ponder.

At this same time, Mother Benedict had to deal with a new
pressure, which came from Archbishop O'Brien. In 1959 he
had given responsibility for the monastery to Monsignor Joseph
Lacy, Vicar for Religious for the Archdiocese of Hartford,[3]
and now, less than two years later, the Archbishop had given
him a mandate. It was to tell Mother Benedict that he wanted
her to build and expand and get out of their present makeshift quarters. As far as she was concerned, at that point Regina
Laudis was in no condition to venture into any kind of building program, and "I told him so, in no uncertain terms", said
Mother Benedict.

"Monsignor Lacy returned to Regina Laudis with the same
message later in that year of 1961, saying vigorously that I had
to do what the Archbishop said. I replied, 'We cannot afford
to approach an architect.' I objected that this was a tall order.
Monsignor Lacy agreed but persisted, and I wondered where
indeed would I ever find such a person. I was caught between

my desire always to be obedient to an order from my superiors in the Church and my practical situation. It was a familiar dilemma. I had been there many times."

Monsignor Lacy turned out to be a godsend. He had been in the war as a military chaplain and had come from a terrible experience—he had had to scale cliffs in Normandy and deal with the horrible deaths caused by war. That experience humanized him. He understood how difficult the task was that Mother Benedict had taken on. When he realized how she and the nuns were struggling, he seemed to be as much at sea as they were with the Archbishop's demands. Monsignor Lacy started coming to Regina Laudis frequently, becoming so sympathetic to their situation that he was willing to challenge the Archbishop, who finally listened to him.

The answer to where Mother Benedict was going to find an architect *pro bono* came unexpectedly and quickly when Father Francis Prokes, Mother Stephen's Jesuit priest brother, approached Mother Benedict with a proposal—would she allow him to be an architectural consultant for Regina Laudis, designing the permanent monastery, but in collaboration with the Community itself, as part of his doctoral thesis?

Father Prokes, a graduate of Notre Dame, at this time was a doctoral candidate in the School of Architecture at Princeton University, studying under the dean of the architectural department, Professor Jean Labatut. Father Prokes had an unusual vision when it came to architecture. He didn't see this as the science of building structures for people to fit into, but the reverse. Modern buildings were to serve the work of the people using them, reflecting the developing world and the overall evolution of society. He saw architecture as art, bringing together all related parts to achieve a wholeness expressive of all that is going on around the structure to be built. Everything had to be taken into consideration in planning a building—the land around it, the history, the water, the adjacent towns, the law, the government.

Most important was that the building be made for the people it would house, allowing for an interdependence. expressed by Pope John XXIII: "Since men are social by nature, they are meant to live with others and to work for one another's welfare", he wrote in his encyclical *Pacem in Terris*, repeating a mandate right out of the Gospels.[4] Thus, for Father Prokes, his doctoral work would have to be comprehensive, focusing not only on the practical ramifications of modern architecture, but also on its theological dimensions, for as he realized, "Any proposed architectural setting is dedicated to the more full experience of what it means to be a man or a woman. This ultimate dimension is intimately theological."[5]

To do proper research, Father Prokes knew he would need to find a client who could participate with him in this task of putting his thesis and beliefs into practice and testing them for validity. Regina Laudis, cramped in space and on the threshold of crucial need when it came to buildings, seemed to be the perfect client.

His proposal appealed to Mother Benedict. She saw this offer of professional help from a person who could also integrate her theological concerns as an answer to prayer. "I understood from the start that he had a special vision and that he was equipped to carry it out to a T. His theology fit like a glove. He always helped draw our attention to what was needed. His influence on the formative level of our building plans was invaluable.

"He never took over. He only advised us. He never could be in the limelight. His contribution was to be in opening aspects for planning buildings that a client never would have thought of. He was also the most cheerful person I had ever known, always thinking life is the greatest, totally optimistic, with a sharp sense of humor, a quality that has always been immensely important to me."

From the beginning, Father Prokes made it clear that he would help them plan their future buildings, but first, he said, "you have to tell me who you are", for the monastery was to be far more than just their permanent home. Intellectually, spiritually and artistically, it was to express a genuine act of integration with the American and the New England milieu. Beyond that, it would express a step in their spiritual development, representing their orientation, self-definition and interior achievement. The center point, as he put it, would be a collaborative "self-exposing analysis" where all would share personal insights into the "history of experience, proposed activity and contemplated purpose"[6] of the architectural plan. The underlying question would continually be, what does it mean to be a Benedictine and a woman in America in the mid-to-late twentieth century?

Father Prokes was very clear on how to approach that question. As he wrote in his dissertation, "Within the twentieth-century American cultural complex, a monastic foundation must be totally unique. Benedictine tradition is to be brought into living expression within a new context of circumstance and need. The objective to be achieved through a client-study of monasticism is thus in no sense an imitation of some past application or interpretation.... Obstinate preoccupation and copy-technique would frustrate the living inheritance to be gained."[7]

It was obvious to Mother Benedict that she had a gigantic task ahead of her in getting each member of the Community to accept the radical change that would eventually be evident in the evolution of Regina Laudis. "I had always been true to the Benedictine Rule and dependent on the Holy Spirit to guide me. Yet I remembered that our Community had once been called 'the most avant-garde batch of nuns in the U.S.'. I wondered sometimes what would next be said about my still young monastery as we pioneered a new path relevant to the changing times", said Mother Benedict.

By September 1961, she began to call weekly meetings of the Community to begin the studies she outlined in consultation with Father Prokes, who continued to live and study at Princeton. Individual nuns were first assigned to study and prepare papers on the meaning and definition of a monastic community, with emphasis on words and phrases like *cloister, workshop, sheepfold, enclosure, novitiate* and *school of the Lord's service*. Then, historical investigations were undertaken, beginning with the geography of Connecticut and a sketch of the settlement of Bethlehem, including research on the people who had lived on the property now owned by Regina Laudis.

In May 1962, two of the nuns began work on the history of the Catholic Church in Connecticut, broadening their scope to include the development of the Puritan churches in New England as a basis for understanding the position of the Catholic Church in the same area. Miss Caroline Ferriday, a socially prominent Bethlehem resident and longtime friend of Regina Laudis, helped in this research. Even in this period of internal study, Mother Benedict allowed for outreach to people beyond the Community, welcoming their contributions to the educational dimension she so strongly espoused for the Community. In the summer of '62, she invited Doctor Lois Hartley, a professor of American literature at Boston College, to give a series of conferences on the development of American thought as expressed in literature. That summer, she also welcomed Father Robley Whitson, a New York Archdiocesan priest who taught at Fordham University and had a home in Bethlehem, to help the nuns assigned to the study of history. Father Whitson also gave fourteen conferences on Puritanism to them, dedicating the last four to the Shakers, a sect that arose in England during the seventeenth century and established communal settlements in the United States in the eighteenth century. He illustrated his talks with some two hundred slides of the New England villages settled by the Shakers, who were dedicated to productive labor and a life of perfection. The nuns could relate to the simplicity and honest craftsmanship that characterized Shaker furniture and products and appreciate why these have had a lasting influence on American design.

The series of studies went on intensely. All of those in the Community began to look at American values and weaknesses, asking how over the decades these ideals have been romanticized, commercialized or betrayed. Mother Benedict had everybody look at these questions in order to consider what, if any, facets of American thinking might be integrated with Benedictine traditions of monasticism and also to find the broadest possible basis for communication with Protestant neighbors or, even more basic, with the world as it comes to the monastery doors. Hospitality was another subject of the study program, with the question of guest houses emerging as a subject very relevant to the architectural project.

Other papers dealt with the theme of how fraternal charity and love should be extended to all those beyond the cloister, springing from the living practice of love within the monastery. Mother Pia presented a heartwarming account of a bicycle trip she had made before entering religious life, crossing towns in the states of New York, Connecticut, Vermont, New Hampshire and Massachusetts, that gave a picture of New England hospitality. The warmth and generosity she met throughout her trip was in sharp contrast to the popular presentation of New England Yankees as being dour and resentful of outsiders. Mother Benedict said she appreciated this insight into the character of people who were their New England neighbors.

The Community had begun this new study phase, but not to the detriment of the regular work that had to be done. Their daily life remained active with the chores of farming and crafts, their routine of prayer and the welcoming of guests.

While the studies went on, the Community also stayed tuned in to what was going on in the world. "It was with sadness that I had to tell them on June 3, 1963, that our beloved Pope John XXIII had died. He had made an impressive mark on both the world and the Church, and I was sure that the Second Vatican Council, which my friend of years back had initiated as Pope, would continue to a fruitful end", Mother Benedict said. "Yet, before the month was over, I could give my Community jubilant news. The man who was elected the new Pope was none other than my faithful mentor and friend Cardinal Montini, who would take the name Pope Paul VI."

As the architectural study program continued, a most important series of studies developed around the theme of woman, and this continued to be an underlying motif in nearly all the subsequent studies, one that continues to this day. Father Prokes, who came as a visitor, sometimes accompanied by his mentor, Professor Labatut, emphasized the feminine realities at the root of this monastery. As he wrote in his dissertation, "The unique aspects of the client's [Regina

Laudis'] individuality as 'feminine' are to be brought into significant expression by 'woman-speaking-as-woman-in-woman's-images'." [8] And he pointed out that buildings that would complement and enhance their contemplative aspirations "must clearly manifest an exemplar feminine purposefulness".[9] Some of the subjects researched by the nuns and novices dealt with the mystery of womanliness, the relationship between the consecrated virgin and the Church, and how the spiritual life is expressed in terms of the virginal, the bridal and the maternal phases of a woman's life. Mother Benedict said often that she felt this was a tremendously important understanding for the nuns to have.

While this study phase was intense and required much of Mother Benedict's attention, she never neglected the other work required of her as head of the Community, especially the importance of being present for individual nuns, whatever their need. In June 1963, she welcomed a new postulant, Dolores Hart, who came to Bethlehem from Hollywood. The young star was leaving an impressive movie career, begun seven years earlier. In that short time, with the noted Hal Wallis as her boss, she had done twelve films and a Broadway show. "By her third visit here, she had talked about her life to me. I knew she needed more time to make a decision of this magnitude. I wrote her a note, which she reminded me of many times in the following years. She said my penmanship was like a doctor's, hard to read, and that when she finally figured out the last sentence, she didn't know quite what to do. I had written, 'I know you're knocking, but you have a lot to do before you'll be ready. You'll have to wait.' By 1963 I could welcome her. I could take a chance that she was ready now." [10]

This was in keeping with the Rule of Saint Benedict, which maintained, "When anyone newly cometh to be a

monk, let him not be granted an easy admittance, but . . .
test the spirits, to see whether they come from God."
"Dolores acknowledged that she had much uncertainty at
that time about entering the religious life, that she had not
yet completed enough professionally and that she 'had to
flower'. I knew that bringing Dolores Hart into the Community would have some ramifications. She had to have a
strong vocation to do it and a strong fiber, along with a
particular capacity to take resentment. I knew she'd have to
learn by experience; there is no other way. Given human
nature, it's very difficult to attempt to be a religious. It's a
frightfully difficult thing to do, so outrageous to our sub-
jective point of view. The hardest thing is to try to establish a way of life that follows the Gospel, because the Gospel
is just an impossible message. Christ had it hard, and if you're
going to follow Christ, you'll have it hard. I knew, of course,
with Dolores' coming there'd be some jealousy. I didn't make
a big fuss over her. I treated her the same as any other
woman coming in. I was realistic about possible reactions.
But that would be nothing new. I was always dealing with
severe issues."

Some of the nuns went out of their way to make the
point that they were not impressed with the fact that the
new postulant was an actress. But they had to respect Miss
Dolores, who, Mother Placid brought out, was "just
unassuming, direct and simple". Yet, curiosity could not be
contained when visitors would come to visit Miss Dolores
at the monastery, honestly out of concern that she was happy
in her choice—celebrities like the late actor Stephen Boyd,
the actress Lois Nettleton, and Maria Cooper, daughter of
the famed Gary Cooper.

Dolores Hart's acceptance came clearly from the foundress.
"Mother Benedict was never locked into an ivory-tower

form of religious life. That's one reason why she could recognize she was dealing with a new age. And she always maintained that different types of relationships were essential. Community life is present to support a relationship of persons, and not vice versa.... She offered us freedom to be in relationships, with our families, with our professions, with one another. Her part was always to see we kept order and balance in these relationships, not to deprive us of them. Lady Abbess had the capacity to incorporate, utilize and expand the relationships that were open to her. I responded to this inclusive way of love."

The Superior also knew that some would misinterpret her emphasis on relationships, wanting to maintain an old, vertical, "God and me" spirituality. Yet "the bottom line in the Gospel message is for someone to give their life for another, and that can be done only in relationship", Mother Dolores affirmed. "Nor can a Community generate life by itself. It needs the complement of lay people. The core meaning of religious life is that you opt every moment for the phenomenon of God's presence, but this can be truthful and real only when we are related to a whole body, as Saint Paul so clearly points out. Our lives are interconnected with a hierarchy, where the Divine and human become one body in Christ."

She went on, "It was clear that Mother Benedict's willingness to help us find ourselves as a Community of women in our own humanity would cause stress in the Community. Nor was it a concept immediately understood by the Church. The concept of Community as a corporate body was consistent with a new age. But there was no model for it, except maybe the idea put forth by Saint Paul!

"The experience of leaving Hollywood and the fast lane to enter a monastery was probably like falling out of a forty-story building and landing on my head. The person who really got me through was Mother Benedict. She sustained me in my vocation.

"Intuitively, I knew that Mother Benedict was motivated by a contemporary grasp of the situation. She knew that a new generation of women would not enter if they were identifying with abstract generalities, but only if religious life corresponded to their own internal sensibilities.

"I was not an anomaly in the '60s. Everyone who came after me needed to find her own identity in the Community, how to serve in specific ways. Obedience was required, yes, but not a mindless obedience. It would require full consent, given in love, in accordance with one's gifts brought by their genealogy and profession. There needed to be mutuality in community living.

"The old concept of religious life, where you were just cut off from everything in the past going back to infancy, was not going to work. The new women coming to Regina Laudis wanted autonomy in collaboration with the others. Mother Benedict knew that this was a principle that needed a valid structure, and she held to achieving this while always remaining a staunch advocate of freedom before God for each individual", Mother Dolores affirmed.

Soon, the "severe issues" Mother Benedict anticipated were going to intensify. The first signs that trouble was brewing surfaced in mid-1963, when Mother Lawrence and Mother Macrina presented their study on the needs of a monastic library. The question that generated heated debate was, what books should the library have on its shelves? Everybody was in agreement that scriptural studies and books on the Fathers of the Church and on theology belonged there, but many thought these subjects were not enough. Mother Benedict pointed out that secular history formed a regular part of the monastic "diet" in the Middle Ages and should have a place in a modern monastery library as well. Others recommended books on Protestant and Orthodox thought, philosophy and social problems as being also appropriate.

But a handful of the nuns were not at all pleased with this. They objected strongly to having books that were not specifically on monastic topics. Mother Benedict responded to their complaints by telling them that a monastic Community such as Regina Laudis must be prepared to meet the world on its own ground. Unfortunately, her answer did not stop the complaints or the underground grumbling that had begun.

The situation soon became heated. The controversy began in a meeting in the parlor with Father Prokes when Sister Mercedes questioned the need for architectural barriers such as the grille and the enclosure walls. Her question challenged the Community to define their purpose as "cloistered" nuns. Mother Benedict rephrased the question, cutting down to the core meaning of what had been asked. "Is enclosure relevant in the contemporary situation, or is it obsolete? Is it a help or a hindrance? Is it doomed to become increasingly incongruous, foreign to the new current of life?"

In the discussion that followed over a period of months, often someone would bring up the reasons why there should be an enclosure: it was a protection; it was a sign of sacredness; it was a separation from the world and a means of assuring concentration on the things of God. This would be rebutted as not reaching the core of the problem they were dealing with and would raise the specific question, what precisely do we mean by the "world", and how are we separated from it? Some felt they should be deeply involved in the world, explaining this did not mean abandoning the cloister or becoming lost in the minutiae of political, social and economic wrangles that fill the newspapers. Rather, it meant that their hearts should be united deeply with the struggles of all mankind. And even more, a nun of Regina Laudis should not merely be aware of the struggles for justice or against poverty but should be vitally concerned that justice be done, that poverty be combatted. How all of this could be an integral part of the true essence and nature of monastic enclosure became a profound study for Mother Benedict, knowing she had to be able to respond to these crucial questions.

The impact of the world's events was to be keenly felt a short time later, on November 22, 1963, when the tragic news of President John F. Kennedy's murder seared people worldwide. "I was profoundly affected by his death. I felt it was linked to the existence of Regina Laudis, which began because of American dedication and service, of American sacrifice for the cause of freedom. I called the Community together and gave them a talk, praising the young, fallen President. I told them what I believed—that the President was called upon to seal with his own blood his great mission of watchman on the wall of freedom. This tragedy brought back vivid memories of my personal experiences in wartime France and the electrifying response I had to the American soldiers who had bought freedom with their own lives."

Unexpectedly, toward the end of 1964, at Jouarre, Abbess Pierre received a notice from a hospital in Paris that Elizabeth Duss, Mother Benedict's mother, had been admitted, and she was deathly ill with cancer. Mrs. Duss had left Bethlehem and taken a trip to Greece. Apparently she had become ill and gone to Paris, where she was hospitalized. In a very kindly gesture, Abbess Pierre contacted Archbishop O'Brien in Hartford to request that he give permission to Mother Benedict to come to France personally to supervise the return of her mother to Bethlehem.

Permission was granted, and after returning from the trip, Mother Benedict was able to get her mother comfortably settled in at Saint Martin's, and the Community took care of her until she died on July 12, 1966. "I was with my mother at the end, and I cherish the love that was silently, but strongly, exchanged between us as my mother passed on. To be shown an emotional expression of love by my mother was not a consolation granted to me, but I recognized the love that was there given to me indirectly. Other people used to tell me that my mother loved my brother more, but I never believed that, and I didn't have dominant feelings of resentment. As her daughter, I really loved her always, and I could intuit what she needed. I took care of her when she needed to be cared for.

"Just before she died, my mother said something that surprised me. 'I've done many harmful things in my life', she said. I think this was a redemptive moment. It gave me consolation. I was always very concerned over how she would meet reality, and to my immense relief, she was coming full circle. The influence of monastic life had been brought home to her in her own moment of need. There was so much of God in her; now she was the mother I would have wanted. We had to bury her in Woodbury, but when Regina Laudis later had a permanent cemetery, we requested permission from the late Ella Grasso, then Governor of Connecticut, to move her body here, and permission was granted."

In all the studies undertaken by the Community in the years from 1961 to 1964, the members were guided by both Mother Benedict and Father Prokes. He was meeting with the Community, attempting always to elicit from them what they determined their needs were for a monastery. "I was really amazed by his sensitivity. He walked the land, slept in the woods, sought to understand wildlife ... all to help us to determine what kind of monastery would fit the people here.

"While our studies and discussions represented original research and thought, I sought constantly to guide the Community so as make sure we did not fall into error. There was and is no given answer to any of the problems that were studied. We were all keenly aware that we were searching together for greater depth and breadth of expression, for a clearer perception of the relation of our monastic life with the life of the modern world. Yet, precisely because I was passionately involved in the search, they could all turn to me with greater confidence as we undertook our individual parts in the study program", said Mother Benedict.

But there was static, and it was getting stronger. For some, the discontent was pointed at Father Prokes, who had come and made waves. Others wanted to go too far in the direction of restructuring the monastery, wanting authority out and democracy in, reducing community life to a fellowship. "When you're first starting a Foundation, so much is evolving. I had come with a vision. Yet everything was leading to what took place in the '60s. If you have new wine, you need new wineskins", said Mother Benedict. "Father Prokes was an amplifier. He put out the new structure—the skin—for the new wine. We needed this; after all, we weren't playing pious dollhouse here. We were going to ask, what does it mean to be a nun in the nuclear age, from locally, to globally, to cosmically?—and find answers.

"Father Prokes articulated another way of getting to the ideal. His vision of religious life is that we're responsible for one another. He had a reinterpretation of everything—and that's when all the upheaval started."

Mother Benedict understood the disruption some of the nuns were feeling. Some came to complain, and she would make every effort to listen carefully. "Some thought it shocking that you had to 'think about' religious life. They had no sense of what could be incorporated into religious life. They had ideas of their own, not tried against reality. I always tried a personalized approach so they could fathom what had to be done. They had to see that each nun had an assignment that related to all the others and that the interrelated activity of each nun would blend to become a living whole. Out of this complementary interrelatedness would come one fabric that would be the life of the Community. Unfortunately, some of the nuns never accepted that structure", she explained.

The next two years were full of pitfalls for Mother Benedict. She had never been in great health, but she wasn't prepared to be hit with sudden, intense pain. It was diagnosed as a gallbladder attack complicated by a hiatal hernia, and she had to undergo massive surgery. She was in the hospital for a month and then hardly able to walk when she returned to the Abbey. The rumblings of discontent that had begun at Regina Laudis were still going on. But there was also some good news. Two new postulants had arrived. One was Helen Boothroyd, who had served as an Army nurse in France during World War II, and the other was Catherine Frenzel from Chicago, a young woman who had just finished college. She later gave them the names, respectively, Sister Irene and Sister Bernadette.

Then a new and distressing situation came up for the Abbey when the town of Bethlehem proposed a development plan and said it was going to expand a path on the Abbey grounds to make it a more important highway. Mother Benedict proposed another solution, to have, instead, a road built that would follow their northern property line. This would be much better for the townspeople and for them.

They agreed to pay half the costs and build half the road. The town was open to that idea; the road was built and named Robert Leather Road.

All the attention given to the road matter was just one more thing to increase the festering aggravation of some of the nuns. They attributed any changes, even the road building, to Father Prokes' influence and resented this. Some said that involving contemplatives with these projects and ideas was exposing them to distractions. They complained, asking, "Why all this emphasis on land?" From this point on, some would attribute any changes proposed as being Father Prokes' idea and would raise objections.

"He became the scapegoat for anything and everything", said Mother Benedict. "Yet, on the other hand, some of the other nuns, like Mother Dolores, took a different position. The new ones didn't want to do tea parties and the nun-things of ten years earlier. They wanted a new analysis of contemplative life, one that cut deeper to where their own issues were. I could see where battle lines were starting to be drawn."

By May 1964, the Community had come to the end of the studies, which had taken three years, and Father Prokes had completed his doctoral dissertation. The Community, responding to his request, had presented him with the practical components they wanted to have for his speculative model of the monastic complex that would fit Regina Laudis.

"As it turned out, I knew the architectural plan originally designed by Father Prokes in his doctoral studies could never be built. It was too expensive. When it came time to evaluate how closely his model achieved what we were asking for, we had to recognize the whole proposal went beyond our expectation and would prove financially prohibitive in view of our resources", said Mother Benedict.

"On the other hand, this long period of study and research left its imprint on the spirit of the Community to the point that it could be said that architecture, as is normal in Benedictine life, has been part of our monastic formation. On our side, a maturation, a strengthening and a capacity for reflection and self-examination had become part of us in a new way because of the architectural program, and this would allow for a more thorough monastic expression within our own development."

A case in point was Mother Placid's response when Mother Benedict asked her what she could do with a cherry tree that had fallen down. An artist, with a belief that everything—and everybody—has an inner "core" connected to God just waiting to be released, she saved that tree, knowing that it could now become something closer to its "true nature". Buoyed by her fundamental conviction that if you can make what's there at the core become visible, that will always be some presence of God, Mother Placid began carving the wood. And something startling emerged—images depicting the pain-filled walk of Jesus to His Crucifixion. When she finished what she started in that midpoint of the '60s, there were fourteen carved cherry wood bas-reliefs, a powerful depiction of the Stations of the Cross, ready to be placed on the walls of the rustic chapel.

Father Prokes left Regina Laudis after completing his studies and obtaining his Princeton University doctoral degree. He was assigned by his Jesuit Superior to teach for a year at a Jesuit college in Detroit. He still retained close ties, however, with Regina Laudis.

One matter that had always remained essential to Mother Benedict was to learn more about the Americans who had liberated Jouarre. In all the years since she had left France, she had never forgotten the sight of American tanks, with their white stars, and soldiers driving up the road near the Abbey at Jouarre. She had always wanted to learn more about who was in charge of the Liberation of that part of France. It was in the early '60s when Mother Benedict heard it was General Patton's Third Army that had swept through that area of France. "I didn't know much about him, except that I had seen an old *Life* magazine at Sheepfold with something on him. But then from June '64 to summer, many publications did stories on the anniversary of the Liberation which documented that it was Patton. I credit this general, who died in a motor vehicle accident in 1945, with figuring directly in the founding of Regina Laudis.

"I'm not sure what would have happened if he hadn't been around", Mother Benedict continued. "He was a vehicle in the call of God to me, in the grace He gave me to start this Community. To see those stars ... as stars in the sky ... that was the Transfiguration ... a Christ-presence. That I can say. I felt that experience and honored it, even though I didn't know at the time what the outcome would eventually be. We have a distaste for war, but in that aura came this monastery. God drew people to Himself from that experience of horror ... perhaps to show that out of tremendous conflict, redemption is possible."

The sense of Regina Laudis' relationship with General Patton deepened when, in the '70s, a lovely young woman named Margaret Patton came to visit Regina Laudis. She was the general's granddaughter. In 1982, she came to stay and was eventually given the name Sister Margaret Georgina.

More and more, however, Mother Benedict was becoming conscious of the underlying unrest that was stirring. After the start of the new year of 1966, she decided to ask Mother Mary Aline to join her in giving conferences on the history of Regina Laudis to the novices. Mother Mary Aline always insisted she was a cofoundress, and Mother Benedict supported that. Mother Mary Aline readily agreed, and the conferences began on February 24, 1966, and ended a year later. Mother Benedict noted:

"The conferences were lively, with touching tales of our monastery days prewar, during the war and postwar. Humorous moments would occur when Mother Mary Aline would say something, and I would have to contradict her, and vice versa. But the goal was achieved. In the end, the novices had heard the somewhat amazing story of how we undertook an incredible journey to found a Benedictine monastery across the ocean from Jouarre."

Also in those early months of 1966, not a day went by in the Catholic Church but that the subject of Vatican II came up. Pope John XXIII had opened the Second Vatican Council on October 11, 1962, with a clear mandate: "'Divine Providence is leading us to a new order of human relations.' It was imperative for the Church 'to bring herself up to date where required,' in order to spread her message 'to all men throughout the world.' While the Church must 'never depart from the sacred patrimony of truth received from the Fathers,' she must 'ever look to the present, to new conditions and new forms of life introduced into the modern world, which have opened new avenues to the Catholic apostolate'." [11]

"In the reports coming through on the debate on religious life, I had felt the tension", said Mother Benedict. Some of the Cardinals were blunt in their assessment that religious renewal was essential, that religious life had to accommodate modern times. They were even more critical when it came to contemplatives, saying that the communities held to an institutional narrowness that was psychologically unbearable. Speaking at the Third Session, Father Joseph Buckley, Superior of the Marist Fathers, said that the truth was that "today's young people don't swallow archaic formulas like 'the will of the Superior is exactly the same as the will of God.' " [12]

Mother Benedict explained, "I had already been facing the dilemmas in religious life raised by Vatican II, particularly the difficult and major challenge of how to move ahead with the new needs while not discarding the essentials of the past. So I was happy to hear from Father Prokes, who contacted me saying he had a new request to ask of me. I respected our Jesuit friend particularly because he had brought a new energy and direction in guiding the Community toward the future. He also had a mature vision that in religious life all were responsible for one another", said Mother Benedict. "Now he asked me if he could take up residence at Regina Laudis. Father Prokes was an Army veteran who had stayed on in Berlin at the end of the war to help rebuild it. He told me he now had been assigned by his Jesuit superiors to work in renewal of religious orders after his ordination. He said he recognized Regina Laudis could be a base for his work. Especially important to him was to be able to help bring to fruition the incipient architectural plans that he had helped the Community to design.

"Father Prokes had never been in residence here and never functioned as a chaplain to the Community. I carefully considered his request and, with the Archbishop's approval, invited him to stay indefinitely at Saint Joseph's as an architectural consultant. He embodied something we didn't have, but something necessary to have a meaningful life. I felt we needed him. Especially helpful to me was Father's insight on the experience of land. He was born on a farm; he lived on a farm as a child and was taught farming. That was extremely valuable to me, especially as I was dealing with a ferment of dissatisfaction within the Community over having to do the farm work.

"He always helped us in a crisis. He helped us architecturally to construct the buildings needed. And the liturgical aspects of our vocation were thoroughly understood by this strong man. I felt he was indispensable. His approach was to 'see one, do one and teach one', that is, he would see the work that had to be done, do it himself and teach others how to do it.

"Yet having Father Prokes back on the scene was like fuel on the fire of unrest that had already surfaced in the monastery. The road we built had become the medium for expressing the problems, and in the next two years the stirrings of discontent became intense. These had a tone of mutiny among some members of the Community, who interpreted Vatican II their way, protesting that the religious habits, Gregorian chant, the Latin Mass and the enclosure should go. High on their list also was their feeling that my tenure as Superior should be ended, aware that a letter from Rome had come saying a Superior's appointment could be only three years.

"Everything started to be discussed at that time. The nuns were having small group meetings, as all communities were doing at that time, and the Community was divided. A lot of the nuns wanted changes that I didn't want—a push for the vernacular, modifying the enclosure, habits off. There was a lot of tension, and I'm sure some of it was good tension. What emerged was that a segment of the Community had very different ideas from mine on the way to go forward. And a lot felt that without me, these changes could be made. They didn't know how to make traditional values relevant.

"Naturally, I felt somewhat betrayed and very saddened by what I was hearing. I also became aware that some of the nuns had written to Rome, complaining about my leadership of the Community. Again, I called on Monsignor Lacy for advice. I made it clear that I had no problem with change, so long as it did not take away the substance of the Benedictine Rule. I knew that things have to be renewed as times change, but I wanted modifications to be done in such a way that the tradition would be intact. I was already incorporating some changes, but always with a mind not to obstruct the vows and to retain a balance as a mode of life. I also felt strongly that I should retain my position as Superior", Mother Benedict explained.

Monsignor Lacy supported her and recommended that she bring her case to Rome, meeting directly with the man who had so admired her for following her call to found this monastery, Pope Paul VI. She met with the nuns, and they voted to give her a chance to see the Pope. Accompanied by Mother Irene, she went to Rome. When Pope Paul saw her, he greeted her with open arms, saying, "You have come to see your old friend."

"Pope Paul told me I needed a forward-looking vision, not a mechanical one. I had to be alive to the change and modifications I would have to follow. He understood that this was an era where it was difficult to live a Benedictine life and that I would have to be striving continuously to find the formulas I would need to adapt to the changing times and adopt the values that in justice and wisdom would have to be introduced. And he told me, 'You need a strong man who will understand your spirituality and support it.' That's what he underscored. This was the Pontiff's unspoken approval for me in my decision to bring Father Prokes to Regina Laudis. And most importantly, Pope Paul VI assured me I could remain as Superior at Regina Laudis. He urged me to go back and have the Community begin working on a constitution that would be tailor-made for Regina Laudis", the foundress related.

By the time the two nuns got back to Regina Laudis, the unrest was surfacing openly. When Mother Benedict reported that the Pope said she could remain as Superior, a few created an uproar. Before the year of 1969 was over, six nuns had left.

That was a very difficult time for everyone. "I think the ones who left wanted to have a say in the decision making . . . wanted more participation. Once you got into a three-year tenure for your Superior, you would have a democracy, with very little authority left in the monastery, because the majority would rule, having their say in just about everything. That wasn't the Benedictine way, and it was not the way Regina Laudis would go. I was very determined in what I felt was the direction of the monastery, and it wasn't a democracy. I knew this was a clash, and it was going to hit us hard", Mother Benedict reflected.

Meanwhile, all were becoming aware that signs of change were now coming from another direction, as two young women, Adele Hinckley and Laura Giampietro, arrived unannounced at Thanksgiving time 1968. They were students at Newton College of the Sacred Heart in Boston, and they had hitchhiked from their campus to Bethlehem. They admitted later this was an idiotic thing to do and said their guardian angels must have been watching over them. They had gotten rides, and the last one had dropped them off in Waterbury. They were still hitchhiking, holding a cardboard sign saying "Bethlehem". By that time it was getting dark, and then a car pulled up with three men. They did have an agreement that they wouldn't get into a car if there were more than two people in it. But they were so lost that they decided to take a chance, hoping the three men were gentlemen. Thankfully, they were. The men actually drove the two of them right to the door, asking them over and over, "Are you going to be nuns?"

Mother Benedict was aware that nothing like these two beautiful young women, arriving in their long, "hippie, Indian-print clothes", had been yet seen at Regina Laudis. As for why they had come, they said it was to "find something". Adele was particularly at a loss. She was not going to church at that time, and while she wanted to find some meaning in life, she didn't have a clue as to what she was going to do with her life. The word she used to describe herself was "miserable". Mother Benedict felt that the story she told had a powerful meaning. Adele had been walking around the campus one night and came upon a big rock on the grounds. She couldn't explain what happened, except that at that moment she got a kind of intuitive message, telling her, "Go to a monastery". She said she didn't even know what a monastery was and thought they existed only in medieval history. Yet the sense of what she felt was urgent enough for her to move on it. Adele then checked with a nun on the faculty, who gave her the names of several monasteries in New England. She wrote to each one. Regina Laudis was the only one that answered. That's when Adele got Laura interested in checking the place out, and the two of them hit the road, thumbs out.

When the three men dropped them off at Regina Laudis, with the hour getting late, the first person they met was Mother Patricia, who came to the door. She took one look at them and asked, "Have you eaten?"—the best question for them at the moment. In their few days at the monastery, they met with Mother Benedict, Mother Placid and some of the other nuns. "I know we impressed them because here they were from a different world, yet we didn't question them, we just accepted them. They said we didn't fit the mold of nuns they had known, and what surprised them was how happy we seemed to be. When they left, they said something here had touched them very deeply and that they would be back.

"At the moment, though," Mother Benedict went on, "I was very concerned about their trip back to Boston. To make sure that they would not be hitchhiking, I arranged that Mother Columba could go at this time to do some research she had been approved to do at Harvard. I had a driver bring Mother Columba to Cambridge—so that Adele and Laura would have a ride back to Boston.

"I have a vivid recollection of that first visit. When I saw them at lunch in the women's refectory, there was something I could sense. I felt it deeply and said it to myself, 'There is the future.'"

Chapter 13

THE GOLDEN YEARS

— After the Sixties
— The First Lay Communities
— The Monastery Becomes an Abbey
— Mother Benedict Is Named Lady Abbess

By the end of the '60s, Mother Benedict had become fully aware that the challenge ahead of her was to help bring about a new consciousness of what monastic life was to be in the post–Vatican II era. She understood that facing the changes looming ahead had been a terrible struggle for the nuns who had left. Some of them had wanted to stay closed in a time frame of monasteries of the past, and some had wanted changes that she felt were superficial and not true to the Benedictine Rule.

"I was trying to introduce a pattern that would include continuity with the past and openness to the future, and the two things appeared to be contradictory. Some people had a problem with that. I was trying every possible route, doing all I could to try to help them exercise their own capacity for being able to accept change, while still corresponding to tradition. At that time we had about thirty-five members, and some of them remained totally closed to anything new. I was deeply pained that six nuns had left in 1969. I felt tremendous human sadness when they left, and yet I had a sense of relief that they were doing what was best for themselves. I long ago learned that you can only propose the way of the Cross. You've got to know it's never going to be the popular idea."

As Mother Benedict explained, no one enters the monastery already having the maturity that the contemporary call requires. Many things have to happen in one's formation that will open one's vision. She would recall an encounter she had with Mother David when she wanted to bring the nuns together to see the movie *Lisa*, which starred Dolores Hart, who was at that time a regular guest at the monastery. Mother David was against movies. It was hard for her to understand how a contemplative could watch a movie. She complained to Mother Benedict, who explained the truth communicated to her by that movie.

"I told her that I saw the whole plan of salvation in that movie, which was about a Jewish woman liberated from a concentration camp. Mother David told me later that she pondered what I said for many years, and one day understood that a contemporary call is to see everything as being in the plan of salvation. Certainly I had to see the coming changes in the Church and our monastery according to that vision."

By the mid '60s a new generation of women had indeed been coming to the doors of Regina Laudis. These were highly professional contemporary women, appropriately named Sisters Dolores, Irene, Bernadette, Maria, Dilecta, Scholastica, Sarah, Ruth, Hildegard and Anne. The signs were strong that they were only the first of the new women to come, all needing to be dealt with subjectively. Theirs was a "show-me" attitude, and Mother Benedict knew without a doubt that to grow in the life here they would have to start from their own experience.

"I fostered this new approach, dependent, as always, on the Rule of Saint Benedict, which always allows you to discern what is of God. You have to ask yourself continually, can you be trusted with that gift? Or are you being taken in by false notions that don't fit with the vocation? I could see that this development was of Saint Benedict. If you allow people to be themselves, then they become themselves in a new way that they had not thought of before", Mother Benedict acknowledged, adding that other major issues had to be dealt with, too, as the '70s began. "Most of the nuns felt very strongly about four of these issues, as I did: that we should retain the habit; keep the Latin Mass and the Gregorian chant; maintain that I, as Superior, have a lifelong term; and insist on respecting the enclosure, seeing this as essential for the survival of Benedictine monasticism.

"The habit is special", she went on. "It signs, seals and encloses you—a constant reminder that you are witnessing to something else. It isn't that wearing it makes you act in a holier—or phonier—way. You know you've been signed as a witness of God in the Church, and you act accordingly. We wear them all the time. When we work, we have work habits. It's total, in everything you do. The habit clearly gives evidence to the fact that a vocation is not a forty-hour week."

Keeping the Latin and the chant was a link to Saint Benedict that Mother Benedict strongly held to, with the support of most of the nuns. Saint Benedict ruled that "you'll sing the Office." He would have known that Saint Augustine said, "Singing is praying twice." And the Psalms were meant to be sung. When the matter of tenure for the Superior came up for discussion, the Community felt strongly that they should adhere to the Constitution from Jouarre that had guided them since the founding, and that was to serve as a starting point for the Constitution specific to Regina Laudis that they were now drafting. The Jouarre Constitution at that time maintained that being named Superior or Abbess would come with a lifelong tenure.

As for the enclosure, Mother Benedict never intended that her Community would live behind medieval grilles, or have impregnable walls, for, she would say, a contemplative nun is not one of the "living dead", but a woman thoroughly alive, connected to all of life and life-giving in her very being, in her relationships and in her work. No way could it be said that to cut people off is a form of holiness!

"We had to define enclosure, emphasizing the difference between a strict enclosure and an extended enclosure. For me, it was very clear that the 'extended enclosure' I chose encompassed the land. Our life is consecrated to God, every phase of it. We must, then, have an extended contact with creation. We draw out of creation our sustenance, and we teach people to reverence that. I don't think you could find a more dismal way of life than living where there was no space and no possibility for the normal life that creation opens."

Essential to her blueprint for an extended enclosure was the land, which she saw as the place holding sacred mystery, teaching them the secrets of struggle and suffering, the rhythm of life, sorrow and joy, death and rebirth. She would say that to be human means to be involved in all these mysteries, an active co-creator in bringing forth new birth, and that "at Regina Laudis, we women, with our hands and feet, bodies and souls, grow to know and love this land, which is holy ground. And from this comes a new and redemptive fertility, whereby our love is not contained but is continually birthing to encompass all living creatures and the One who initiated life itself, the Creator."

Mother Stephen oversaw the development of the farm, which grew widely with the coming of women into the Community who centered their love on a particular area of farm work that, in turn, became a vehicle for their professional development. Thus, Mother Ruth took on the garden and the sheep; Mother Telchilde took over the care of the pigs; Mother Thérèse, Mother Scholastica, Mother Dilecta and Mother Noella began the dairy.

There is a "powerful relationship between the monastery and the land", Mother Stephen would say. "The land becomes a part of you, and you are part of it. From here, the next step is your relationship with other members of the human family. You have found something wonderful, and you want to share it. You can dialogue and extol the land, but unless you taste it—taste the rain and the dust—you haven't got it. When you are this involved, it becomes your way of responding to God, Who put it there. Your prayers are of thanksgiving, because the land inspires that."

It was with the foregoing decisions and premises in place that the '70s began, launching a decade and a half that the nuns would remember as "the golden years".

Adele Hinckley and Laura Giampietro kept coming back as often as they could. These young women had been scandalized by the lack of morality, the worldliness, the whole mindless environment into which they had been born. They weren't pious or prudish, but they were trying to find a place of sanctuary and a meaning to life.

Adele would later explain that this drive to find meaning in their lives, to become who they could become, was the root of their contemplative call. They responded to something at the monastery but could not articulate what it was. They only knew that it came from a deep place, and they had not found this anywhere else. They worked on the land

and spent time with Mother Placid, who welcomed them with open arms. Soon they were bringing friends with them, and friends of friends came. Mother Placid met with all of them, recognizing that they were all seeking help for the confusion they were feeling from the explosive '60s. Some in the Community, like Mother Benedict herself, were pleased, some outraged by the welcome Mother Placid was giving these young people. She was called by some "ahead of her time", and by others, a disrupter letting in "beatniks" and "hippies". Mother Placid knew it was good for the Community to see the young ones coming in and affirming what was there.

"As we opened a hope to them, they opened a hope to us", Mother Placid affirmed. "Many of the customs of our life, which were on the fire within the Community, were totally welcomed by these 'beatniks', for whom traditional religious life was not supposed to be relevant any longer."

Before long, thirty or forty young adults, many of them men, around the same age as Adele and Laura would be visiting Regina Laudis every chance they got, seeing Mother Placid and working together with Father Prokes. Laura entered Regina Laudis in 1972 and was later named Sister Perpetua. Adele entered soon after, in 1973, and was given the name Sister Telchilde. Among the young people coming to join them were three other women who also found their true vocation at Regina Laudis: Martha Marcellino (Mother Noella), who entered in 1973; Nancy Collins (Mother Augusta), who came in 1975; and Patricia Kuppens (Mother Lucia), who arrived in 1979, after taking the time to get a doctoral degree in English, with an emphasis in Shakespeare, at Yale University.

"These women represented a whole new wave of vocations. Some thought that taking these women in was a scandal. The old way of religious life would have been, you don't get involved with people who don't present a conventional Catholicism. You pray from a distance for these unconventional types. But we were asking, how do you integrate them?—which was really a revolutionary question", said Mother Benedict. "The incredible gift we were able to give these young women was that the monastery saw something good in them. We weren't put off by their long hair and strange clothes. They were being received by a strong Community. They knew we respected them and would work with them where they were. We opened a door for them to be able to become who they could be. Some of those coming had tried different lifestyles, such as living in communes, and found these empty. Adele told me later that this was the only place where the intensity they were feeling was being tapped so that they could go somewhere good with it. There was something here they responded to, and they went for it in a big way. For them it became being in the right place at the right time."

Mother Telchilde, looking back on her first encounters with Mother Benedict, spoke of the special way they were welcomed by the Superior. "I was always incredibly struck by Mother Benedict's capacity to incorporate any honest, authentic human expression or desire. There was nothing threatening to her. She had a way of putting everything into the context of humanity. This breadth of vision and sensitivity made her unafraid of any expression of humanity or of body. Hers was one of the strongest educational influences in our lives. Her extravagance is phenomenal in allowing whatever is needed to bring a person into what she is meant to be. Probably because of this incredibly sensitive perception that she has, from her experiences with Christ, once she knew that letting us be here was the thing to do, no matter how much turmoil this would cause, this was the way to go. What I have understood the most from her is that everything is blessed in some way."

Father Prokes spent a lot of time with these new nuns. At times, some would admit, they didn't understand what he was saying, because he had a disciplined, systematic, analytical, professional training, and they were still at the intuitive and "feeling" level, unprofessionally trained as yet. But his words resonated with the truth of their experience. He had a gift with the young, and they flocked to him. These relationships endured.

"As for my own inner feelings about the 'flower children' now being regulars at the monastery, I was moved by their energy and goodness, yet a bit worried", Mother Benedict would admit. "I saw them as the future, but with the restriction that they would have to accept a severe formation. I didn't know if they could accept what was ahead. They wanted hands-on reality and substance. They would have to go through very real obstacles. For me, professional development had always been the road to legitimate formation. Did they know what they meant when they said they wanted a vocation? You can be turned off by what you encounter on the way. That whole projection of what they could be had never been tested. They were totally unprepared for the struggle—and yet I found they had an honest response."

To help these new candidates in their struggle, Mother Benedict asked Mother Dolores, who had been finally professed in 1970, to work with them. She knew this nun was professionally equipped to deal with the instinctual level because of her training as an actress. She also had the gift of being analytical, and as such she could identify with the goodness in each and project a context for that goodness to come forward and be developed and formed.

In 1972, Mother Benedict appointed Mother Dolores to be Dean of Education. Mother Benedict had established four deaneries, based on the Rule of Saint Benedict, which recommended deaneries be formed so that the Abbot might, without anxiety, share his burdens among them. The deaneries were to work on the specific interests and needs of the Community: Education, Formation, Liturgy and Choir. Mother Dolores' role as Dean of Education was not academic, but a means of helping to lead these young ones so they could be ready for monastic life. Mother Benedict told her, "You're an actress. You can identify with them." And she did understand this new generation. She knew that by their teens some of them had been hurt badly. The monastery now had to deal with American women who were coming out of the violence of a Vietnam-era society. Regina Laudis could not ignore the pain and the process these new seekers would have to deal with in entering a religious community.

One of the young men in the group that had been coming regularly to Regina Laudis was Kevin Thornton, who later became a lawyer. After many trips to the monastery, he realized that alone, he was no match for the outside society that he reentered when he left Regina Laudis. He could not sustain his good resolutions alone. The nuns knew that only in community would any of these young people coming here have the support they needed. One day Kevin articulated the obvious question that all had been considering, whether consciously or unconsciously: why couldn't the young people start their own community? The idea did not originate with him. Laura had inherited the idea of a Christian artists' community from her Italian father, and there was a strong contemporary impetus toward the development of communes, which had affected all of the young people at the time. But Kevin's question galvanized the group to act. Mother Placid related this to Mother Benedict, who remarked that she had been silently considering that all along. With the help of Mother Placid, the young people then arranged for everyone who was asking to be in a community to come on one weekend to explore the question, "How can we be a community as men and women facing what we have to face?"

"What the young people had come to was an inner response to the values they had been exposed to at Regina Laudis", said Mother Benedict. "It was very basic. We asked, could you start living the Commandments? Later a major point of contention came up about sex. We weren't going to accept free sex. Our values were clear—sex belongs in a marriage, which must be monogamous. Some got really involved; some said, 'I'm out' and left. Some got hostile, especially over the issue of sexuality. There were different degrees of responses.

"But something important came out of these meetings, and it was another major step in the development of Regina Laudis. Many of the young people from this group wanted to form a community associated with the monastery, and we welcomed them. They got their name in a funny way. Because they held firm to their principles and values, they were dubbed very 'closed' by the mother of one of them. The word caught them for having a truth in it. They wanted their own 'enclosure', and so they called themselves from then on, the Closed Community."

This was the first of many communities that eventually formed around the monastery. Lay professionals began coming to Regina Laudis looking for a reference point for the moral and spiritual components they were searching for as a complement to their professions. Lucille Matarese, a member of the Connecticut Bar Association, had entered in December 1971, bringing with her nearly fourteen years of professional training and a wide range of experience in law, government service and politics, including a term in the Connecticut State House of Representatives. With her colleagues, who specialized in different aspects of law, she formed the Advocate Community. The Physicians' Community was formed for doctors, the Healing Community for therapists and the Montessori Community for educators, as some examples. Each focused on a different need within society.

"There was nothing esoteric about them. They were asking, what does it mean to be a Christian as a doctor, an actor, an educator, etc., in this society today? Always they were seeking new ways of living the Ten Commandments", Mother Benedict said. "The communities affiliated with Regina Laudis are the lay priesthood in action, a witness to the statement of the Second Vatican Council that 'the lay apostolate ... is a participation in the saving mission of the Church itself.' "

The development of the lay communities became a most important work at Regina Laudis. One or more of the nuns belonged to each group, working in tandem with the members. The emphasis was always on how to live the Gospel values more fully and deeply in relationship with all persons encountered in daily life. The goal was always to work corporately as members of Christ's body to help bring His salvation to the world. As Mother Dolores put it once, "At Regina Laudis, we are mothering the life of the lay priesthood into the twenty-first century."

In the last years of the '60s, important work for the structure of the monastery had been steadily going on. Mother Benedict knew they had to have their own Constitution, and in the late '60s, she and several of the nuns, and even some novices, had worked on drafts. She invited some of the younger members to participate in drafting the Constitution because she was open to what they wanted to say. Mother Dolores, who was only a Sister in first vows at that time, was one of them. The fact that Mother Benedict would include a younger member was very threatening to some of the long-professed nuns, who didn't think the younger members had the right to be included in the thinking process and in presenting ideas.

But the foundress was very clear in what she was trying to do. She wanted to propose a Constitution that would fit Regina Laudis as the monastery moved into the next phase of its development. She was more concerned about the fullness of spiritual expression while knowing, of course, we must have laws. Yet here was their golden opportunity to have an official document expressing everything they stood for. In the first draft, they attempted to pull together the values they had talked about and were determined to retain—like maintaining the Latin, the chant, their habit, the enclosure and the life term for the Superior—which had brought such a tremendous upheaval among a few.

They also wanted to retain the ceremony of the Consecration of a Virgin, something very important to Mother Benedict because of what it meant, that a woman is promising that she will now totally give herself to God, that she will be "sealed for God", but in a "spousal relationship" that will be continually fertile and life-giving, bringing Christ's love to all. In Jouarre, on the day a nun was professed perpetually, the rite of consecration immediately followed. At Regina Laudis, in 1970, Mother Benedict returned to the earlier, long-held monastic tradition of separating the two rites, in order to increase appreciation for both as "two stages" in a nun's life. The two rites were seen to "call forth and complete" each other. Following the ceremony of perpetual profession, a nun should have the time to be assured that she can, with a new consciousness and fruitfulness, live the life of virginity that she has promised in her profession. When the Abbess sees that this promise of spousal fidelity has been stabilized, she may determine a candidate is apt for the blessing of the Church in the Consecration of a Virgin.[1]

In Rome they had a problem with this rite and said it was out of fashion, that not many today are interested in virginity. "But I never ask if they are virgins. That question belongs in the secret of the confessional", Mother Benedict noted. "The promise being made is to a life of virginity, from this day forward, because the nun is now entering her new life of a 'spousal relationship' with Christ, pledging fidelity to Him forever. I was determined to keep this ceremony in our Constitution."

Another change in the draft of the Constitution was her decision officially to specify what they had been living for some time: that they would no longer call those members of the Community who could leave the enclosure of the monastery Oblate Sisters. They would now be called *Missae*, "those who could be sent out" on whatever mission was needed, and they would have equal status with the choir nuns. Mother Benedict also felt the need to express Regina Laudis' identity with the land, which was a completely different frame of reference for a contemporary women's monastery.

When they felt the draft was completed, it was time to get it to the Sacred Congregation for Religious in Rome for approval. Accompanied by Mother Placid, Mother Stephen, Mother Jerome and Mother Irene, Mother Benedict traveled to the Vatican and personally presented the draft to the head of the Sacred Congregation. That was in 1970. It was two years before she got a response on the draft of the Constitution for Regina Laudis, and then she was told by Rome that they needed something more basic and simple.

By this time, they had an in-house lawyer. Lucille Matarese, now Sister Maria Immaculata, accepted the foundress' request that she work on the Constitution with a lawyer's touch.

In those first years of the '70s, the monastery seemed to be abuzz with new life and the energy such fertility brings. Mother Dolores, skilled with a camera, took action films of the Community at work—cultivating the land, caring for animals, milking the cows, haying, baking, preserving, making cheese and ice cream. The camera also captured the buoyant spirit of nuns chopping trees and wood-chipping, gathering honeycomb, painting, sewing, making perfume, weaving, bookbinding and perfecting photography skills, including those needed in a darkroom.

Mother Benedict expressed her delight that there was such a variety of activities at Regina Laudis. She felt this was in keeping with the Benedictine Rule, which maintains that a community should try to do every aspect of work within the enclosure; therefore, she now encouraged the nuns to develop thriving "industries" that would keep Regina Laudis self-sustaining.

"I had long believed that every person entering should be given an area of work and accomplishment that was matched to her own talents. Now I was acting on this. If someone was gifted in an area, we were able to 'set up shop' for her. The survival works (like gardening, cooking, preserving, laundry and sewing) always had to be done, but this was in combination with letting individuals work at projects that fit their particular gifts. I had always been enthralled by a garden, and so I made sure to find the time to cultivate flowers so I could take care of the sanctuary flower arrangements. I felt individuals should be assigned to works that they could respond to, that they would love doing so that they could develop personally. I couldn't see any holiness in doing something for God that you hated, except for the times you had to. Everything has to have meaning because if you feel you are engaging in meaningless action, that's the worst. It brings you to the height of emptiness.

"I had been encouraged by Pope Paul VI to seek women who had some basis of professional excellence in their life, because without that professional base, they would not be able to connect with the world in a way they could trust. And I accepted the value of any profession that I could see relating to the underlying rhythm of Benedictine life, which accounts for why so many varied works emerged at Regina Laudis. The monastery wasn't to be a structure that women would be poured into. What we built here had to reflect externally the inner life of the Community. You build a monastery for the people who really live there. If we had an Olympic swimmer, we would have built a swimming pool!"

An example of her determination to work with each individual nun according to her professional talents and personal needs was the construction of an Italian woodburning kiln, specifically for Laura Giampietro, who was now Sister Perpetua. She needed the kiln for firing the pottery she created in the studio that had been set up for her at Saint Martin's farm. Her involvement with pottery had begun at an early age, an interest "inherited" from her father Alexander Giampietro, a sculptor, potter and professor at Catholic University in Washington, D.C. As a student, she had been able to accompany her father to southern Italy, where he was studying the ancient craft of pottery practiced there. While there, Laura learned about many ancient methods of pottery making from the noted expert Emmanuele Rondinone. Everyone was so pleased when Signor Rondinone said he would come to Bethlehem to supervise the building of a high-temperature, wood-fired kiln, based on a design thousands of years old.

The entire Community, and the young people of the Closed Community and other communities, celebrated the first firing of the new kiln with Sister Perpetua and Signor Rondinone. It was an exciting day for Mother Benedict when she took out the finished pieces, holding them up for all to see, as everyone cheered, rejoicing at the accomplishment. The pottery produced by Sister Perpetua, and later, her novice apprentices, was recognized as special and became permanent best sellers at the monastery's annual fair and in the art shop.

Mother Dolores herself made an unusual request, that a carpentry shop be set up so that she could be trained in woodworking skills. The idea had come unexpectedly after hearing from Mother David that her father, a Peruvian Indian, who was dying, had asked the family to bury him in a plain wooden box. They had been unable to find one. Mother Dolores said she could make one if she had the equipment. Mother Mary Aline had shown her pictures of the coffins, shaped like the body, that were made at Jouarre, and Mother Dolores said she knew she could learn to make them.

With Mother Benedict's blessing, she was able to get lessons from Brother Jerome Blackburn, an Oblate of Mary Immaculate and a master carpenter who was staying with the monastic community for a period of spiritual and religious renewal. Together they set up a carpentry workshop in an old garage, and with Brother Jerome as her teacher, Mother Dolores was in training to become a master carpenter, specializing in coffin-making.

When the foundress saw the first finished coffin, recognizing talent, she told Mother Dolores she was to take this on as one of her special works. She made the coffins for eighteen years, until Mother Mary Aline died. Then the former Hollywood star was asked to take over Mother Mary Aline's job as guest secretary, and the coffin-making was turned over to Richard Beauvais, an Oblate. Mother Dolores taught him how to make coffins that would fit the body. A very interesting footnote to this is how Mother Dolores found out during a visit from her grandmother, Nellie Bowen, that she had, surprisingly, a coffin-making link in her heritage. Mother Dolores had been terrified to tell her that she was making coffins. But her grandmother didn't blink an eye. She told Mother Dolores that her great-grandfather had made coffins for a poorhouse in Illinois and that her great-grandmother had made the burial clothes!

Young people were now a frequent sight on the monastery grounds. They were asking for a direction that respected them as persons and striving to find ways that they could relate to one another. These young men and women were getting received in a way never before experienced, and this drew them like a magnet to returning as often as they could to Regina Laudis.

As part of their community formation process, the members of the Closed Community would come for the entire month of August to work on their spiritual development, personal relationships and group dynamics, for which challenging manual work provided a grounding. One thing the monastery had always wanted was a "chapter house", where Mother Benedict could meet with the nuns for Community meetings. She was very happy when, encouraged by Father Prokes, the members of the Closed Community came up with a proposal to build a chapter house. With Mother Benedict's approval, they began to plan a structure to be built on the hill where one day she envisioned their new church would be erected. They decided the building would be a circular tower of stone, and to determine its size, the young men and women and a few of the nuns held hands and formed a ring. The circumference of the circle they thus made was marked, and this outlined the boundary of the walls of the building, which was modeled on a medieval dovecote.

They envisioned a stone archway that would serve as the entrance to this circular chapter room, and with Father Prokes' guidance, assisted by Professor Giampietro, Mother Perpetua's father, they built this according to an ancient manner of construction in which a wooden frame is set up to support the placement of rocks and mortar. Peter Pettingell, an architect and master stonemason, was key in getting this work done. When the mortar has set, and the wooden support removed, if all has been done correctly, the arch "groans" and is set forever. When this moment came, the whole Community as well as the young ones from the lay community gathered to watch, and when the arch held, everyone shouted with an explosion of joy—and they danced!

The young people said over and over that it was a privilege to work on something so much beyond themselves. They dug the foundation by hand with shovels, gathered stones on the property and learned how to work with cement. Father Prokes worked with them. They worked on the structure for a month each summer for about ten years, but it did not receive a roof until the '90s, in the last year that Father Prokes was at Regina Laudis.

The chapter house wasn't the only building going up. Another group of young people had been coming to the monastery, and they formed a complement to the Closed Community, taking the name the Associate Community. They took on the mission of building a new barn near Saint Gregory's, with Father Prokes as their consultant, under the direction of Brother Jerome Blackburn. This barn became especially valuable during the Abbey Fair days, which had become extremely popular, now being held every year in August, with the invaluable assistance of lay people who formed a Regina Laudis Fair Committee.

The nuns never knew who would be coming to the monastery, but visitors were continually arriving and always welcomed. Among the more notable guests in these early '70s were the famed architect and inventor Buckminster Fuller and the environmentalist René Dubos. Mr. Fuller drew so much interest that the only place big enough to accommodate both the Community and guests for his lecture was the loft of the monastery barn. As listeners sat on bales of hay, the noted visitor spoke hour after hour on the need for comprehensive vision in the crucial matter of conserving the earth's resources.

Other notable guests were the celebrated aviator Charles Lindbergh and his wife, Anne Morrow Lindbergh. Anne came many times and found strength and solace at Regina Laudis. She and her husband participated in one of the professional seminars the Abbey hosted and worked on the land, helping to plant pine seedlings for Christmas trees. Other guests included the opera singer Veronica Tyler, who taught polyphonic singing to the Community; and Major General George S. Patton, son of General George S. Patton, Jr. He came several times to the monastery, once by helicopter, when he arrived to keep a commitment to the Associate Community to give them a seminar on America's relationship to Vietnam.

His first coming to Regina Laudis had to do with his daughter, Margaret Patton. In 1972, Margaret, an eighteen-year-old freshman at Bennington College in Vermont, nominally Episcopalian, had come with a roommate to spend a weekend at this Catholic monastery of Regina Laudis. She knew nothing of the Patton connection to the founding of this place and was, in fact, trying to obscure the fact that she was part of the Patton legacy. These were the Vietnam years, and being General Patton's granddaughter was something she wanted to forget about.

The apparent coincidence of General Patton's granddaughter showing up in Bethlehem was not lost on Mother Benedict. Yet, when she spoke to Margaret about how she had learned that her grandfather figured directly in her decision to establish a monastery in America, the young woman responded negatively. "She said, 'I absolutely hate him. Do not talk about him.'"

Still, intrigued by her weekend stay, Margaret Patton returned that summer for a longer visit. Mother Benedict spoke to her again about her grandfather and this time asked her if she would raise the American flag at an event they were planning to honor General Patton and his soldiers. Margaret was "dumbfounded", she said later. She felt strangely moved and began trying to understand the many levels in the complex life of her grandfather.

That fall, her father was ordered to Germany, and the whole family went. At Christmastime, Margaret and her brother wanted to go to Paris. As she explained: "I felt we couldn't be that close and not go to the places Mother Benedict was talking about. My father and I were driving in France early one morning, through lots of little towns, and we finally saw the tower of Jouarre! In my brazen way, I went up to the monastery door and opened it. I kept opening doors. All of a sudden I saw nuns and a priest. Something was going on. They were all facing me. I closed the door and started to run. Then I heard a tap, tap, tap and someone say, 'Mademoiselle.' It was a nun. I stammered something like, "*Je suis Regina Laudis*" (I am Regina

Laudis). Her name was Mère Jean Marie. She and my father, who speaks very good French, had a great conversation. She was very gracious. As we drove off, Mère Jean Marie waved and called out, "Vive Patton, Vive Patton!'"

Before the end of 1973, Margaret Patton began taking instruction in the Catholic faith. She came back to Regina Laudis with her father that year. She converted to Catholicism in 1976, when she was twenty-two, and in 1982 entered the Community as a postulant. It never struck her, or Mother Benedict, as a coincidence that she came here. Eventually, she came to respect her grandfather. "I gave her the name Sister Margaret Georgina. And her special work is as a professional horticulturist."

Two other visitors who came to Regina Laudis in the early '70s were Evelyn Jantzer, a New York–based teacher of dance, and June Christian, a noted teacher at the Royal Academy of Dance in London. Mother Benedict thought it would be a great idea to have them teach the nuns basic ballet techniques. It would be a way for learning grace, dignity and stature. It would be great recreation for the Community and also make everybody more able to move in unison during liturgical processions and ceremonies.

She had the nuns design a special habit, with black tights and a scapular; they then put up a barre, and these dance masters gave them basic ballet techniques. They choreographed a dance to Beethoven's Eighth Symphony and even did folk dance. But the truly memorable accomplishment of the dance adventure was when they took *The Dream of the Rood*, a mystical poem that tells the story of the Crucifixion from the point of view of the Cross itself, set it to Mahler's First Symphony and then added choreography. This poem was translated from the Old English by Mother Columba, the Community's author and scholar.

Mother Dolores spoke of this "dance adventure", saying, "For me this was a paradoxical experience. I never thought leaving show business, I'd find something like this in a monastery. But this was in 'synch' with the basic premise of Mother Benedict—that if our own cultural expression is not met, then we have nothing to take to church with us. It was a fruitful experience for the Community, many of whom had never had the chance to dance. We were dumbfounded at the hidden giftedness and talent we found. Everyone can sing and dance. Even Mother Ida, who was then in her eighties, insisted on being part of this ballet corps." And Mother Dolores added, "A most important part of contemplative life is to witness to the human, which is so well expressed in dance."

Another development in this golden period of the '70s was the coming of nuns from different religious orders to make retreats at Regina Laudis, or simply to find some clarity from the confusion many had felt about what Vatican II meant or didn't mean in its statements on updating convents and monasteries. One group belonging to the Franciscan Sisters of Perpetual Adoration in the Midwest came looking for a new experience in how religious life could meet the needs of the modern world. They were welcomed by Mother Benedict and Father Prokes, who always maintained that all orders needed to relate to the others. "Father Prokes was always trying to build the corporate body of Christ by finding ways to bring the body together so all could work in complement with each other", she explained.

The Franciscan Sisters received permission from Rome to leave their motherhouse and establish a province of their own, with a new name, the Franciscan Sisters of the Eucharist. They worked closely with Regina Laudis during this change. Their main work was in counseling, and they developed centers to provide this service in five states and overseas in Italy. In Connecticut, they found property in Meriden, where the Franciscan nuns have since expanded their work to include programs for children and a housing community for the elderly.

The timing was perfect for Regina Laudis to have a complementary relationship with nuns who were trained in counseling. The people coming to the monastery then did not come from a place where family life or the Church had prepared them for growing into a mature life. Some had suffered abuse, had been hurt badly by drugs or had been left in pain from the other disorders of the society in which they had been raised. How could the Community send them away? The Franciscan Sisters of the Eucharist, trained in counseling, became indispensable to the nuns in their work of formation and hospitality.[2]

Mother Benedict had given the job of completing the final draft of the Constitution to Sister Maria Immaculata, and by early summer of '74, she had gone over it carefully with Abbot Augustin Mayer, the Secretary for the Congregation of Religious in Rome, and Franciscan Father Basil Heiser, the Undersecretary. She had also sent a copy of the draft to the Archbishop of Hartford. All summer she worked on the revisions they had suggested and had it ready to go back to them in early fall. Accompanied by Mother Mary Aline, Mother Luke and Sister Maria Immaculata, the foundress took the document to Rome. On November 21, 1974, they were told it would be approved, since only a few very minor corrections were now needed. When the three nuns returned with the good news to Bethlehem, some of the members of the Community greeted them with a dance! Getting their Constitution approved meant that the next step was now on the horizon—the elevation of their

Foundation from a monastery to an abbey, a request that would have to be sent to Rome with the approval of Archbishop John Whealon. The word came shortly after Christmas that the Constitution was approved, and the Archbishop set the formal date for the establishment of the Abbey—the Feast of Saint Scholastica, February 10, 1976.

"When the approval came through, I had an immense sense of relief. This is what I had been after ever since the inception of the Foundation. After getting the freedom to come to the United States, I had continually contemplated what would be the proposal I could make for a Foundation that would respect American principles and yet incorporate all the demands of the Holy Rule. Only a sense of the Beatitudes allowed me to resolve this very real conflict and not succumb to arbitrary pressure. For the Beatitudes open you to the gifts of the Holy Spirit and give you freedom to make decisions that have to be made. What I had established was a place where, through that freedom, I had to live to serve others in their vocation, respecting our relationships", said Mother Benedict.

The approval of the Constitution meant the foundress now had the verification that their mission would now be accepted by all, from the Vatican to the State of Connecticut—and worldwide.

When the great day came for the ceremony establishing Regina Laudis now as an abbey, the jubilation was contagious. Maria Cooper Janis, who came frequently to the monastery, did on-camera interviews that day and called it "one of the most transforming experiences of my life". She interviewed many of the two hundred–plus smiling people who attended, and the universal feeling was one of sharing "the spiritual blessing of family".

The celebrant, Archbishop Whealon, noted that it was fitting that the Abbey be established in the year of the celebration of the nation's bicentennial, for this was the first Abbey of its kind founded specifically for contemplative Benedictine women on American soil. The Archbishop questioned Mother Benedict, as the Abbess-elect, asking if she was willing to take on the burden he was about to ask her to accept—that of the role of Abbess, "the Good Shepherd", in Saint Benedict's words, and be at the service of each member of the Community.

"Will you do it?" he asked, directly. She said yes, proclaiming her faith in the Roman Catholic Church, which the Archbishop called "the rock ... the quarry from which you were cut". He bestowed upon her the title of Abbess, giving her the crozier symbolizing her leadership and emphasizing that her responsibilities would be to teach, give good example and be faithful in love to her Community and the Church, as in the marriage ceremony, till death. He then extended his hand and gave her the blessing of the Church. It would have been impossible for her to express her feelings at that moment, she later said, being so overwhelmed, both with joy and the knowledge that her responsibilities were now heavier than ever.

At the end of the ceremony, Archbishop Whealon told the Community and crowds of guests how the election of the Abbess underscored that "a new moment in the life of Regina Laudis and in the life of the Church is now beginning." After that, each of the postulants, novices and nuns, radiating joy, came to their "Lady Abbess"—as she would from then on be called—to receive her kiss of peace and her blessing.

"I knew to be chosen Abbess meant I would continue to do as I had done as the Superior, but with a deeper responsibility. It means being absolutely available at all times and that people can bother you and interrupt you. You need the discipline to be able keep a balance between what these members of the Community need and your work that has to be done. In this position, you have to be calm for all those who are not and accept that they're flustered. You work very hard because your whole life is one of service.

"You also have to know that you are not automatically loved. You can be hated your whole life long by one person or a group. You can be subject to jealousy. And worse, you have to keep moving in the face of the power of evil, for the devil sometimes uses people you would not expect to attack and break you down. But always the monastery is a school of the Lord's service, where you constantly work out, 'How do I give my life for someone else?' And this is the work the Abbess accepts as a lifetime commitment, to be carried out with dedication and fidelity, knowing that somehow from this comes the redemptive mystery of the Abbey."

That February day in 1976 was a momentous and memorable one for Mother Benedict, Mother Mary Aline and all the nuns. But it also signaled new beginnings. By the end of the '70s, the nuns were noting how many changes had taken place. They had lost some people close to them. On January 13, 1979, Fanny Delehanty, their longtime friend, died. Lauren Ford, Regina Laudis' dearest friend, had died six years earlier, on August 30, 1973. Mother Assumpta died at the Abbey from a fatal brain aneurism on August 23, 1979.

On the plus side, every aspect of work in the Abbey was flourishing. They had welcomed a confessor who would be with them for years to come, Father Robert Tucker. Four more professional women had entered, given the names Sisters Rachel, Praxedes, Michael Mary and Felicitas, bringing to eleven the total number who had entered in the '70s.[3]

And the summer Abbey Fair had taken off, already becoming a yearly event drawing thousands of people from far and wide.

One of the attractions at the fair was the theater, which began in a tent. Because Mother Dolores could understand and speak the "language" of theatrical professionals, the Abbey felt free to build a theater. She not only attracted other actors to the contemplative life but was able to coordinate and consult on their professional offerings, making it possible for the Community to integrate a wide spectrum of cultural events that would otherwise have been beyond their capacity to manage or contain. This was in keeping with the concept that Mother Benedict had long espoused— that each member of the Community would find her place, allowing her to fulfill her own needs and to keep herself connected to people who share her profession. It was a complete surprise to people that the Abbey would have a working theater on the premises.

Two people who assisted Mother Dolores in developing the theater at Regina Laudis were James Douglas, a movie actor who became especially well known for his television role in the long-standing series *Peyton Place*, and his wife, Dawn, an actress and dancer. "I was in Hollywood and didn't know many actors who were Catholics", said Mother Dolores, who at that time had starred in two movies with Elvis Presley, *Loving You* and *King Creole*, and was much in demand as an up-and-coming young actress. "When I heard Jim was a Catholic, my ears went up. It was difficult to find someone in that town with whom you held a common basis."

The friendship that developed between Dolores Hart and the Douglases grew into a real mutuality of love and trust, and in the '70s, the couple, seeking a deeper meaning for their lives, moved east and settled in Bethlehem to be near Regina Laudis. They helped Mother Dolores establish the theater, where a variety of works—from Shakespeare to musical revues—have been held over the years. Stars such as Patricia Neal (who later wrote her best-selling book, *As I Am*, which she dedicated to Mother Benedict, from a base at Regina Laudis), actress Gloria De Haven, opera singer Veronica Tyler and many others came to perform at the Abbey's theater.

"We have a naturally inclusive approach to religious life at this monastery. To be able to receive people who can complement us in our professions on site is a practical demonstration of religious witness to what the Abbey was envisioned to be", said Mother Dolores. "You build a monastery for the people who really live there."

As the '70s came to an end, the golden period was still intact and thriving. But while good work would remain the mark of Regina Laudis, the '80s would also bring an unexpected, briefly painful time to the Abbey.

Chapter 14

GROWTH AND DIFFICULTIES

— Seeds of Trouble as the Abbey Flourishes
— The New Buildings on the Hill
— Questions from Rome
— An Abbey Church at Last

Not long after the Foundation had achieved this momentous state of becoming an Abbey, Mother Benedict received an unexpected invitation from a monk of the Abbey of Mount Angel in Oregon, Dom David Nicholson. One of his good friends was a man named Henry Ellis, who owned property on Shaw Island off the coast of the state of Washington. Mr. Ellis, a convert to the Roman Catholic faith, wanted to offer his land and the building on it to a monastery that would come and start a Foundation there.

Dom David came to Bethlehem to pay Regina Laudis a visit. He stayed two or three days, observed the Community and then told Mother Benedict about Mr. Ellis, who had said to him, "You've got to find a community to appreciate and accept the property." He invited her to come and see the property, but she did not want be involved that way. She sent Father Prokes to give her a professional opinion, knowing he had sound judgment. He went and came back saying he felt it was something Regina Laudis could take on. In some sense, it reminded him of Regina Laudis. It

326

had a good building, with decks. Mr. Ellis had never lived in that house, though he had invited friends to live there.

Father Prokes had such a positive response that Mother Benedict said she'd consider accepting the property to start a Foundation and met several times with the Community to discuss the implications of this. It could not be an arbitrary decision. It became important to her to take a look at the property, and so she made a visit. At that point, she and Mr. Ellis—whom she now called Henry—got along quite well. He said he was offering this land and building, no strings attached. She took a lot of photos, and when she came back to the Community, she showed the nuns a number of slides, and then they took a vote. It was a communal decision to accept the property.

They had to obtain permission from the local bishop, Archbishop Raymond Hunthausen, as well as permission from Rome to go there. Archbishop Hunthausen, who knew Henry quite well, was cordiality itself. Henry went with Mother Benedict, and the Archbishop welcomed her to come and start the Foundation on Shaw Island. "I knew we needed a period of time for things to settle in and to adapt the building, and so I sent Mother Luke to stay there to record her impressions of what we would have to do. Mother Luke is of Italian heritage, very affable, and the Shaw Island people and the workmen were very happy for her to be there. They appreciated her vision and her courage. It was a terrible financial struggle to make ends meet, and Henry helped somewhat with this", said Mother Benedict. She added, "We wanted to choose a name that would evoke the area. The main building was built around a mesa, the rock formations so common to the West. That became the Priory. We figured the chapel could be in the furnace room, where space was available. The view outward from here was beautiful because it looked out to the rock formation surrounding the building. We knew then we had our name—Our Lady of the Rock."

Brother Jerome Blackburn, the carpenter who had often done work at Regina Laudis, went to Shaw Island to make the altar and the furniture. He made everything from beachwood. This was the most economical way to do it, and the expense ended up being relatively small. Brother Jerome found a large group of trees that had grown together, fallen into the water and then washed ashore. This massive driftwood became the altar. Then he made the benches for the chapel out of the huge deposits of wood he found on the beach. The wood had a particular beauty because worms had eaten at it, leaving a lace effect on the wood.

In 1977, Mother Thérèse Critchley, Mother Miriam Benedict and Mother Prisca Dougherty were sent to start the Foundation on Shaw Island.

Father Prokes, meanwhile, had been working with the Franciscan Sisters of the Eucharist, who had come to Connecticut because of Regina Laudis, and, as Mother Benedict recalled, "His enthusiasm for the Foundation out west was catching." There were two "openings" on Shaw Island: the country store was for sale, as was the operation of the ferry slip. Father Prokes suggested the possibility of the Franciscan Sisters buying the store and the Mercy Sisters running the ferry slip. Archbishop Hunthausen thought it was a great idea to bring the Franciscan apostolate to Shaw Island. And Father Prokes envisioned that the different work of the three orders would be a complementary apostolate, though, as it turned out, the Mercy involvement did not materialize as a mission.

"All was blissful at that point", Mother Benedict would later say, calling the '70s "a time of flourishing". "We experienced a steady growth and development of the corporate structure and intercorporate life of the community. We had moved from a pre–Vatican II atmosphere of being what might have been thought of as 'correct', to a post–Vatican II atmosphere of freedom to grow. Father Prokes' contribution was invaluable, especially in sharing with us his vision of renewal of religious life, where he emphasized that we are responsible for one another. I believe his being here was essential for bringing the Abbey into the future and helping to give us the structure that everybody wanted but didn't know how to achieve."

On the practical side, Regina Laudis was "still making it financially only by the grace of God. Ahead of us was a task we knew we had to carry out—the erection of buildings that were sorely needed by our Community, which had outgrown the space we had in the former factory that had become our monastery. Yet we couldn't go ahead with building on our own. Permission had to come from the Archbishop, who oversees our finances. By 1986, Archbishop Whealon thought we were in sound enough financial position to think about building", the Abbess reported.

Almost a decade before that, they had begun a forestry development program for their land, especially in relation to the hill. They had the state forester, Harold H. Sweeton, come to speak to them in the '70s, and following that, Mother Stephen presented a projected program for the following four years. "That's when we started having what we called 'corporate work days', which involved pruning and forestry work on the hill. When we finally began constructing the first building, in the late '80s, the nuns themselves had cleared the land and felled the trees that were then sent to a lumber operation to be cut, cured and aged. When this lumber was subsequently returned to us, some of it was used for our first new building, the six-sided wooden building on the hill, which was to be our novitiate.

"It was because of the architectural program that Father Prokes had initiated, at my invitation, that the Community was able and ready to take on its own building plans", Mother Benedict continued. "I had chosen three of our Sisters, two of them architecturally gifted and the third competent in legal and financial matters, to become a 'building triad'. They were Mother Telchilde, an art historian with a particular knowledge of medieval art; Mother Praxedes, an artist accomplished in almost every possible medium; and Mother Maria Immaculata, an attorney with experience in regulations and codes. I felt that with their training and gifts, they were eminently suited to design and oversee the construction of our buildings."

The foundress would later say they reached a milestone in the fulfillment of the vision for this Foundation when the walls of the circular stone building that would be their Chapter House was completed. On the floor at the entrance was a large fieldstone star that they called the Epiphany Star. "I had been baptized on the Feast of the Epiphany, and so this star had a particular significance for me as a symbol leading to a universal meaning about our existence and our call. Yet I have to give full credit to Mother Mary Aline for insisting the star be placed there. I'm grateful to her. She saw the star as an architectural expression of what this monastery stands for. That star on the floor, shaped in stone, is not only a reminder of the white star we saw on the tanks of General Patton's army the day Jouarre was liberated. Moreso, it reminds us first of the morning star, a symbol of the faith, pointing to the mystery of Christ. But seeing the white star on the tank was for me an apocalyptic moment," she admitted, "for it was a new revelation in the

perennially transcendent orientation of my whole life—
that God was calling me, and I had to follow."

As the '80s progressed, Regina Laudis was becoming ever
more noticed. Lay people kept asking how they, too, could
live according to Benedictine principles. The nuns had long
had Oblates associated with the Community. Now many of
these people wanted to have a stronger, more consistent
commitment to Regina Laudis. It was clear there had to be
levels of Oblates, with a core group that would see their
commitment to Benedictine principles as a lay vocation,
praying part of the Divine Office and observing the spirit
of monastic life. But all the Oblates, and the lay people in
any of the communities associated with Regina Laudis, would
participate in the corporate work to be done, engaging in
any aspect of development needed, from tending the gardens to working in the art shop.

Only one venture relating to the Abbey ever backfired a
bit, and it made local news. It was undertaken by Oblates who
had taken the name the Healing Community, and it led to
some misunderstanding. The members had taken a great interest in property in the nearby town of Bridgewater, both
because of its locale and its history as the former home of Connecticut Native Americans. They bought the property, which
was known traditionally as Promisek. It had several buildings
on it, and in the late '70s, the Healing Community agreed to
have one of these buildings used to house a nondenomina-
tional Montessori school. It was to be founded and staffed by
Montessori teachers who belonged to a Montessori Community associated with the Abbey. These Montessori teachers had found a spiritual center at the Abbey, and they saw
that Benedictine life had much in common with the Montessori way of education. They felt that establishing their school
near the monastery could be mutually enriching.

Margaret Patton, the granddaughter of General Patton, had been trained as a Montessori teacher and became a cofoundress of the school with the Montessori Community. It seemed fitting that the school would be named after her grandmother, General Patton's wife, Beatrice Ayer Patton. The Montessori Community also felt that would be a good name for the school. After Margaret left to enter Regina Laudis, the Abbey remained marginally associated with the Montessori school, which was becoming more and more of a financial drain.

In the early '90s, the owners of Promisek also felt it was too unprofitable to keep the Montessori school going, and they closed it. "The original teachers from the Montessori Community had all left, and actually, it had come to the point where Regina Laudis was subsidizing the school. Becoming responsible for someone's else's project is not what we were supposed to be doing as a contemplative community of Benedictines. Yet, in actual fact, I was not part of the decision to close the school", said Mother Benedict.

Phyllis Beauvais, the spokesperson for the Promisek owners, tried to explain to the parents and the press why the school had to close. But the media tried to make Regina Laudis the scapegoat, saying the nuns had much to do with closing the school. "None of that was true, but this was not the first time we had been the victims of unfair reporting and the stories had nothing to do with the truth", the Abbess commented.

The darkest time for the Abbey came in 1987, when it was criticized in newspaper and television stories, with accusations running a gamut of claims—that they were a cult, that they demanded rich people give them their fortunes, that they broke up families, that they told people to put their children up for adoption. "Apparently the stories were being widely reported before we even heard about them. Mother Mary Quentin, who headed the Mercy Sisters of Alma, was probably the first to tell me about the mess. The trouble had begun on Shaw Island. So we were dependent on information coming in. And we weren't the only order getting assaulted. The Mercy Sisters and the Franciscans were also under fire", Lady Abbess said.

"As I look back, I can see where the problems escalated. The Mercy Sisters had put up a building to which the residents on Shaw Island objected, saying it violated their building codes. The Franciscans were running the only store on the island. And we had our Foundation, Our Lady of the Rock. We also had a problem with Henry Ellis, who had promised us we'd have three hundred acres but then told us we could have only one hundred fifty acres. All three hundred acres were essential for the support of the monastic farm, animals, enclosure and community life. The Foundation could not have been continued without them. The Community had invested much and labored hard over ten years of time to develop that land, and the Foundation was made in reliance upon Henry's promise to give the three hundred acres to us. Because he was now set to give away one hundred fifty of the three hundred acres to a group that was not compatible with monastic life, and this transfer was imminent, we had no alternative but to seek injunctive relief, which asked only that the one hundred fifty acres be transferred to us as had been promised. After hearing all sides, the court ruled that the one hundred fifty acres be transferred to us." Since all three communities were linked to Father Prokes, he came under fire, too.

"The people on Shaw Island didn't know the difference between us, the Franciscans and the Mercies, who were in

the active, fast lane and not contemplatives. So these people made accusations about 'the nuns', putting us all in the
same box. There was no differentiation among the three
communities for Shaw Island people, and they just felt the
intensity of having an influx of nuns on their tiny island,
which is only 7.7 square miles and has a population of around
two hundred people.

"If we had maintained only the Benedictine and Franciscan presence, I think the people would not have created
the explosion. As a matter of fact, it was only a few who
were making a fuss in the name of the whole Shaw Island
community. Actually, we never felt a grass-roots rejection.
If we had, as a Benedictine, I would have closed up, and all
of us would have left. Saint Benedict makes it clear that if
the earth rejects you, you can't stay. That's not to say that
the mudslinging didn't hurt.

"Yet," she went on, "in retrospect, I hand it to the people. They did have a lot to swallow. What was especially
painful for us, however, was Henry's actions. He was so
bitter after losing the lawsuit that he went to Rome to complain about us, and he proceeded to get the media to attack
us, even to getting a devastating and false story about us on
television's *20/20* show."

Mother Benedict felt that Henry expected he would be
a leader of the Benedictine Foundation on Shaw Island.
When he went to Rome, it was clear that he definitely felt
he was the patriarch. "Then he started courting a handful
of people who had disconnected from us, for their own
reasons. He found a nucleus of discontented people, among
them one of our former nuns who felt she had grievances,
had left secretly in the night and identified with the opposition. They went to the press with bizarre stories, many of
them accusing Father Prokes of having a dictatorial control

over us and loading his sermons with sexual images. None of this was true, but it got a lot of attention, and many people probably believed what they read. Henry was blatantly open about his agenda that he had taken to Rome. He wanted Father Prokes—and me—out of Regina Laudis."

Not surprisingly, Mother Benedict started getting calls from reporters, but she could not respond. She had contacted the Apostolic Delegate, Pio Laghi, and he had put her under orders not to talk to anyone in the press. He reminded her, "They have been throwing Christians to the lions for centuries." He told her, "Your path is going to be strewn with obstacles. Don't read, don't know what they're blaming you for. Ignore it completely." She very much appreciated that "order".

Fortunately, there was a trust between the Community and their Abbess. They considered the issues of their monastic day to be more critical than thinking about the criticisms. She reminded them that you're never without crisis day by day when you choose a life for God. It puts you into a continuous struggle between good and evil. The lies they were being subjected to were part of this struggle.

But she did acknowledge that bad publicity is always a problem, and any scandal hurts the morale of a community. "But eventually it gets through to you that this is the Christian life. I take it in stride; it's part of a package. If we weren't challenged, we wouldn't be doing something significant", she said, wisely.

Mother Dolores asked Hollywood film editors to collaborate in examining one of the television stories aired on the 20/20 program and reported that "they said it was put together as a propaganda piece. They showed Mother Jerome in sunglasses, commenting, 'Something shady is going on here.' Then they showed some novices in a truck on their way to church but labeled this, 'A number of nuns have left.' " Mother Dolores said, "I contacted our friend Roone Arledge, who was then the president of ABC News, and asked how it was that they could put something like this on national television. He sent a personal message to Lady Abbess and apologized but said he didn't have the power to pull it, because of the terms of the First Amendment. If we wanted commensurate air time, he said, we could have it. But we said no. We didn't want to be put into the denigrating position of having to defend ourselves, and besides, we were being obedient to the Pro Nuncio, Pio Laghi, who spoke for the Church." [1]

Mother Benedict had hoped that when the publicity died down, the matter would be put to rest, but the damage done by the lies against them surfaced again a few years later, and this time, from Rome.

The Abbess felt she had always had a good relationship with Rome. She had cherished her friendship with Pope Paul VI, and all were all terribly saddened when he died in 1978, but they were pleased when Pope John Paul I was elected and very happy when John Paul II was named to head the Church on October 16 of that year.

In 1984 Mother Benedict went to Rome, and while there she was invited by Archbishop Vincent Fagiolo, who was the Secretary of the Sacred Congregation for Religious in Rome, to spend some time with him. He said they were all fascinated with Regina Laudis and all thought highly of the nuns.

The following year, he came to America, and he stayed at Regina Laudis for a week. He was very much in favor of the Abbey and gave the nuns conferences on canon law and on the renewal of religious life. He was extremely friendly, especially at seeing they were happy in religious life and completely submissive to Rome. He saw no problems, and in fact, he registered great admiration for the nuns and acceptance of their work. He called the nuns very respectful, very refreshing and affirmative.

This became a time of respite. The nuns had never let those dark events of the late '80s block them in carrying out either their practical or spiritual work at the monastery. The Abbey Fair was getting ever more popular, with a great deal of help coming from lay people who called themselves Friends of Regina Laudis and many residents of the nearby communities, whose efforts were all coordinated by a devoted Oblate and friend of many years, Dorothy (Dot) Eichelman. They had an active theater group, and, with the professional help of Mother Dolores, they put on high-quality performances, even of Shakespeare's plays. Mother Praxedes, an artist and sculptor, became trained as a blacksmith and, with the coming of a master, Jeff Havill, set up a functioning blacksmith shop on the Abbey grounds. Their tree nursery was doing well enough to bring in brisk sales of Christmas trees, and their crafts and other products produced by the nuns were selling well in their Little Art Shop.

They had also taken another big step for the care of their land. Mother Benedict felt that for the nuns to be able to do the agricultural work needed for today's world and the future, some would need to be highly trained in specific areas of agriculture. She didn't want Regina Laudis to be thought of as just nuns with a farm. "We are professional women in everything we do, and it became clear to me that some of the nuns had to have higher degrees in agriculture if we were going to meet the future demands of the land. And so I encouraged four of the nuns here to apply for admission first to the master's program, to be followed by the doctoral program at the College of Agriculture and

Natural Resources at the University of Connecticut. Mother Telchilde, Mother Noella, Mother Augusta and Mother Jeanne-Yolaine began doctoral studies in animal science, microbiology, agronomy and plant science. To our surprise and joy, Mother Noella received a Fulbright Scholarship in 1994, allowing her to study the microbiology of cheese[2] in France", Mother Benedict said, noting that the University of Connecticut would often tell them they had been over-joyed to have the nuns in their agricultural programs.

She acknowledged that it was highly unusual for cloistered nuns to get permission to go outside the monastery and back to school to get an advanced degree. "But I never had any doubts about this. I knew it was the right thing. In fact, this decision to have some of our nuns get Ph.D.'s in agriculture is in keeping with Saint Benedict's Rule, which says we must be of help to whomever comes to us, a rule we have incorporated in our Constitution. Their experi-ence will definitely be of help to others", she explained.

In the late 1980s, motivated by a desire to teach others how to care for the land according to Benedictine prin-ciples, the Abbey, with the encouragement of Father Prokes, began another unusual venture, the International Student Land Program. Young men and women had by this time been coming for years as guests of the Abbey, often par-ticipating in work on the land. The idea was to build on this and offer a more formally structured year-long Land Program, which could be recognized by other schools and employers as a valuable educational experience. A year would be a long enough period for the students to gain new insights about what they could do with their lives in the future. Father Prokes felt this would be a remarkable thing, and he was right. For the past twenty years, young men and women have been hearing about the program, now called the Monastic Internship Program, and asking to come to participate. They go through the four seasons working in this natural environment. They are housed and fed, and for those who need it and qualify, the Abbey can arrange to get them college credit for their fieldwork. Everyone who has completed his full land program has called this an invaluable time of growth.

Mother Benedict would call 1988 "a personal time of happiness" "because that year I celebrated my Golden Jubilee, marking fifty years that I had been a Benedictine nun. We had an outdoor Mass on the vigil of Pentecost that year, and Monsignor Lacy was there and Father Robert Tucker officiated. Father Louis Aufiero gave the homily. I'll never forget his consoling words. Referring to the lies and slanderous publicity of the year before, he said, 'God made you face that opposition to make you strong.' I pondered his words many times in the coming years."

The year 1989 also marked an important milestone for the Community. They had finally achieved a decades-long goal—the dedication of their first residential building on the hill. "It was May 11, and intermittent rain kept the weather raw, but nothing dampened our spirits. This was a day we had longed for, waited for and prayed for", said Mother Benedict. "This first building was to be the novitiate, the home of the novices. All of us who were involved in planning the structure agreed that it would have an exterior built of wooden logs and be hexagon-shaped. This is a figure of perfection, and the form is a sign of Eternity, and so this becomes an analogy for what this Benedictine monastery is about. The hexagon is the shape of many crystals and cells, too. It is a fundamental form of nature."

Archbishop Whealon, who had visited Regina Laudis regularly, came for the dedication and said what they were

doing gave witness to the enduring values of faith and goodness rooted in Catholic tradition. "He was a zealous and
vigilant shepherd who took to heart his responsibility in
our regard. Though sometimes severe and exacting, Archbishop Whealon unfailingly supported and encouraged our
monastic life and acquired a real esteem for our Abbey. After
leading the introductory prayers for the dedication ceremonies, he went to each of the rooms in the new building and
gave a special blessing. With good humor, he even blessed
the furnace in the basement. It was an awesome day for all
of us. It had taken over forty years of preparation to come
to this day", the Abbess said.

The '90s began on a low note for Mother Benedict, not
only because of rumblings of opposition, but more so because
her dear and faithful friend of the past fifty years, Mother Mary
Aline, was dying. This was a very difficult time for the Community to see such an esteemed elder so ill and to know that
she would not be long on this earth. Mother Mary Aline
wanted Mother Benedict with her constantly, and so often
Mother Benedict would sit near her, keeping vigil and remembering their days at Jouarre, the dangers they had faced in wartime France and how they had come to America together,
following the charge of starting the Foundation here.

The Abbess was concerned for her friend because Mother
Mary Aline had always been so afraid of death. "Actually, it
was a terror of death that she felt, and I had always been
aware that she had this terror. We had talked about it for
years. It had surfaced strongly when her mother died, years
ago, on a Christmas Day. Mother Mary Aline had hated
Christmas ever after that because she associated it with death,
and she was so afraid of death. I don't know what it was
from her childhood or her past that left her with this terrible condition. The reason was totally unknown to me,

but I was always praying that this burden could be lifted from her and that she wouldn't need to be so afraid. I gave up talking to her about it because she was in a panic if you talked about death. How she clung to life!

"I was with her most of the time in her last days", Mother Benedict went on. "I was the only one she wanted. She was dependent on my presence, and she called for me constantly. She had always been herself, a person with no pretenses and a very orthodox faith. I think these fine qualities stayed with her and somehow helped her to carry through serenely at the end. I was so relieved to see this. Her last moments were amazingly peaceful. She died on March 26, 1990. She was eighty-five. I have missed her very much."

One memory that remained strong for the Abbess was how much Mother Mary Aline loved the owl, the snowy white owl in winter and the speckled owl in spring. In her office, she had symbols of the owl, and everybody used to think of her as a "wise owl". After she died, Mother Benedict related that she was in a car going up the hill and there was an owl, in broad daylight, flying in the same direction. She felt her friend's presence when she saw the owl.

The Abbess would later say that Mother Mary Aline's concern about death forced her to think about what she might be feeling herself if she were facing her own death. "It's normal to be afraid of death, but I know it is just a climax of trusting God to accept death, and I hope I'm going to be able to do that when my time comes. Many saints put all their focus on that very point so that when the moment came, they would be prepared to leave everything in God's hands", she acknowledged. "But no matter what you do to prepare, you always know you haven't done enough. At the same time, if you have done all you could, God will do the rest. He will do in you what you can't do for yourself, and so you can trust that God will receive you.

"The contemplative prays incessantly that everyone would receive the grace to believe in God's love. You try to counsel a dying person who is a nonbeliever to open his capacity to trust in God's love even when he can't believe. You carry out actions yourself for the faith of others, that they may be open to receive the gifts of faith, hope and love.

"It's the grace of God that opens the heart", she went on. "The pursuit of grace is spontaneous, from within. But we have ways of blocking it. Yet that blocking is never completely total. Grace is always available. We can ignore it, defy it and bury it, but God's grace is His handprint on our souls, and His love that put it there is permanent. Unbelievers can't change this, and death can't erase it. That's why I say that death is just the climax of trusting God, and it should bring no fear if you have lived according to this trust, believing that He will receive you after your last breath, bringing you into the new life He promised."

They buried Mother Mary Aline in their cemetery on the hill, and this was a very emotional time for everyone. Then, along with the pain of missing Mother Mary Aline, 1990 brought Lady Abbess a personal trauma—when she discovered a mass in her breast and, being a doctor, knew this was a potentially serious tumor. She had to have a mastectomy right away. A short time later, she had to have a hysterectomy. She would say firmly that her support in this difficult time was her Community.

"But even more fortunately, I've been spared much of the anguish that comes with severe illness because I have had a particular grace as a contemplative, meaning that I had the habit of remaining in God's holding. Knowing you are held by God becomes a form of stability. Because this relationship with God is continually on my mind, it protects me from all sorts of wandering, or anguish, normally associated with the kind of physical trauma I was undergoing. And so illness doesn't distract me from the positive mental attitude that comes from the gift of contemplation.

"I think because I've been through the medical profession, this has helped me keep a stable attitude about the presence of God", she continued. "To see people on stretchers, over and over, helped me think of God. That person lying there could be me, except for the grace of God. The contemplative life never allows you to forget any of that. In the contemplative life, you check out everything. It actually goes hand in hand with the medical profession, where you also check out everything. This is a habit of mind you acquire as a doctor, and it is the basis, too, of being a contemplative. And so I keep going back to square one—God created me, and He loves me—and this gives me a stability that never allows illness and pain to become overly important and distracting."

Getting the news on May 18, 1990, that Monsignor Lacy had died was a very painful time for the Abbess. He had been such a true friend for so many years, so she felt the loss keenly. "This was a time when we needed the support of friends who had a history of coming to Regina Laudis and understood what we had tried to accomplish here. Monsignor Lacy had always intervened for us when we had been subject to misunderstandings. Now I was really aware that the climate had changed for us in Rome because, I found out later, Rome was being besieged by people in opposition to us, who were not only being heard, but were being believed."

And the Community's work went on. At the end of 1990, a second structure, Saint John's Tower, built in proximity to the novitiate, was completed, now giving them the space they needed for an infirmary and a residence for Lady Abbess and some of the older nuns. This too was a wooden building, hexagonal in shape. "We felt these two buildings were a creative expansion of the classical image of the 'log cabin', which maintains the character of poverty but is decidedly charming", the Abbess said. "At this point we now had a trio of buildings on the hill, the two new ones and the circular stone Chapter House. And we were well into the planning of our church on Robert Leather's hill, the gift he gave us, telling me, 'I have this beautiful hill, and the view is so beautiful. It should be a place where people could come to worship God.'"

Then, in 1991, Mother Benedict faced two major changes. Archbishop Whealon, who had always supported the nuns, died; and Archbishop Fagiolo was replaced as Secretary of the Sacred Congregation for Religious by Archbishop Errázuriz Ossa.

That summer, only a few weeks after Archbishop Whealon's death on August 2, which was another great sadness for the Community, Mother Benedict got a letter from Archbishop Errázuriz Ossa telling her that he was sending two representatives to Regina Laudis to conduct an apostolic visitation. She was surprised and confused by this. "I just couldn't put this all together to get a handle on what was going on."

On September 24, Bishop Joseph Gerry and Dom Adelbert Buscher, both Benedictines, arrived. They seemed friendly, but also uneasy. They stayed for four days, and during that time, they spoke to everyone at the Abbey, from top to bottom. They had a list of questions about life at Regina Laudis and asked some questions that were disturbing to the nuns. "They were, I think, trying to see if there was any justification to the accusations that had been made about Father Prokes, specifically bizarre ones saying that his sermons were about sex and about having sexual feelings at Mass. It was very difficult for all the nuns, pledged to a life of chastity, to be subjected to this line of questioning, and it was especially difficult for the younger ones," said Lady Abbess.

By the end of the four days, the two Visitators saw that the spiritual life of the Benedictines at Regina Laudis was above reproach. The Visitators seemed friendlier and commended the Community for their missionary zeal, their work and their way of fulfilling their monastic obligations. "We couldn't have been more assured that all was well, and we had every reason to believe that we had been exonerated from the flimsy complaints", said the Abbess. At this point, she still believed they were "hand-in-glove" in a dialogue with the Sacred Congregation for Religious, which is the central organization in the Church that focuses on religious life, and that all could be resolved by speaking about the problems.

Mother Benedict went to meet with the new Secretary for the Sacred Congregation for Religious, Archbishop Errázuriz Ossa, in Rome on November 21, 1991. While he was cordial, he made her uncomfortable because he immediately brought up Father Prokes, asking in very broken English, "What about Father Prokes?"

Not understanding what he meant, she repeated his question, "What about Father Prokes?"

"I got the sense that he didn't want an open dialogue because he immediately dropped the subject completely and went on to another subject", she recalled. "This subtle hostility toward me was very hard for me to understand, especially after having had such a great relationship with Archbishop Fagiolo. All we could figure was that the two Visitators must have added on their report that they had some questions about Father Prokes.

"We knew in that moment what we had been suspecting. Our enemies had made inroads, even threatening lawsuits, and the door was being shut to Regina Laudis for some reason", said Mother Benedict.

"Up until the late '80s, the Community had always had the assurance that they were completely in line with Rome, submitting to all they were asked. It was a shock to them to find out in 1991 that they were being negatively criticized at the Vatican by hostile persons.

"I planned to send Mother David and Mother Dolores to Rome to respond to further questions about Father Prokes and also to present the draft for our revised Constitution containing the changes Rome required for us to be aligned with the new Code of Canon Law. The major complaint about our Constitution seemed to be that the Community had chosen to have an Abbess for life, which was revered as a tradition written into the Constitution. They also kept complaining about our insistence on the value we placed on the ceremony of the Consecration of a Virgin. Again, I couldn't understand their objections to this, since the consecration is a rite that exists in the Roman Pontifical, which is part of the revered books of the Church."

Mother Benedict contacted the Sacred Congregation for Religious in Rome to get an appointment, and when one was definitely set up, she sent Mother David and Mother Dolores to Rome to keep it, carrying a letter from her responding to Archbishop Errázuriz Ossa's questions. When the two nuns arrived for the scheduled appointment, on November 8, 1992, a secretary handed them a note written that morning, saying they couldn't keep the appointment. It was "inopportune". The secretary was obviously embarrassed. There was nothing Mother David and Mother Dolores could do except go home. They were never told beforehand that this was an inopportune time for Archbishop Errázuriz Ossa to meet with them. They had traveled from Bethlehem to Rome only to be told the appointment had been canceled.

After that visit to Rome by Mother David and Mother Dolores in 1992, it was clear that some persons had sullied Regina Laudis' reputation with the Vatican. The nuns thought that what they were doing at Regina Laudis was established and accepted. They had no idea the criticisms had gone that far.

"We were accused by enemies and then asked by Rome to prove ourselves innocent! That sense of questioning us came as a complete shock. We had no idea of the damage that had been done. Our critics were taking sections of Father Prokes' homilies and distorting the message. What they said about these was so bizarre, I can see why Rome would have wondered about them", Mother Benedict said. "Soon, however, we could begin to see this denigration as, in fact, an amazing gift of the Holy Spirit. If Regina Laudis is worth its salt, we have to face that we will not be spared crisis. Yet we must always believe that out of crisis comes a new birth. That's the mystery of redemptive salvation within the heart of the Church. I trusted that out of the crisis we then faced would come a new and positive relationship with Rome."

It wasn't her way to focus just on bad news! The following February, they received a great gift—and an honor—from the Province of Manche, in Normandy, France. After a series of negotiations, they were given the privilege of caring for an apple orchard in the French village of Néhou. This orchard, located a short distance from the beaches of Normandy, had been the command post for General George Patton in the summer of 1944 as he was in hiding, awaiting

the orders to enter the battle for France. When Lady Abbess
first heard the history of this orchard and the response of
the village to their distinguished guest, she immediately felt
there was a relationship between Regina Laudis and that
orchard. She had offered that the abbatial Community would
assume the ongoing restoration and care of this orchard as
an expression of gratitude for the Liberation, and now the
response of the Manche officials was yes. "I felt personally
honored when they decided to transfer the care of this historic property to Regina Laudis, asking that we maintain
and cultivate it 'in perpetuity'", Mother Benedict said.[3]

"To help us be good stewards of the orchard, we acquired
an abandoned eighteenth-century house in the village of
Néhou to be a center for study, work and meditation", she
continued. "This came about with the help of my brother,
John Duss. He was a lawyer in Jacksonville, Florida; his
wife had died. He told me he was going to France. I asked
him to look and see if he could find us a house in Normandy. He did. He found a really quite lovely house that
was not at all expensive. We decided we should get it. We
called it 'The Living Flame'. Helen Patton, General Patton's granddaughter and the blood sister of Mother Margaret Georgina, worked very hard with us to restore the
house and the orchard so we could develop the center. She
got the neighbors to help her, and together they planted
over 130 apple trees, thriving today in the orchard." The
Province of Manche, Normandy, later purchased the field
next to the orchard and established the two fields as a memorial of this phase of the Liberation. It was given the name
Camp Patton. Lady Abbess attended the dedication of Camp
Patton in June 1994. It was an incredible event for her. A
U.S. military color guard was there, along with many of
her friends.

After the formal ceremony of dedication, all in attendance were invited to a dramatic presentation at "The Living Flame", directed by Helen Patton, an actress and director. The program included Academy Award–winning actress Patricia Neal reading from the memoirs, poems and diaries of General Patton.

Meanwhile, the work of planning their Abbey church on the hill had never ceased, and the construction of a building the nuns themselves designed, with Father Prokes' professional architectural guidance, was under way in late 1993. This was to be a simple structure, with an exterior of plain wood. But on the inside, it would be unusual, very spacious, with the walls mostly of clear glass so light could stream in, quite in contrast with the first chapel. The monastic enclosure, where the nuns pray, would be separated from the rest of the church by an open grille and a stone altar on a raised platform in the center. Because the walls were to be mainly of glass, everything outside, from the stones on the ground to the birds, the maples, pines and other vegetation—all would be part of the interior. The outside landscape would be, in effect, inside.

It was one of the happiest days for the nuns when, in April of 1994, the church was finally completed and they were able to celebrate the Rite of Dedication for their first Abbey church. They named the church *Jesu Fili Mariae*, or Jesus, Son of Mary, choosing this title because it emphasizes the humanity of Christ and the monastery's reverence for the Incarnation. It also maintains harmony with its location—Bethlehem.

"The name—Jesus, Son of Mary—relates very obviously to the mission of this Abbey", said Mother Benedict. She chose to emphasize Jesus' relationship to Mary "because, even though a man, He has all the qualities of His Mother.

And the appeal of Mary is that these qualities of hers will be heightened in his relationship with us. So it's very simple. We need His humanity as well as His Divinity to be completely disposed to support and fill this church with that kind of presence where people can, hopefully, feel something here not found elsewhere.

"Not that we were trying to do something theatrical", she quickly added. "But if there is any way through the Holy Spirit to establish a climate where something of God's goodness could go out to the people who will visit this church, then this is what you accent. That is why we always saw our church as a sanctuary for people who feel tossed around in a world of constant flux and a witness for eternal truths and values that remain unchanging and ongoing. Central to Benedictine spirituality is the tenet that guests should be received like Christ. This is sometimes difficult to do, but we strive to do it. For indeed, it is the Holy Spirit moving to lead us to go beyond what we might have thought out and unconsciously wanted to force in our own limited way."

Their church was consecrated on Thursday, April 28, 1994, by the head of the Archdiocese of Hartford, Archbishop Daniel Cronin. More than twenty priests were there, as well as two abbots from other New England monasteries. Part of the ceremony included installing first-class relics of several saints inside the granite of the altar. One of these was a relic of Saint Benedict. The Archbishop, on his knees, with the help of a stonemason, installed these relics. The nuns, and they numbered more than forty, sang the chants for the ceremonies, including the Mass. They presented the Archbishop with a book showing the construction work in progress and with the names of all the workers recorded in it.

At the end of the Mass, the Blessed Sacrament was taken to a standing stone tabernacle at the side of the altar and placed within it. The candle hanging over the tabernacle was lit, signifying the presence of Christ in this newly consecrated church. "We were all very moved by the beauty of the day, and I was truly at peace for what had been achieved at Regina Laudis after nearly a half century. It was a day of complete fulfillment, really", Mother Benedict commented. "Some people told me afterward that they feel the church looks like a ship and that this is a dynamic image. While I would hope always for a 'bon voyage', I know the journey will not be without peril."

In fact, a new challenge was already at their door. Just before the consecration of their new church was to take place, Mother Benedict had gotten word that Father Prokes was being reassigned by the Jesuit General at the request of Rome.

Chapter 15

FINAL YEARS

—Father Prokes Reassigned
— The Future as Seen by the Foundress
— A New Abbess Is Installed
— Mother Benedict Dies at Ninety-four
— October 2, 2005

Mother Benedict did speak about her confusion over how it had happened that the Abbey had become the victim of such bad publicity. She felt there had been "extreme hostility to Father Prokes, which I never understood". The Sacred Congregation for Religious had, without explanation, ordered him to be reassigned. Mother Benedict felt "completely in the dark" and wished for some "recognition for [all that] Father Prokes had done here".

He had a "magnititude of vision" that matched Pope Paul VI's recommendation for them, she said. "He was always humble. He never focused on his own worth. He stressed the renewal of community formation according to Vatican II, and he integrated a masculine influence in a very discreet way. He believed in something that people rejected—a modern conception in which society was called to collaborate in the work to be done. He had a vision of how scientific and technological progress was included in what would come to pass. But he knew that many would not accept modern technology as a sign of God at work, because history has shown that people become frightened when something new is being introduced and incorporated."

What was especially difficult for the Abbess was that Father Prokes was never called to Rome to be given an explanation for why he was being removed. What she learned was that Father Prokes' Jesuit Provincial in Milwaukee, Father Bert Thelen, had been contacted by the Jesuits' Father General in Rome suggesting that he reassign Father Prokes. [1]

What was clear was that much of the animosity of the Abbey's detractors was aimed at Father Prokes. Yet, in an interview (by this author) with Father Bert Thelen, it was evident that he thought highly of this priest. He took issue with the *Courant* story, which implied that the late Archbishop of Hartford had asked for an investigation of Father Prokes.

"That's false", Father Thelen told me. "Archbishop Whealon was completely supportive of Father Prokes and the Abbey. Even when all the bad publicity came out in '87, he never wanted to do anything on this. . . . I think he knew the criticism was coming from some alienated people", who perhaps felt they had been given some bad advice from the Abbey.

The Jesuit Provincial said he reluctantly transferred Father Prokes when his Superior in Rome suggested reassignment on the basis that "it was unusual for a Jesuit to be out of his own community so long, working with another community." There was "no other tone" but this in the letter, said Father Thelen, who emphasized the "good achieved" by Father Prokes in his thirty years of working with the nuns at Regina Laudis. And he strongly commended Father Prokes for the work he had done at the Abbey, saying, "Probably the world and the Church will never know the extent of the good you have achieved and the blessing you have been for the Sisters and the lay associates.... I know of no one, at least in the American assistancy, who has come close to achieving what you have achieved in the work of the renewal of religious life so crucial to the future of the Church and the vitality of collaborative ministry."

Father Prokes had already moved out when the Abbess received a letter from the Sacred Congregation for Religious telling her they wanted Regina Laudis to assume their own governance, with no interference from an outsider. Rome then informed the Lady Abbess that they had appointed a Delegate from the Holy See to come to Regina Laudis. He was a Benedictine, Abbot Matthew Stark, and they would have to answer to him. Mother Benedict was confused by this. "They had told us to be free, and then they took away our freedom. No wonder we asked, what was going on."

Then new problems came. The Sacred Congregation for Religious questioned Regina Laudis' revised Constitution that had been sent to them for approval. "Two specific items in our Constitution were causing the criticisms. One was that they objected to the life-term for the Abbess. They wanted me to resign, but I couldn't in conscience. My hands were tied because the Community chose to have an Abbess for life, and it was in our Constitution. The Sacred Congregation admitted they had no grounds for asking me to resign, but they made a big issue over a life-term for the Abbess.

"The other matter was our insistence that we retain the ceremony of the Consecration of a Virgin. At Jouarre the final profession and the consecration were both done on the same day, and at Regina Laudis I had separated these two occasions to bring a new emphasis to the beauty and importance of the consecration."

She went on to explain that the consecration is the Church blessing a woman in her resolve to give herself to God. It is not her asking for the blessing of the Church. Rather, it is the Church offering to consecrate her. The witness for that is the Abbess. And she underscored that never in her prior experience had the Sacred Congregation for Religious had to say anything or approve anything about this ceremony in order for it to take place.

"Father Abbot Matthew was going to officiate at the rite of Consecration of a Virgin for five of our professed nuns in '94. But first he was taking a trip to Rome", the Abbess related. "When he got back he told us he couldn't do the ceremony. There would be no consecrations for the time being." The Sacred Congregation also required them to study further the issue of the consecration. "The effect on the Community was tremendous suffering", she continued. "Some worried that the Vatican would shut Regina Laudis down, but they don't do that when there are no grounds for this kind of action."

Mother Benedict's outlook in the face of all the misunderstandings and false accusations was the following: "Opponents have no power over what is deeper here. Certainly, all the hurt has made us stronger. If we're going to stick to our guns and our vocation, we have to stand up against the assaults. It's not very uplifting, but we have to remember, our Lord was also falsely accused."

From 1994 through 1997, the dialogue with Rome and the arduous process of *conversatio* continued, stretching the Community to a new degree of spiritual engagement with aspects of their life they once might have taken for granted: the Consecration of a Virgin, and Abbess for life. After many months' work, the Community submitted a study of the Consecration of a Virgin, outlining their understanding of this rite and their reasons for seeking it. Finally, in February 1997, a letter from the Sacred Congregation arrived announcing that the 1991 revision of the Constitution could be provisionally lived by the Community. Consecration of a Virgin was once more to be celebrated at Regina Laudis. On the Feast of Saint Benedict, July 11, 1998, nine professed nuns who had been awaiting this day for many years received the solemn rite of Consecration to a Life of Virginity from Abbot Mark Serna of Portsmouth Priory. Joy knew no bounds that day.

In these years, much progress had been made by the Community at Our Lady of the Rock on Shaw Island. On February 27, 1997, the newly completed chapel was dedicated, and Mother Benedict was invited to be with them for the celebration. In her words, it was "very impressive to see what has been accomplished there. Besides Mother Thérèse, the Prioress, there are seven nuns, and all of them work very hard on the land. Besides sheep and cows, they have llamas, and they take these beautiful animals to shows."

They had begun the chapel in November of '95, their architect being Joseph Giampietro, the brother of Mother Perpetua. Everything was done Japanese style, to be in keeping with the land, including Japanese gardens. It was very special for Mother Benedict to be there to see their chapel completed. She said she was pleased that the crucifix on the altar was one that had been given to them in the beginning by the late Henry Ellis, before he went to Rome to complain about the nuns. She prayed that he had found peace. This was her first time back in four years. To see the new compound, with the library and a music room, gave her great happiness that became even greater when they had an open house on the Sunday of the dedication, and one hundred fifty people came—almost the whole of Shaw Island!

Another highlight for her came in 1997, when the Abbey produced its first CD, called *Women in Chant*, with the nuns' choir singing a most unusual repertoire of Gregorian chant pieces reflecting on the virgin martyrs and Our Lady of Sorrows.[2]

"I have pursued the study of chant for most of my life", said Mother Benedict. In the interview conducted by Tom Pomposello for the CD booklet, she elaborates, "I think there is something evocative and archaic, something above time, that resides in the chant and is waiting to be picked up and used, even though for the time being it has been discarded.... I do believe chant is a medium that has the power to release and strengthen people.... When I hear the chant, I hear people at peace together.

"I have been asked why we chose the particular chant pieces from the repertoire of the virgin martyrs and Our Lady of Sorrows. That's easy to answer. It's because we're a women's community, and we thought it would be good to choose texts that exemplify what we are trying, in our own way, to actually live. Our Lady of Sorrows embodies the consummate expression of a consecrated feminine response to God. The Virgin Martyrs all share a common response to Christ, yet each one is an original woman, and her music is original."

Commenting on the CD's success, Mother Benedict reflected, "We must have done something right with this CD because the response has been phenomenal. I think we should do another one to herald the new millennium!

"I don't think too much about the fact that we are coming to the end of the century, though I do wonder sometimes what Regina Laudis will be like in the future. That, of course, will be in the hands of others."

In spite of the Community's repeated efforts to retain in its Constitution the practice of electing an Abbess for life, the Sacred Congregation ruled that at age seventy-five a resignation must be offered and that Mother Benedict was therefore no longer able to hold her office. In 1996, the Community received a visit from Pro Nuncio Archbishop Cacciavillan, who announced on behalf of the Vatican that Lady Abbess Benedict Duss would from then on be Abbess Emerita. Though this decision was a crushing blow for her, Mother Benedict once again gave her "yes" to the Holy Spirit speaking through Rome. She knew the members of the Community must go forward, and they did, showing the strength and resilience she had formed them to bring to whatever challenge they faced. The Community continued its efforts of appeal on behalf of its beloved foundress.

In 1997 Mother David Serna was appointed as Administratrix of the Community. Shortly after that came the news that the 1991 revision of the Constitution could be lived provisionally. Finally, on July 11, 2000, the final revisions of the Regina Laudis Constitution were approved. The Foundation Mother Benedict had given her life to bring to birth was established. The Community was ready for the blessing of succession to pass to a new Abbess.

As described by the nuns, the announcement on January 25, 2001, of the election of Mother David Serna as the second Abbess of Regina Laudis was greeted by an outpouring of gratitude and profound joy. On May 13, Mother's Day in 2001, amid irrepressible acclaim, she was installed as the new Abbess, receiving the Rite of Blessing at the hands of the Hartford Archbishop, Daniel A. Cronin. At the ceremony,

Mother Abbess David was "assisted" by Mother Benedict, now ninety years old and called "Abbess Emerita", a title of continued respect accorded a former abbess. Mother Abbess' second assistant was Mother Dolores Hart, whom she had appointed Prioress,[3] the title given to a nun having the major responsibility of totally supporting the Abbess from her complementary gifts.

Bells tolled, and the voices of dozens of nuns chanting sounded within the beautiful new church. Nearly two hundred people, including many priests, had come for this joyful event, a ceremony of the ages, where the Abbess-elect attests to the Archbishop her devotion to the Rule of Saint Benedict and her fidelity to the Church, to the Holy Father, to the Archbishop and to a life of holiness. After the Liturgy of the Eucharist, celebrated in Latin, Archbishop Cronin gave a pontifical blessing to Mother David. Each nun went before the new Abbess and received from her the kiss of peace. In his homily, the Archbishop urged Catholics to persevere in their faith, to renew life and love one another. Mother David, thanking him and everyone responsible for her election, asked for prayers "every day".[4]

⚜ ⚜ ⚜

Mother Benedict, then approaching ninety-one, continued to work in the gardens—work she had always loved—and to receive visitors, who often traveled great distances to see her and speak with her. In the last years before her death, the life of the Community continued to intensify and evolve, but she no longer had to be actively engaged to be at its center. After suffering a stroke, she became more the contemplative than ever, witnessing to the redemptive value of suffering by her daily physical ordeal. The members of the Community who were able to assist her in her illness speak of the privilege of this direct encounter with her fierce and unquenchable spirit as she longed for her return to the Father. As Mother Maria Immaculata so precisely expressed it, "Lady Abbess is revered for all she has done but is loved for who she was, a woman totally feminine and maternal, without guile, who always met you at the core of your being." Then Mother Maria Immaculata captured the gift of Lady Abbess in five words: "She could read the heart."

⚜ ⚜ ⚜

On October 5, 2005, a brilliant autumn day, bishops, abbots, monks, clergy, religious—notably the Franciscan Sisters of the Eucharist—and hundreds of lay people, including many who had once spoken out against Regina Laudis, gathered at the Abbey to pay tribute to Lady Abbess as she was buried in the Abbey cemetery on her beloved hill.

Excerpts follow from an article carried the next day by the local newspaper, the Waterbury *Republican American*: ▸

Abbey founder laid to rest
300 celebrate life, legacy of Mother Benedict Duss

BETHLEHEM—*The founder of the Abbey of Regina Laudis was laid to rest Wednesday on the pine-studded hill where she launched her dream 57 years ago. . . .*

Archbishop Henry J. Mansell, who heads the archdiocese of Hartford, officiated at a traditional Benedictine funeral mass in Latin, enhanced by female voicing of Gregorian chants, for which the Abbey has gained worldwide acclaim.

Archbishop Emeritus Daniel Cronin, who led the archdiocese through the period when Mother Benedict retired in 1995, also participated in the service.

"This was a great woman of faith, who had a spousal relationship with God," the Rev. Robert Tucker of St. Anthony's Catholic Church in Litchfield said in the homily.

"She was the contemplative center of our community and she always will be," Mother Benedict's successor, Mother David Serna, said after the service. . . .

Tears mixed with laughter throughout the four-hour ceremony, which began at midmorning, shortly after a bright sun burned away a heavy shroud of fog. . . .

Sunlight, candlelight and incense filled the barn-shaped structure, while the body of the "Lady Abbess" lay in the sanctuary in a simple pine-and-cedar coffin made by one of the sisters. It rested on two stools covered by sheepskins.

Two black-and-white oxen from the abbey farm—Belted Dutch steers . . .—pulled a cart carrying the coffin up the hill to the cemetery, accompanied by a procession of priests, nuns and worshipers. . . .

With the blessing of the Vatican, the devotion and work of determined proteges and the help of many benefactors, the dream (of Lady Abbess) became a reality. On Wednesday, it became a woman's legacy.

News of Lady Abbess' passing was broadcast on local radio and television networks and was reported in news publications throughout the country, including the *New York Times* and *Time* magazine.

A beautiful tribute to her, written by Mother Lucia for the Monastic Burial Book given to those attending the Mass and services for their beloved Lady Abbess, was entitled simply, "Lady Abbess, Gardener". She writes:

"One story out of the hundreds of stories recalled in these days: One year during Easter week, Mother Mary Aline, frantic and ferocious as only a co-foundress and exasperated

portress could be, was searching high and low for Lady
Abbess, who was urgently needed for some official business. At that point, Mother Mary Aline no longer moved
easily, and she had had a chance to get very indignant before
she finally discovered Lady Abbess unhurriedly walking down
the road toward her flower garden. Surely at the moment
she was not consciously echoing Mary Magdalene when,
drawing herself up to her full height, she growled, 'Lady
Abbess, are you a gardener or are you an abbess?' But the
poignancy of the echo reverberates still. Anyone who has
ever waited for Lady Abbess to arrange a bouquet or seen
her painstakingly place tulips in the sanctuary after the long-
est Easter vigil, has known the question and the answer to
it: she was both. And so she embodied the paradox of unstop-
pable drive to be about the Father's business and the slow
loving care of one who listens to the earth and lives by its
rhythms. . . .

"This gift of unshakable faith in the goodness of God, of
knowing how to start with nothing, of just being able to
'do the next thing' was learned from the soil but bore fruit
in the soul, the souls of countless people who were touched
and changed forever by Lady Abbess Benedict Duss, O.S.B.,
M.D., Foundress of Regina Laudis, gardener."

⚜ ⚜ ⚜

REFLECTIONS OF
LADY ABBESS BENEDICT DUSS, O.S.B.

I
VOCATION

I had often wondered how Mother Benedict can know if a woman asking to enter the Abbey has a true vocation. She shrugged when I asked and explained:

"When a woman comes to the door asking if she can be accepted into this Community, it is a question mark. The big thing is to know if God is sending her or not. Of course, God is sending her, but for what purpose? I have to try to stay as open as possible. Very often we have been able to steer people to what they're made for—this life, or, we steer them to another path. The more I grow, the less I worry. Something much bigger is at stake. We have to be available to whatever God wants for this person. I can't think—Is she good for us? But rather—Is it right for her? That's hard to tell. Most have no idea of what community [life] entails, and that's a good thing. Nobody enters very easily. Sometimes I knew that a candidate would one day leave. I knew, but the Community voted her in, and I would not veto that. There's no point in saying no. It always works out as it was meant to.

"People who want to try the religious life often have a very hard time with the faith condition. In very few cases of those leaving was there enough faith. One might have a great enthusiasm to join the Community, without a grasp of the complexities ahead. Those who left had no concept of what it would mean to enter the culture of the monastery honestly and to meet the hurdles as they came. They had no concept of how much energy would have to go into trying again and again to win against the hurdles. There are nothing but crisis points in religious life, and we can continue in this life only if the spiritual dispositions are there. If not, it can't work. You have to be stable in the spiritual life to be able to withstand the changing tides, the contagion of the culture and the attacks of evil spirits. The belief that a vocation is a privilege given to you by God has to go deep enough so that it can't surface for debate. It has to be invested in your person constantly. This is possible only for a person who is living in the faith dimension.

"The role of a Superior is to be at the beck and call of each member of the Community. You must be such that you are loved by them, and yet be tough with them. Your responsibility for each parallels the parenting role, for they are members of your body by faith.

"The attempt to speak of Gospel life and to live the Gospel life requires that you, as a Superior, have a stable manner of being always attuned to that moment that is ahead of us. The progression of time is certainly difficult, because you have to meet—for the sake of a whole generation—the problems of that age and solve them in your behavior in such a way that what happens then to the Community is relevant to every person, because each is under the same obligations. To be able to do this presupposes that you have a contemplative dimension and can look at things in each moment, knowing they don't really change in time, but only in color. The life of God is always the same, and this is what I must introduce to others in such a way that they can be drawn to live in the society of God. If they have a contemplative capacity, they can understand that because they are held by the stability of God, they can handle the next hurdle. They'll have the resources to meet every new event that calls on them.

"Some come here and have difficulty understanding what I'm trying to do, but I can't worry about that. To live the Benedictine life, you have to stay in that contemplative attitude all the time, and this is very difficult. You can't tire of it or say 'I'm through', because the constant challenge is to meet creatively the newness of the next phase you must enter. This involves deep reflection. You can't get by with an irrational unfolding of your thinking. There has to be a supra-intelligent capacity to interpret what keeps you creatively on the path of the contemplative, spiritual life.

"If someone can do this, honestly, it becomes a means of their developing their own freedom. But some people never really get this, so there's an incompleteness, a lack of getting to the point of what the spiritual, contemplative life is really about. It's human nature to be afraid, and some people would rather be shackled than be free.

"That's the challenge—and if you don't get it, you're never going to make it as a Benedictine religious."

II

CONSECRATED VIRGINITY

"Some people are called in a specific way to be ever-present, faithful witnesses to what Christ has done and what

He has asked of us. To follow this call, they enter monasteries and do more than accept the requirement of celibacy,
which means not to marry; they choose to go to a deeper,
richer place for their lasting rendezvous with Christ; they
choose virginity. For women called to the religious life as
lived at Regina Laudis, this means literally to enter into the
most intimate relationship possible with Christ—to become
the spouse of Christ, to become two-in-one-flesh with Christ
in a relationship that is virginal precisely because they have
chosen to go all the way in aligning themselves as partners
with Christ in His mission of bringing all people to His
Paradise restored. They put their bodies on the line in this
merging with Christ, and Christ becomes incarnated—
becomes flesh—in them. To be the spouse of Christ is a
full-time job. The woman is forever fertile, pregnant with
the seed of Christ, bringing forth the new life of Christ to
be shared with all others.

"That's the theology. But what does it mean in everyday life?" Mother Benedict asked. "To begin with, most
people can understand that to live life as a community of
women in a monastery would have to require celibacy,
certainly for logistical reasons, but even more because it
is impossible to be true to the transcendent call of being
available to others as Christ "in the body" if a nun is
married. Not so easy to understand is how one can
choose to surrender a sexual relationship for life to
the hope of Eucharistic, sacramental fulfillment. The archaic
idea of religious life was that a monastery was after
the inexperienced girl, who had a bodily purity that
came from ignorance. But an ignorant life is an untested
life, and the would-be nun was often unprepared
by life to grow in the intensely difficult path of religious
life.

"This sometimes led to immature development of the person, resulting in personality, psychological or emotional disorders. Regina Laudis could not settle for immaturity. I readily welcomed professional women who, not finding substance and body-soul nourishment in the world, came here to find what it means to live in a state of purity and innocence, linked to God. The purity they sought was not the kind that comes from ignorance, but choice. After much awareness for what the world held, its sin and pain and ugliness, its false promises and shallow pleasures—and its beauty and love, too, but incomplete—they made a conscious choice for Christ and came to Regina Laudis.

"Strongly attracting them was the enclosure. These women had learned the importance of boundaries. From personal experience or otherwise, they had seen how letting down boundaries could make them vulnerable to the negative and destructive forces of the world. Therefore, without boundaries, there is no freedom, and without freedom the path to Christ is blocked. After all, He was the one who said, 'I have come that you might be free.'

"This is not the way of the world, which understands selfishness, but not otherness. And so, like our Spouse, Christ Jesus, we nuns are a contradiction to this world, which can't really understand how women can choose values that put love and service to others before wanting fun, money, sex, power and prestige. Like Christ, we are subject to ridicule, lies said about us, betrayals by one-time associates and to being victims of those who would destroy us.

"All this fertility is possible because I established a structure within this Community that allows the life of each person to be released from within."

III
DE PROFUNDIS

Mother Benedict one day spoke from her heart about what she felt had been an injustice done to her and her Community by the actions of "enemies" who turned the Sacred Congregation for Religious against them. In her words:

"But what can you say about it? The truth is that what they do doesn't alter at all what our mission is. Yet it's normal to feel discouragement. All this shows that when something is right, the world is there to try to destroy it. The principles of religious life are always under threat. The powers of evil will do their level best to destroy you—even finding a way to work through the institution that's supposed to support you. I take it all in stride. As I said before, our Lord was treated exactly the same way.

"I have a tendency not to think of obstacles. That doesn't mean I don't understand the complications of obstacles. But I couldn't let them become a big deal for me. I've had obstacles surround me all my life. I long ago realized I'd have to face them and go through them. I was never under any illusions.

"There is a crisis in the Church herself. Our Community can't do much about that, but we can continue what we're doing here. Maybe the role of the contemplative is to be the last resort for a Church in crisis. The Church has been in a bad way chronically throughout the centuries. For some obscure reasons that no one understands, the Church can be allowed to look so bad. But she still holds. And yet God never came down to protect the Church in troubled times. She righted herself through other media.

"One of the hardships of faith is that no external influence comes down from Heaven to straighten the Church out. It's done internally. There's where contemplatives come in. I'm convinced that a very small number of contemplatives can make a difference. But you can't describe why or how because this is a mystery, deliberately hidden, probably because God wants us to do our part.

"I can say with confidence that [the authenticity of] Regina Laudis can never be questioned. I knew fifty years ago that what I was offering was ridiculous, and I needed courage to go ahead. I was totally clear about the human aspects, that I was onto something that people would laugh at. But I know I was called; I can't question that. I had no idea then of what I'd have to do. What's here today is not at all what I envisioned—because I had nothing in mind. I simply wanted to begin with what would be suitable. I didn't start with an image.

"Founding a monastery is a continuous process of sawing to build your design and trying to dispose of the sawdust while you're always being forced to reconstruct. It's all so difficult, you don't know how you're going to do it. You're at square one all the time, trying to include each new move and activity of the monastery, each new candidate. You have to give it your all, and it's never done. You have to keep thinking about it all the time.

"We're still formulating the principles as we face each new phase. You can't suppress a phase; the soil in each is different; the process is different, but you have to go through it in whatever form it takes. To understand and know authentically what you are building, you have to bow to each step in the process. The Holy Spirit does the work, actually. Our work is to submit to what is given to us at each phase and to have faith that we are being obedient to the moment, even though we can't have absolute predictability about the outcome.

"In my personal reflections, I think that I have nothing now, except the joy of knowing God still exists. Saint Benedict foresaw the destruction of his monastery, and one of his monks found him crying in his cell. At that moment it didn't even look like Benedict, who through his tears said, 'The Lord has shown me what will happen.' The only thing he asked was for God to protect the monks and take them somewhere else. After Saint Benedict died, an invasion of barbarians destroyed Monte Cassino. The monks had to go to Rome. After things calmed down, they started a Foundation in Rome and stayed there until they could rebuild Monte Cassino.

"You see, you have to go through the tearing-down process—in order to rebuild. All has to be done in a new form that works for the whole Church. We have to go through all the phases Christ had to endure Himself—die and be resurrected, sending the apostles to carry on His work. It all starts from scratch, and we have to repeat the process to get the new picture.

"I can't forget what the point is, that I'm trying to go to God. I start from scratch every day. When He takes away what I had hoped to accomplish, I don't understand it, but I accept it. I lean on one of Saint John of the Cross' basic principles. He said, in a situation where there is no love, you put in love and love will be there. That's not a high-faluting description, but when I face discouragement, I like to relate to that simple statement.

"I started something here, and for it to continue it's going to depend on those who come after me. I believe the women of the Church will hold to what I started. Someone will follow me as Superior of this Abbey, and I pray that person will be responsible and have an even more enlightened attitude than I've had, always able to accept the fact that you can't do everything.

"The only failure is to let your personal feelings of hurt take over. Humility is the principal thing Saint Benedict expects, and it takes a real capacity for dissection of your motives to maintain that. It's something you work on all your life.

"I'll pray for my successor. That person will need a lot of help. It's certainly a difficult experience she'll have to go through."

APPENDIX:
MOTHER BENEDICT'S FAMILY

1. Vera Duss—Mother Benedict Duss, O.S.B., Abbess
   Born: November 21, 1910, Pittsburgh, Pennsylvania
   Died: October 2, 2005, Bethlehem, Connecticut
   Brother—John Duss, III
   Born: February 12, 1912
   Died: March 15, 1990, Florida
   (Sons: Robert and John, both of Florida)

2. a) Father—John Duss, Jr.
   Born: March 25, 1885, Red Cloud, Nebraska
   Died: January 28, 1961, Florida
   (Sister: Vera Duss Houston)

2. b) Mother—Elizabeth Vignier
   Born: June 17, 1891, Geneva, Switzerland
   Died: July 12, 1966, Bethlehem, Connecticut

3. a) i. Grandfather—John S. Duss, Sr.
   Born: February 22, 1860, Cincinnati, Ohio
   Married: July 17, 1882, Keokuk, Iowa
   Died: December 14, 1951

3. a) ii. Grandmother—Susanna Creese Duss
   Died 1946
   (Sister: Kate Creese)

3. b) i. Grandfather—Charles Vignier
   Born: Paris
   (Sister: Alice Vignier Densmore. Alice's
   daughters: Marianne, Yvonne. Yvonne
   married Abel Luthy)

3. b) ii. Grandmother—Ianthe Densmore Vignier

MOTHER BENEDICT'S ANCESTORS

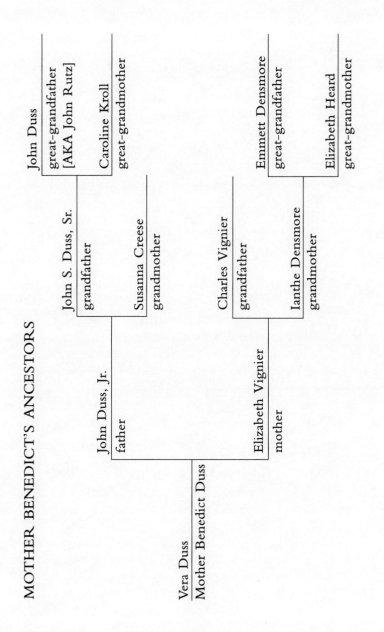

NOTES

CHAPTER ONE
THE EARLY YEARS IN AMERICA

1. John S. Duss, *The Harmonists: A Personal History* (1943; repr. Ambridge, Penn.: Harmonie Associates, 1970), pp. x–xi.
2. Ibid., pp. 119–20.
3. Ibid., pp. 123–24.

CHAPTER TWO
CHILDHOOD AND YOUTH IN FRANCE

1. Mont-Saint-Michel is a towering abbey on a rocky islet off the coast of Normandy, France, built in the thirteenth century. Most of the time it is surrounded by sand banks; it becomes an island only when the tides are very high. It has a colorful history but is mainly known today for its spectacular architecture, which down through the centuries has earned the monastery the name of *La Merveille* (The Wonder). It is now one of the most popular tourist attractions in France.
2. St. Thérèse of Lisieux was born in France in 1873, the youngest of nine children, only five of whom survived. She was raised by her father and sisters after her mother died when she was five. She, like three of her sisters, became a Carmelite nun (the fourth sister became a Visitation nun). Professed in 1890, she took the name of Thérèse of the Child Jesus. She very soon became ill with tuberculosis, but she was such a model of patience and virtue that she was told by her

Prioress she must write about her childhood and her life. Obediently, she did, and this book became an extraordinary work. It is known as *The Story of a Soul*, a story, not of events, but, as Thérèse herself put it, of grace at work in all the little things of life. The book became widely popular after her early death, at age twenty-four, as did her promise to "spend Heaven doing good upon earth". So many miracles were attributed to her that she was canonized a saint in 1925 by Pope Pius XI. St. Thérèse became a strong spiritual force for Catholics in the first half of the twentieth century because people related so well to her message that the way to God is by our simple and ordinary, everyday tasks.

CHAPTER THREE
VOCATIONS

1.   The Abbey of Notre-Dame de Jouarre was founded in the seventh century, during the reign of King Dagobert, by one of his nobles and his family. It was at first a double monastery comprised of monks and nuns living in separate enclosures under the Rule of St. Columban. This arrangement lasted two centuries, then disappeared. The Rule of St. Benedict was then introduced by the nuns, and it gradually became the norm of observance.

One of the most remarkable features of this ancient abbey is that the first examples of Merovingian funereal sculpture and architecture are still extant there in the form of a crypt for the founding family, a number of bishops and local saints. From the beginning, Jouarre gave a procession of saints and bishops to the Church.

2.   In order to preserve a sense of Mother Benedict's French cultural heritage and spiritual formation, she is

referred to by her French name as long as she was at Jouarre. "Benoît", the masculine form of Benedict, was an unusual name for a woman to receive and a great honor. However, apart from Mother Benedict, all the other nuns in the story are called by the names that were familiarly known to Mother Benedict and the rest of this Community. So, for example, Mother Mary Aline is always referred to as she was known in America. There is a mixture of French usage and English in the names themselves because there was a certain blending of the two cultures. Mother Ethelburga, for example, is referred to by her English name, and Mother Jean Marie by her French name. Some of the nuns who came from France to Regina Laudis changed the pronunciation of their names immediately; for some the shift was more gradual. This mixture is true to the lived experience and therefore was kept in the telling of the story.

CHAPTER FOUR
FRIENDS AND ENEMIES

1.   At the Abbey of Jouarre, where Mother Benedict began her monastic life, there were three classes of nuns: choir nuns, Lay Sisters, and Oblate Sisters. The choir nuns were obligated to the choral recitation of the entire Office. The Lay Sisters did much of the manual labor and had limited participation in the choir. Though they lived inside the enclosure of the monastery, they did not live in the same quarters as the choir nuns. The Oblate Sisters, a category introduced in the 1930s in order to provide a "bridge" between the monastery and persons outside, were responsible for all the work needs outside the enclosure (maintenance of guest houses, etc.). Even if finally professed, these

Lay Sisters and Oblate Sisters were always called Sister, rather than Mother, and they were not eligible to vote in the monastic chapter or to be elected Abbess. Choir nuns were given the title of "Mother" after making final vows.

2.   Jacques Maritain was a French philosopher and writer whose democratic political philosophy is credited for greatly influencing Catholic social thought after World War II. Born in 1882 and raised as a liberal Protestant, he studied under the philosopher Henri Bergson. He and his wife Raïssa, a Russian Jewish poet, converted to Catholicism in 1906 and became strong followers of Thomas Aquinas. Maritain taught in Paris and Toronto and in the United States at Princeton University, Columbia University and Notre Dame. He was the French Ambassador to the Vatican from 1945 to 1948, and after his wife's death in 1960, he lived with the Little Brothers of Jesus in Toulouse, joining their order in 1970. Author of sixty books, Maritain died in 1973 at the age of ninety-one.

3.   David Schoenbrun, *Soldiers of the Night* (New York: E. P. Dutton, 1980), p. 35.

4.   Ibid., p. 40.

CHAPTER SIX
FACING DANGER AS AN AMERICAN
IN WAR-TORN FRANCE

1.   St. Jean-Baptiste Marie Vianney (1786–1859), known as the Curé d'Ars, began life as a shepherd on his father's farm and never was a good student. His goodness was seen to offset his deficiencies as a scholar, and he was allowed to be ordained. He was sent to serve in the town of Ars in France in 1818, and he remained there for the rest of his life. He was tireless in warring against the frivolities, the

religious indifference and the immorality he found in Ars. Eventually, he made a difference in reforming the town, even finding a way to open a shelter for orphans and deserted children. He became famed as a spiritual counselor and confessor, sometimes spending up to eighteen hours in a day hearing confessions. He was canonized in 1925 by Pope Pius XI, who made him the patron saint of parish priests in 1929; his feast day is August 4.

2.   This is the same Sister who was later known as Sister Genevieve at Regina Laudis. She had come to Jouarre from Maradret in Belgium, where she had been Sister Geneviève. Since there was already a Sister Geneviève at Jouarre, she was given the name Sister Solange. When she came to the United States she was free to use her first religious name, which she did; however, she took the American pronunciation of the name. She was a lay Sister and always remained Sister Genevieve.

CHAPTER SEVEN
GOD CALLS FOR A NEW MONASTERY IN AMERICA

1.   Olga Afanacieff, the schoolgirl who rang the bells on liberation day, became a lifelong friend of Mother Benedict, and she visited Regina Laudis many times.

CHAPTER NINE
GETTING STARTED IN AMERICA

1.   Gregorian chant, the plainchant of the Roman rite in the Church, was named after Pope Gregory the Great, who

is credited for wanting music in the service of God to be distinctly sacred, sounding a harmonic view of the universe that would reflect the Divine order of creation. But Gregorian chant, which had a substance entirely different from secular music, unfortunately suffered major changes, alterations, innovations and revisions in the 1,200 years following the death of Pope Gregory in the year 604. Then, in the nineteenth century, the French Abbey of Solesmes initiated a liturgical revival, and the monks, under the direction of Dom Mocquereau and Dom Pothier, began editing chant books based on a careful and thorough analysis of ancient manuscripts. Solesmes became noted worldwide for this work and in the early 1900s was charged by Rome to be the principal editors of the official Roman rite chant books. Most of the chant books in use today reflect the scholarship and advances made by Solesmes in its faithful pursuit of the study and interpretation of ancient chant manuscripts.

2.   In the late 1980s, I personally interviewed Mr. Crane, who provided this firsthand information.—A. B.

CHAPTER TEN
BUILDING A CLOISTER

1.   *Regina Laudis* means "Queen of Praise". Mother Benedict explained that even before she and Mother Mary Aline had left France, they had chosen this name precisely because they wanted to give the new Foundation a name that would proclaim their identity. Queen of Praise did this, for it defined the spirit of their mission. "Mary is the exemplar of praise for the Lord, for she did nothing else but live to meet God's terms. She was the most important ally God had in the work of redemption. We would try to grow into

what she was—to be the complement of the great plan of God for salvation", said Mother Benedict. She explained that the Benedictine spirit fosters a form of spiritual centering that can meet the crises of every successive generation, while preserving what needs to be recognized as essential for salvation and redemption. Like a continual rebirth, through grace and the Holy Spirit, the Benedictine spirit opens ways to overcome the terrible liability of original sin, so as to free man from this fallen state, restoring everything lost, so as to return to God. "This is all so much bigger than what people can comprehend", Mother Benedict affirmed.

The foundress also explained that when a foundation is made, it is first called a "house", or monastery, without any specification. As the order becomes more clear, the foundation then enters the phase of becoming a priory, which is a lower stage than an abbey, not yet having the prestige of that title. "St. Benedict had a very comprehensive view of what a Benedictine monastery had to be. That's clear in the way he wrote the Rule, which is a blueprint for the institution, which must be a constant search for order", Mother Benedict commented.

2. Secular Oblates, now known more simply as Oblates, are lay people who wish to dedicate themselves to living the spirituality of St. Benedict in the world. In order to do this, their promise of dedication has to be "received" or accepted by the Superior of a particular Benedictine community. There were many committed lay people gathering around Regina Laudis from the very beginning of the Foundation, including some people who knew Father Damasus Winzen from Keyport Priory, which had closed. They were looking for a new center, but until Regina Laudis was officially established, it was not authorized to receive the commitments of lay persons. To overcome this obstacle, the Abbot

of Monte Cassino allowed these people to dedicate themselves to Regina Laudis by officially becoming Oblates of Monte Cassino. The ceremony, which was fairly formal at that time, involved each person "offering himself to God, the Blessed Virgin Mary and our Holy Father St. Benedict" and promising "reformation of life" according to the "spirit of the Rule and the same most holy Father Benedict, and according to the Statutes of the Oblates". A record of the oblation was kept at the monastery.

3.   Before long the nuns were able to sing the full Divine Office, adding the "little hours" of Prime, Terce, Sext and None to the hours of Matins, Lauds, Vespers and Compline. The times of each of the canonical hours has stayed more or less the same, but with slight variations over the years.

4.   The "choir" is the section of the chapel occupied only by the nuns, separated from the visitors and others by a grille. The choir is made up of rows of stalls with seats and a place provided for holding books. In the middle there may be a lectern. It is in the choir where the nuns chant the prayers at specified times of the day and night and gather for Mass.

5.   The chapel and choir at this time was very "rustic and rudimentary. It was a fundamental structure that had the basic ingredients for a place of worship. But we were always conscious of what it yet was not", Mother Benedict emphasized.

CHAPTER ELEVEN
THE NUNS' LIFE IN THE FIFTIES

1.   In 1945–1946 and again from 1954–1959, as a way of thanking America for its participation in World War II,

France sent a boxcar filled with gifts for each state. The gifts ranged from extravagant heirlooms to the offering of a pair of worn shoes. The bell Mary-Eugene-Benedict was on that first train and found its way to Regina Laudis through the assistance of Father Eugene Moriarity.

2.   Caroline Woolsey Ferriday, who inherited the Bellamy-Ferriday House, known as "The Hay", in the heart of Bethlehem, was a philanthropist whose good deeds crossed international borders. She greatly admired the nuns of Regina Laudis and remained a friend of the Abbey until she died in 1992. Today, her home is a museum maintained by the National Antiquarian Landmark Society. Open to the public at posted hours, it is especially noted for its spectacular rose gardens.

3.   The Crèche contained in the one-time Bellamy-Ferriday barn was made by eighteenth-century craftsmen in Naples. It consists of about sixty figures representing groups of people from all walks of life moving toward the center of the Nativity scene—Mary, Joseph and the Child. The Holy Family rests in the ruins of a miniature Roman temple, which is set within a three-dimensional landscape constructed to look like a typical hill town between Rome and Naples around the year 1770. The figures are about twelve to eighteen inches high and are in the dress of the period. They include children, old and young women bearing gifts, merchants, peddlers, a princess, the Three Kings and their retinue, shepherds, peasants and their farm animals.

CHAPTER TWELVE
CHANGES IN THE SIXTIES

1.   When Mother Benedict began Regina Laudis, she carried over the designation for Oblate Sisters (see chap. 4,

n. 1), but with the intention of emphasizing that they would have equal status with the choir nuns. From the first, her vision was that there would not be two classes of nuns, but one. She had to await the directive that came through Vatican II that there would be one class of nuns.

With the writing of the Regina Laudis Constitutions in the 1970s came the opportunity to articulate further Mother Benedict's vision: there would be one class of nuns, with two accents of call. Those who habitually go out, in response to various needs of the community, would be called *Missae*, Latin for "sent". Those who habitually remain in the enclosure would be known as "enclosed". These two groups would live and work in a complementary relationship.

Since that time, this concept has evolved further. The final revision of the Constitutions (2000) defines the vocation of Regina Laudis in accordance with paragraph 15 of *Perfectae Caritatis*, the Decree of Vatican II on the Renewal of Religious Life. In effect, the Constitutions say that in the Regina Laudis Community there is "one class of nuns—*moniales*—with only that distinction of persons which corresponds to the diversity of works for which the nuns are destined, either by special charism and vocation from God or by reason of special aptitude". In the early days of the Foundation, Mother Prisca, Mother Maria Joseph and Mother Jerome, for example, were all originally Oblate Sisters, but they were part of forging the new understanding of their call and made the transition to being known as *Missae*.

2.   Angelo Giuseppe Roncalli (1881–1963) was one of thirteen children born to a tenant farmer and his wife near the city of Bergamo in Italy. In his seminary years, he was drafted into military service, and later, as a priest, he was again in service, first as a hospital orderly, then as a military chaplain with the rank of lieutenant. The steps in his career

included getting a doctorate in canon law, being a seminary theology teacher and spiritual director, directing the Italian organization for the support of foreign missions, and serving as a Vatican diplomat in Bulgaria and then as an apostolic delegate to Greece. His biographers say he was stunned when, at the end of 1944, he was named Papal Nuncio to Charles de Gaulle's newly liberated France. The French post was a particularly delicate one at the time because Msgr. Valerio Valeri, Roncalli's predecessor, had been close to Philippe Pétain, the general who had collaborated with the Germans. De Gaulle insisted he be replaced, as the French detested people they viewed as former collaborators. Roncalli turned out to be exactly the right person for soothing the ill will that had been created by Valeri. His success was rewarded by Pope Pius XII, who made him a Cardinal in January 1953.

At age seventy-one, Cardinal Roncalli was appointed patriarch of Venice. He may have been the one most surprised when, after the death of Pius XII on October 9, 1958, he was elected Pope. Very soon after his coronation as Pope John XXIII, he announced he would call a meeting of the Bishops of the Church for an ecumenical council, saying the idea had come to him in a "sudden inspiration". From the beginning, he said the purpose of the Council would be an *aggiornamento* ("to bring the Church up to date"), and he sought, he said, a new outpouring of the Holy Spirit. By the time the Council, in session from 1962 to 1965, ended, sixteen documents had been agreed upon.

3. Msgr. Joseph R. Lacy was born in Hartford in 1912 and was ordained in 1938 as a priest of the Archdiocese of Hartford, leaving Connecticut on July 17, 1943, to serve as a chaplain in the U.S. Army. On June 6, 1944, Father Lacy participated in the historic D-day invasion of France,

walking under heavy fire with the young soldiers to the Normandy shore. There, he waded up and down the beach, ministering to the wounded and dying soldiers. In a story commenting on his heroism, the Army newspaper *Stars and Stripes* later wrote: "On the beach, pinned down when no one could move, it was the padre who moved from man to man despite the barrage of the German 88s and all the machine gun fire in the world. He took care of the dying and helped the wounded to live." Fr. Lacy was given the Distinguished Service Cross for his courage. After the war, he studied canon law in Rome and was named a Papal Chamberlain and, later, a Domestic Prelate, with the title Right Reverend Monsignor bestowed by Pope Pius XII. Upon his return to Hartford in 1955, Msgr. Lacy was named Chancellor of the Archdiocese by Archbishop Henry J. O'Brien. In 1970, Archbishop John Whealon named him pastor of St. Luke parish in Hartford. He died on May 18, 1990, a much beloved and honored priest.

4. See the reference from the encyclical of Pope John XXIII, *Pacem in Terris*, as quoted by Francis Prokes, "The Theological Dimension of Architecture: An Investigation of Implications: Theoretical; Theoretical-in-Collaboration; and Collaborative-Practical." (Ph.D. diss., Princeton University, 1964), p. 62.

5. "Theological Dimension of Architecture", p. 15.

6. Ibid., p. 27.

7. Ibid., p. 93.

8. Ibid., p. 95.

9. Ibid., p. 96.

10. In 1961, while she was in Arizona making a film with the late Jeff Chandler, Dolores Hart faced her moment of truth. "I looked in a mirror, and I knew my career in movies would be short-lived. I felt a desire to enter Regina

Laudis, yet I didn't know really what that meant. I just knew I had to submit to God teaching me how my life is to be." That is what the young actress told Mother Benedict when she arrived and was welcomed in June 1963, the very month Cardinal Montini—who had given a strong mandate to Mother Benedict to seek professional women, the best in their fields—was made Pope, taking the name Paul VI.

Looking back now, Mother Dolores reflects on why she was drawn to the monastery. For a long time an uneasiness had settled in her. "To be seventeen years old, with three thousand dollars a week in your pocket, makes you ask, 'What's going on here?' I had been given the whole thing so fast, with such generosity, I had to question, what is my part in all this? What is God asking?" God was not a stranger for young Dolores, because as an only child of divorced parents, vacationing with them in California and living with her grandparents in Illinois, she learned quickly to make her own decisions. She attended St. Gregory's grammar school in Chicago and found herself drawn to spend a lot of time in the local Catholic church. "I had a very intense realization of the presence of the Lord in the sacrament of the Eucharist", she recalls, adding that she became a convert to the Catholic faith when she was only nine years old.

A major influence in her decision to enter religious life after seven very successful years playing in movies such as *Loving You* and *King Creole* with Elvis Presley, *Where the Boys Are* with George Hamilton, *Francis of Assisi* with Bradford Dillman and *Lisa* with Stephen Boyd was a painful family situation. "My father's sister, Betty Hicks, married Mario Lanza. When my Uncle Mario died tragically in 1960, followed a year later by his wife, both victims of the Hollywood star system, I was deeply sobered. I had to question the superficial values in my industry and to seek answers to life through the mystery of redemptive love and faith in Christ. I led an active social life in Hollywood and seriously considered marriage twice. However, I was held to my religious call by an overriding consciousness of an inclusive fidelity to Christ and the need of redemption within a society which was overwhelmed by moral and sexual degradation."

11. Taken from Xavier Rynne, *Vatican Council II* (New York: Farrar, Straus and Giroux, 1966; Maryknoll, N.Y.: Orbis Books, 1999), p. 49.

12. Ibid., p. 391.

CHAPTER THIRTEEN
THE GOLDEN YEARS

1. See *The Monastic Ritual for English-speaking Nuns of the Order of St. Benedict*, printed at Stanbrook Abbey, February 1984 and approved by the Sacred Congregation for Divine Worship in 1983, pp. 3–19.

2. In Mother Benedict's words: "In asking the Franciscan nuns to work with me in the task of continuing formation by being available for counseling, I was open to misunderstanding and evil interpretation. People who don't know the value and benefits of complementary life turn this into a Frankenstein. Some actually said that we were trying to supplant the Spirit, when all of this was meant to provide a solid substructure for religious life, where the human and Divine could come into relationship with the person. I held my ground on this.

"The other nuns who became closely associated with Regina Laudis were a group of Mercy Sisters who had broken away from their order in Grand Rapids, Michigan. They worked mainly in health care and had property, but their own mission had not yet taken root. The Mercies set up their main location in Alma, Michigan, and called themselves the Mercy Sisters of Alma. Father Prokes, always opting for corporate relationships between religious communities, worked with them both at Regina Laudis and in Michigan, coming up with a plan for them to set up a health service in Bethlehem. I could see the value in this and approved it. Eventually, a group of the Mercy Sisters, choosing to remain in Bethlehem, was able to occupy a house, which was, in part, a gift to them from George and Isabelle Zifcak, a couple from the Closed Community. The Closed Community itself had bought from Lauren Ford's daughter, Dora, forty-two acres of land across the street from the Zifcak property. However, when they found they were having difficulty handling the mortgage, the Mercy Sisters agreed to take it on. Dora Stone then forgave the loan and in effect gave the Mercy Community the land.

3.   Mother Philip Kline, O.S.B., now at the Abbey of San Vincenzo al Volturno in Italy, was among those to enter in the decade of the '70s.

CHAPTER FOURTEEN
GROWTH AND DIFFICULTIES

1.   At the time these allegations surfaced, I [the author, Antoinette Bosco] was the executive editor of the *Litchfield County Times*, a secular weekly newspaper published in the same county where the Abbey of Regina Laudis is located. I contacted the office of the papal ambassador, Archbishop

Pio Laghi, in Washington, D.C., asking if the stories saying he had asked for an investigation into the charges being levied against Regina Laudis were true. Fr. Dennis Schnurr, then the spokesman for the papal embassy there, said no and told me that Archbishop Laghi's role in this "somehow, someplace got misconstrued".

2.   Mother Noella began making the Abbey's Bethlehem cheese in 1977 according to an ancient technique taught to her by a native of the Auvergne in France. While pursuing a Ph.D. in microbiology at the University of Connecticut, she received a Fulbright Scholarship to France in 1994 and a subsequent three-year fellowship from the *Institut National de la Recherche Agronomique* (INRA). She traveled 30,000 km. through traditional cheese-making regions collecting native strains of cheese-ripening fungi to access their biochemical and genetic diversity. A documentary film about this journey, *The Cheese Nun: Sister Noëlla's Voyage of Discovery*, produced by the Paris American Television Company, has been shown in film festivals and aired nationally on PBS Television in 2006.

3.   In 1988, the people of Néhou, France, dedicated a small monument to General Patton in the center of their village. The plaque reads as follows:

> *The village of Néhou had the honor to receive a prestigious guest,*
> *General George S. Patton, Jr.*
> *His headquarters had been established in this village, where he stayed in absolute secrecy from the 6th of July to the 2nd of August, 1944.*
> *It is from this place that he prepared and commanded the historic "breakout from Avranches", a decisive victory for our liberation.*

This came to the attention of Lady Abbess when the Patton family was invited to attend the dedication.

CHAPTER FIFTEEN
FINAL YEARS

1.   In November 1994, when Fr. Francis J. Prokes, who was then seventy, was removed from Regina Laudis by an action from the Vatican in Rome, this news was reported in the press. A story in the *Hartford Courant* of Connecticut and picked up by the Associated Press regurgitated the old finger-pointing with a headline saying, "Vatican Intervenes at Abbey in State; Cloister Accused of Cult-Like Practices". The old '87 allegations were repeated in the new *Courant* story with vague unnamed and unidentified sources. At the time, as a newspaper editor, I investigated the allegations and again found them to have no truth. One of the people I interviewed was Fr. Robert Tucker, pastor of St. Anthony of Padua in Litchfield, who has been confessor to the nuns at the Abbey since 1971. He said, "The point of a cult is to have everyone act, be and do the same thing. One only has to know the individuality of the nuns to know how false this accusation is. Each woman there is unique. They have no common ground other than faith."

After my editorial in the *Litchfield County Times*, entitled "The Abbey of Regina Laudis—Not a Cult, a Spiritual Community", appeared, Mother Benedict wrote me, thanking me "warmly ... for the courageous response you have written.... There is a special tone to your article, and it breathes in the spirit of freedom and absolute firmness. Once again, it is in moments like these that one can name true friends."

Fr. Matthew Stark, a Benedictine priest and Abbot Emeritus from the Abbey of St. Gregory the Great in Portsmouth, R.I., was appointed by the Vatican for a three-year term to oversee the Community.

2.   *Women in Chant: Gregorian Chant for the Festal Cel-ebration of the Virgin Martyrs and Our Lady of Sorrows*, sung by the choir of the Abbey of Regina Laudis, Bethlehem, Connecticut, was produced in 1997 by the late Tom Pom-posello, proprietor of Pomposello, Inc., a music production company in New York City. He collaborated on this project with the nuns and their chant master, Dr. Theodore Marier. The result of this work is a sixty-minute CD, recorded on location at the Abbey. It includes the Gregorian chant for the feasts of Sts. Lucy, Agnes, Cecelia, and Agatha and Our Lady of Sorrows, as well as a recording of the Kyrie, Pater Noster and Collect and an abbatial blessing by Lady Abbess herself.

Accompanying this CD is a forty-eight-page booklet including an interview with Lady Abbess, new translations of the original Latin texts, a brief history of the Abbey, a biography of each of the virgin martyrs and original photographs.

In 2001, the nuns released a second CD, titled *Women in Chant: Recordáre; Remembering the Mysteries in the Life of Jesus, Son of Mary*, and in 2004, they released *A Gregorian Chant Master Class*.

3.   The Prioress is the person who assists the Superior—or Abbess—by being very present to the Community and its needs and is able to represent those needs to the head of the Community. The Prioress thus facilitates the work of the Superior, or Abbess, and acts in her place should she become ill or have to be away from the monastery.

4.   As part of the program booklet, Mother David wrote a brief autobiography telling of her family and the journey that led her to the monastery. She indicated that God must have been the matchmaker for her parents, both of whom were immigrants. Her father had come from Lima, Peru,

and her mother was an immigrant from New Castle, England. Both were working for wealthy American families when they met, and their marriage, blessed with four children, was defined by their Catholic faith.

Her concern for others began early. As a student, commuting from her home in Greenwich, Connecticut, to the College of New Rochelle in New York State, she had helped aid people migrating from Puerto Rico to New York. After graduation, she spent a year in Puerto Rico. Back in the States, she continued to aid poor families and worked at the New York Foundling Hospital, caring for abandoned babies. But all the while, she was feeling an internal restlessness. "I wanted somehow to be able to do something totally, but needed another dimension to do it", she told me. By coincidence, she visited the Abbey of Regina Laudis and knew she belonged here. She entered in 1959.

I had had the privilege of interviewing Mother David back in 1990 for a feature I was doing on the Abbey for a Connecticut newspaper. Remembering how she impressed me with her down-to-earth presence, permeated with an undeniable spirituality, I applauded the wisdom of the Community in choosing her to follow Mother Benedict.

Now her wisdom is guiding the nuns of the Abbey as they continue to work in collaboration with one another, all for the cause of ever underscoring the simple, profound truth that we belong to God and we live in a holy place, His world.

INDEX